Praxis 0089

Middle School Social Studies

Teacher Certification Exam

By: Sharon Wynne, M.S.
Southern Connecticut State University

"And, while there's no reason yet to panic, I think it's only prudent that we make preparations to panic."

XAMonline, INC.

Boston

To obtain permission(s) to use the material from this work for any purpose including workshops or seminars, please submit a written request to:

XAMonline, Inc.
21 Orient Ave.
Melrose, MA 02176
Toll Free 1-800-509-4128
Email: info@xamonline.com
Web www.xamonline.com
Fax: 1-781-662-9268

Library of Congress Cataloging-in-Publication Data
Wynne, Sharon A.
Middle School Social Studies 0089: Teacher Certification / Sharon A. Wynne. -2nd ed.
ISBN 978-1-58197-263-4
1. Middle School Social Studies 0089. 2. Study Guides. 3. Praxis 4. Teachers' Certification & Licensure. 5. Careers

Managing Editor	Dr. Harte Weiner, Ph. D.
Senior Editor	Janis Mercer, Ph. D.
Copy Editor	Ira Glasser, B.A.
Assistant Editor	Kerrie Forbes, B.A.
Production Coordinator	David Aronson

Disclaimer:
The opinions expressed in this publication are the sole works of XAMonline and were created independently from the National Education Association, Educational Testing Service, or any State Department of Education, National Evaluation Systems or other testing affiliates. Between the time of publication and printing, state specific standards as well as testing formats and web site information may change that is not included in part or in whole within this product. Sample test questions are developed by XAMonline and reflect similar content as on real tests; however, they are not former tests. XAMonline assembles content that aligns with state standards but makes no claims or guarantees teacher candidates a passing score. Numerical scores are determined by testing companies such as NES or ETS and then are compared with individual state standards. A passing score varies from state to state.

Printed in the United States of America   œ-1

PPST: Middle School Social Studies 0089
ISBN: 978-1-58197-263-4

About the Subject Assessments

Praxis™: Subject Assessment in Social Studies 5-9 examination

Purpose: The assessments are designed to test the knowledge and competencies of prospective secondary level teachers. The question bank from which the assessment is drawn is undergoing constant revision. As a result, your test may include questions that will not count towards your score.

Test Version: There are two versions of subject assessments for social studies tests for Praxis. Although both versions of the test emphasize conceptual comprehension, synthesis, and analysis of the principles of the social studies, the major difference between versions lies in the *degree* to which the examinee's knowledge is tested.

Version 1: **Social Studies 6-12** This version requires a greater depth of comprehension in US History, world history, economics, geography, political science, anthropology, and psychology. The social science 6-12 guide is based on a typical knowledge level of persons who have completed a *bachelor's degree program* in social science.

Version 2: **Social Studies 5-9** This version test the examinee's knowledge level in less detail than the first version of the subject assessments. The degree of knowledge required is typically based on completion of *introductory-level course work* in the same areas mentioned above. Although US History remains the focus of both tests, fewer questions on that topic are included in Social Studies 5-9.

Taking the Correct Version of the Subject Assessment: While some states offer just one test called a social studies test, Praxis breaks out those topics into two tests. You would take the 5-9 to become a middle school teacher and the 6-12 if you plan on teaching at the high school level. However, as licensure requirements change, it's highly recommended that you consult your educational institution's teaching preparation counselor or your state board of education's teacher licensure division to verify which version of the assessment you should take. We have not mentioned a history test. If you plan on applying for a position in another state, consider a history option. Visit the XAMonline.com web site for information about becoming certified in any particular state.

Time Allowance, Format, and Length: The time allowance and format for both versions are identical; you will have 2 hours to complete the test and the questions are presented in a 90 question, multiple-choice format worth 75 percent of the total score and three constructed response questions worth 25 percent of the total score.

Content Areas: Both versions of the subject assessments share a degree of commonality in that the test content categories are divided into (6) broad areas that roughly overlap between test versions. Version (1) has a narrower focus on specific disciplines than does version (2).

	Content Category	Number of Questions	Percentage of Total Score
I.	United States History	22-24	18-20%
II.	World History	16-19	14-16%
III.	Government/Civics	13-15	11-13%
IV.	Geography	14-16	11-14%
V.	Economics	12-14	10-12%
VI.	Sociology and Anthropology	0-6	0-5%
VII.	Short Content Essays	3	25%

Test Taxonomy: Both versions of the subject assessments are constructed on the comprehension, synthesis, and analysis levels of Bloom's Taxonomy. In many questions, the candidate must apply knowledge of more than one discipline in order to answer the questions correctly.

Additional Information about the Praxis Assessments: The Praxis™ series subject assessments are developed by the ***. They provide additional information on the Praxis series assessments, including registration, preparation and testing procedures, and such study materials as topical guides—about 30 pages of information including approximately 25 additional sample questions.

Table of Contents

Great Study and Testing Tips!

What to study in order to prepare for the subject assessments is the focus of this study guide but equally important is *how* you study.

You can increase your chances of truly mastering the information by taking some simple, but effective, steps.

Study Tips:

1. **Some foods aid the learning process.** Foods such as milk, nuts, seeds, rice, and oats help your study efforts by releasing natural memory enhancers called CCKs (*cholecystokinin*) composed of *tryptophan*, *choline*, and *phenylalanine*. All of these chemicals enhance the neurotransmitters associated with memory. Before studying, try a light, protein-rich meal of eggs, turkey, and fish. All of these foods release the memory enhancing chemicals. The better the connections, the more you comprehend.

Likewise, before you take a test, stick to a light snack of energy-boosting and relaxing foods. A glass of milk, a piece of fruit, or some peanuts all release various memory-boosting chemicals and help you relax and focus on the subject at hand.

2. **Learn to take great notes.** A by-product of our modern culture is that we have grown accustomed to getting our information in short doses (i.e., TV news sound bites or USA Today style newspaper articles.)

Consequently, we've subconsciously trained ourselves to assimilate information better in neat little packages. Scrawling your notes all over the paper fragments the flow of the information. Strive for clarity. Newspapers use a standard format to achieve clarity. Your notes can be much clearer through use of proper formatting. A very effective format is called the *Cornell Method.*

Take a sheet of loose-leaf lined notebook paper and draw a line all the way down the paper about 1-2 inches from the left-hand edge.

Draw another line across the width of the paper about 1-2 inches from the bottom. Repeat this process on the reverse side of the page.

Look at the highly effective result. You have ample room for notes, a left hand margin for special emphasis items or inserting supplementary data from the textbook, a large area at the bottom for a brief summary, and a little rectangular space for just about anything you want.

3. <u>Get the concept then the details</u>. Too often, we focus on the details and don't gather an understanding of the concept. However, if you simply memorize only dates, places, or names, you may well miss the whole point of the subject.

A key way to understand material is to put it in your own words. If you are working from a textbook, automatically summarize each paragraph in your mind. If you are outlining text, don't simply copy the author's words.

Rephrase them in your own words. You remember your own thoughts and words much better than someone else's and subconsciously tend to associate the important details to the core concepts.

4. <u>Ask Why.</u> Pull apart written material paragraph by paragraph and don't forget the captions under the illustrations.

Example: If the heading is "Stream Erosion," flip it around to read "Why do streams erode?" Then answer the questions.

If you train your mind to think in a series of questions and answers, not only will you learn more, you will reduce test anxiety because you are used to answering questions.

5. <u>Read for reinforcement and future needs</u>. Even if you only have 10 minutes, put your notes or a book in your hand. Your mind is similar to a computer; you have to input data in order to have it processed. *By reading, you are creating the neural connections for future retrieval.* The more times you read something, the more you reinforce the learning of ideas.

Even if you don't fully understand something on the first pass, *your mind stores much of the material for later recall.*

6. <u>Relax to learn so go into exile</u>. Our bodies respond to an inner clock called biorhythms. Burning the midnight oil works well for some people, but not everyone.

If possible, set aside a particular place to study that is free of distractions. Shut off the television, cell phone, and pager and exile your friends and family during your study period.

If you really are bothered by silence, try background music. Light classical music at a low volume has been shown to aid in concentration better than other types. Music without lyrics that evokes pleasant emotions is highly recommended. Try just about anything by Mozart. It relaxes you.

7. <u>Use arrows not highlighters.</u> At best, it's difficult to read a page full of yellow, pink, blue, and green streaks. Try staring at a neon sign for a while and you'll soon see that the horde of colors obscures the message.

A quick note, a brief dash of color, an underline, and an arrow pointing to a particular passage are much clearer than a horde of highlighted words.

8. <u>Budget your study time.</u> Although you shouldn't ignore any of the material, *allocate your available study time in the same ratio that topics may appear on the test.*

Testing Tips:

1. Get smart, play dumb. Don't read anything into the question. Don't make an assumption that the test writer is looking for something else than what is asked. Stick to the question as written and don't read extra things into it.

2. Read the question and all the choices _twice_ before answering the question. You may miss something by not carefully reading and then re-reading both the question and the answers.

If you really don't have a clue as to the right answer, leave it blank on the first time through. Go on to the other questions; they may provide a clue about how to answer the skipped questions.

If later on, you still can't answer the skipped ones . . . **_Guess._** The only penalty for guessing is that you _might_ get it wrong. Only one thing is certain; if you don't put anything down, you will get it wrong!

3. Turn the question into a statement. Look at the way the questions are worded. The syntax of the question usually provides a clue. Does it seem more familiar as a statement rather than as a question? Does it sound strange?

By turning a question into a statement, you may be able to spot if an answer sounds right, and it may also trigger memories of material you have read.

4. Look for hidden clues. It's actually very difficult to compose multiple-foil (choice) questions without giving away part of the answer in the options presented.

In most multiple-choice questions you can often readily eliminate one or two of the potential answers. This leaves you with only two real possibilities and automatically your odds go to Fifty-Fifty for very little work.

5. Trust your instincts. For every fact that you have read, you subconsciously retain something of that knowledge. On questions that you aren't really certain about, go with your basic instincts. **Your first impression on how to answer a question is usually correct.**

6. Mark your answers directly on the test booklet. Don't bother trying to fill in the optical scan sheet on the first pass through the test.

Just be very careful not to miss-mark your answers when you eventually transcribe them to the scan sheet.

7. Watch the clock! You have a set amount of time to answer the questions. Don't get bogged down trying to answer a single question at the expense of 10 questions you can more readily answer

DOMAIN I.   **UNITED STATES HISTORY**

COMPETENCY 1.1   **PHYSICAL GEOGRAPHY OF NORTH AMERICA**

Skill 1.1a   **Demonstrate knowledge of North America's location in the world and of the continent's rivers, lakes, and important land features**

North America consists of Canada; the United States of America; Mexico; the Caribbean island nations of the West Indies including Cuba, Jamaica, Haiti, and the Dominican Republic; and the "land bridge" of Middle America, including Panama, Honduras, El Salvador, Nicaragua, Guatemala, and others.

At its most northern extreme, Alaska and Canada border the Arctic Ocean. At its most southern extreme, the Isthmus of Panama borders Colombia. The west coast borders the Pacific Ocean, while the east coast borders the Atlantic Ocean, the Caribbean Sea, and the Gulf of Mexico, further southeast.

The major freshwater bodies are the Great Lakes—Huron, Ontario, Michigan, Erie and Superior—which lie between Canada and the United States. The Mississippi River is the longest North American river, extending from the U.S.-Canada border to the Gulf of Mexico, draining the Ohio River from the east and the Missouri River to the west. Other significant rivers are the St. Lawrence, which connects Lake Erie to the Atlantic Ocean, and the Rio Grande, which forms most of the border between Mexico and the United States.

The three most significant mountain ranges are the Appalachian Mountains, which extend from the Canadian Maritime Provinces south to Georgia in the United States along the eastern seaboard; the Rocky Mountains, which extend from west-central Canada through the United States to Mexico; and the Sierra Nevada cordillera, which extends from Alaska in the United States, through Canada, through the west coast of the United States, and through Mexico and Mesoamerica to South America.

Skill 1.1b   Demonstrate knowledge of broad climate patterns and physiographic regions

Climate is average weather or daily weather conditions for a specific region or location over a long or extended period of time. Studying the climate of an area includes information gathered on the area's monthly and yearly temperatures and its monthly and yearly amounts of precipitation. In addition, a characteristic of an area's climate is the length of its growing season. Four reasons for the different climate regions on the earth are differences in the following:

Latitude,
The amount of moisture,
Temperatures in land and water, and
The earth's land surface.

The earth has many different climates. It is most unusual if a country contains just one kind of climate. Regions of climates are divided according to latitudes.

0 - 23½° are the "**low latitudes**"
23½° - 66½° are the "**middle latitudes**"
66½ ° to the Poles are the "**high latitudes**"

The **low latitudes** are composed of the rainforest, savanna, and desert climates. The tropical rainforest climate is found in equatorial lowlands and is hot and wet. There is sun, extreme heat and rain every day. Although daily temperatures rarely rise above 90° F, the daily humidity is always high, leaving everything sticky and damp. North and south of the tropical rainforests are the tropical grasslands called "savannas," the "lands of two seasons" – a winter dry season and a summer wet season. Further north and south of the tropical grasslands or savannas are the deserts. These areas are the hottest and driest parts of the earth, receiving less than 10 inches of annual rainfall. These areas have extreme temperatures between night and day. After the sun sets, the land cools quickly dropping the temperature as much as 50° F.

The **middle latitudes** contain the Mediterranean, humid-subtropical, humid-continental, marine, steppe, and desert climates. Lands containing the Mediterranean climate are considered "sunny" lands found in six areas of the world: lands bordering the Mediterranean Sea, a small portion of southwestern Africa, areas in southern and southwestern Australia, a small part of the Ukraine near the Black Sea, central Chile, and Southern California. Summers are hot and dry with mild winters. The growing season usually lasts all year and what little rain the region gets falls during the winter months. What is rather unusual is that the Mediterranean climate is located between 30 and 40 degrees north and south latitude on the western coasts of countries.

The humid subtropical climate is found north and south of the tropics and is moist indeed. The areas having this type of climate are found on the eastern side of their continents and include the southeastern coasts of Japan, mainland China, Australia, Africa, South America, and the United States. An interesting feature of their locations is the warm ocean currents. The winds that blow across these currents bring in warm moist air all year round. Because of the long, warm summers and short, mild winters, these regions have a long growing season, which means that different crops can be grown several times a year. All contribute to the productivity of this climate type, which supports more people than any of the other climates.

The marine climate is found in Western Europe, the British Isles, the U.S. Pacific Northwest, the western coast of Canada, southern Chile, southern New Zealand and southeastern Australia. A common characteristic of these lands is their proximity to water. The ocean winds are wet and warm bringing a mild, rainy climate to these areas. In the summer, the daily temperatures average at or below 70 degrees Fahrenheit. The temperatures rarely fall below freezing during the winter because of the warming effect of the ocean waters.

In northern and central United States, northern China, south central and southeastern Canada, and the western and southeastern parts of the former Soviet Union, the "climate of four seasons" is found. This humid continental climate has spring, summer, fall, and winter. Cold winters, hot summers, and enough rainfall to grow a variety of crops are the major characteristics of this climate. In areas with the humid continental climate, some of the world's best farmlands and important activities such as trading and mining are found. Differences in temperatures throughout the year are determined by the distance a place is inland, away from the coasts.

The steppe or prairie climate is located in the interiors of the large continents such as Asia and North America. These dry flatlands are far from ocean breezes and are called prairies or the Great Plains in Canada and the United States and steppes in Asia. Although the summers are similar to the humid continental climate, the big difference is in annual rainfall. In the steppe climate, rainfall is light and uncertain, 10 to 20 inches a year, mainly in spring and summer, is considered normal. Where rain is more plentiful, grass grows; in areas of less rain, the steppes or prairies gradually become deserts. These are found in the Gobi Desert of Asia, central and western Australia, southwestern United States, and in the smaller deserts found in Pakistan, Argentina, and Africa south of the Equator.

The two major climates found in the high latitudes are **tundra** and **taiga**. The word tundra meaning marshy plain is a Russian word and aptly describes the climatic conditions in the northern areas of Russia, Europe, and Canada. Winters are extremely cold and very long. For most of the year, the ground is frozen but becomes rather mushy during the very short summer months. Surprisingly less snow falls in the area of the tundra than in the eastern part of the United States. However, because of the harshness of the extreme cold, very few people live there and no crops can be raised. Despite having a small human population, many plants and animals are found there.

The taiga is the northern forest region and is located south of the tundra. The world's largest forestlands are found here along with vast mineral wealth and fur bearing animals. The climate is so extreme that very few people live here; they are not able to grow crops because of the extremely short growing season. The winter temperatures are colder and the summer temperatures are hotter than those in the tundra because the taiga climate region is farther from the waters of the Arctic Ocean. The taiga is found in the northern parts of Russia, Sweden, Norway, Finland, Canada, and Alaska with most of their lands covered with marshes and swamps.

In certain areas of the earth, there exists a type of climate unique to areas with high mountains, usually different from their surroundings. This type of climate is called a "vertical climate" because the temperatures, crops, vegetation, and human activities change and become different as one ascends the different levels of elevation. At the foot of the mountain, one finds a hot and rainy climate and the cultivation of many lowland crops. As one climbs higher, the air becomes cooler, the climate changes sharply, and economic activities change to such endeavors as grazing sheep and growing corn. At the top of many mountains, snow is found year-round.

COMPETENCY 1.2   NATIVE AMERICAN PEOPLES

Skill 1.2a   Demonstrate knowledge of Native American tribes living in the various regions of North America

Strong archaeological evidence supports the contention that the ancestors of today's Native Americans and Latin American Indians crossed the Bering Strait from Asia to Alaska, eventually settling in all parts of the Americas; and evidence suggests that some may have arrived from Asia and the Pacific islands via a more southerly transoceanic seafaring route.

Indigenous peoples of North America have been traditionally divided by anthropologists and ethnologists into mutually unintelligible linguistic groups.

Inuit—In the north, from western Arctic Alaska, across Arctic Canada to the Canadian Maritimes;
Dineh—From interior Alaska to the Sonoran Desert in Mexico (Athapaskan, Apache, Navajo, etc.);
Anishinabe (Algonquian)—Eastern woodlands United States and Canada (Ojibwe, Mohican, Abenaki);
Siouan—Midwestern and western Great Plains of the United States and Canada (Lakota, Dakota, Nakota);
Iroquoian—Northeastern United States and southeastern Canada woodlands (Seneca, Oneida, Mohawk, Onondaga, Cayuga);
Nahuatl—Central Mexico (Aztec);
Mayan—Southern Mexico and Mesoamerica; and
Northwest Indian—Southern Alaska Panhandle through Pacific Coastal Canada to the Oregon coast (Tlingit, Haida, Tsimshian, Nitnat).

Skill 1.2b   Demonstrate understanding of the political, economic, social, and cultural life of Native American peoples

Native American tribes lived throughout what we now call the United States in varying degrees of togetherness. They adopted different customs, pursued different methods of agriculture and food gathering, and made slightly different weapons. They fought among themselves and with other peoples. They had established varying degrees of culture long before Columbus or any other European explorer arrived on the scene.

Perhaps the most famous Native American tribe is the **Algonquians**. We know so much about this tribe because they were one of the first to interact with the newly arrived English settlers in Plymouth, Massachusetts, and elsewhere. The Algonquians lived in wigwams and wore clothing made from animal skins. They were proficient hunters, gatherers, and trappers who also knew quite a bit about farming. Beginning with a brave man named Squanto, they shared this agricultural knowledge with the English settlers, including how to plant and cultivate corn, pumpkins, and squash.

Other famous Algonquians included Pocahontas and her father, Powhatan, both of whom are immortalized in English literature, and Tecumseh and Black Hawk, known foremost for their fierce fighting ability. To the overall Native American culture, they contributed wampum and dream catchers.

Another tribe who lived in the Northeast was the fierce fighting and forward thinking **Iroquois**. They lived in long houses and wore clothes made of buckskin. They, too, were expert farmers, growing the "Three Sisters" (corn, squash, and beans). Five of the Iroquois tribes formed a Confederacy, a shared form of government. The Iroquois also formed the False Face Society, a group of medicine men who shared their medical knowledge with others but kept their identities secret while doing so. These masks are one of the enduring symbols of the Native American era.

Living in the Southeast were the **Seminoles** and **Creeks**, a huge collection of people who lived in chickees (open, bark-covered houses) and wore clothes made from plant fibers. They were expert planters and hunters and were proficient at paddling dugout canoes, which they made. The bead necklaces they created were some of the most beautiful on the continent. They are best known, however, for their struggle against Spanish and English settlers, especially led by the great Osceola.

The **Cherokee** also lived in the Southeast. They were one of the most advanced tribes, living in domed houses and wearing deerskin and rabbit fur. Accomplished hunters, farmers, and fishermen, the Cherokee were known the continent over for their intricate and beautiful basketry and clay pottery. They also played a game called lacrosse, which survives to this day in countries around the world.

In the middle of the continent lived the Plains Tribes, such as the **Sioux, Cheyenne, Blackfeet, Comanche, and Pawnee**. These peoples lived in teepees and wore buffalo skins and feather headdresses. (It is this image of the Native American that has made its way into most American movies depicting the period.) They hunted wild animals on the Plains, especially the buffalo. They were well known for their many ceremonies including the Sun Dance and for the peace pipes that they smoked. Famous Plains people include Crazy Horse and Sitting Bull, authors of the Custer disaster; Sacagawea, leader of the Lewis and Clark expedition; and Chief Joseph, the famous Nez Perce leader.

Dotting the deserts of the Southwest were a handful of tribes, including the famous **Pueblo**, who lived in houses that bear their tribe's name. They wore clothes made of wool and woven cotton, farmed crops in the middle of desert land, created exquisite pottery and Kachina dolls, and had one of the most complex religions of all the tribes. They are perhaps best known for the challenging vista-based villages that they constructed from the sheer faces of cliffs and rocks and for their **adobes**, mud-brick buildings that housed their living and meeting quarters. The Pueblos chose their own chiefs. Their government was perhaps one of the oldest representative governments in the world.

Another well-known Southwestern tribe was the **Apache** and their famous leader **Geronimo**. The Apache lived in homes called wickiups, which were made of bark, grass, and branches. They wore cotton clothing and were excellent hunters and gatherers. Adept at basketry, the Apache believed that everything in Nature had special powers and that they were honored just to be part of it all.

The **Navajo**, also residents of the Southwest, lived in hogans (round homes built with forked sticks) and wore clothes of rabbit skin. Their major contributions to the overall culture of the continent were in sand painting, weapon making, silversmithing, and weaving. Navajo hands crafted some of the most beautiful woven rugs.

Living in the Northwest were the **Inuit**, who lived in tents made from animal skins or, in some cases, igloos. They wore clothes made of animal skins, usually seals or caribou. They were excellent fishermen and hunters and crafted efficient kayaks and umiaks to take them through waterways and harpoons with which to hunt animals. The Inuit are perhaps best known for the great carvings that they left behind. Among these are ivory figures and tall totem poles.

COMPETENCY 1.3   EUROPEAN EXPLORATION AND COLONIZATION

1.3a   Identify the major explorers and the reasons for European exploration

A number of individuals and events led to the time of exploration and discoveries. The Vivaldo brothers and Marco Polo wrote of their travels and experiences, which signaled the early beginnings. Survivors from the Crusades made their way home to different places in Europe. They brought new information about exotic lands, people, customs, and desired foods and goods such as spices and silks.

The Renaissance ushered in a time of curiosity, learning, and incredible energy sparking the desire for trade to procure these new, exotic products and to find better, faster, cheaper trade routes to get to them. The work of geographers, astronomers and mapmakers made important contributions; many studied and applied the work of such men as Hipparchus of Greece, Ptolemy of Egypt, Tycho Brahe of Denmark, and Fra Mauro of Italy.

Portugal made the start under the encouragement, support, and financing of Prince Henry the Navigator. The better known explorers who sailed under the flag of Portugal included Cabral, Diaz, and Vasco da Gama, who successfully sailed all the way from Portugal, around the southern tip of Africa, to Calcutta, India.

Christopher Columbus, sailing for Spain, is credited with the discovery of America although he never set foot on its soil. Magellan is credited with the first circumnavigation of the earth. Other Spanish explorers made their marks in parts of what are now the United States, Mexico, and South America.

For France, claims to various parts of North America were the result of the efforts of such men as Verrazano, Champlain, Cartier, LaSalle, Father Marquette and Joliet. Dutch claims were based on the work of one Henry Hudson. John Cabot gave England its stake in North America along with John Hawkins, Sir Francis Drake, and the half-brothers Sir Walter Raleigh and Sir Humphrey Gilbert.

Actually the first Europeans in the New World were Norsemen led by Eric the Red and later, his son Leif the Lucky. However, before any of these, the ancestors of today's Native Americans and Latin American Indians crossed the Bering Strait from Asia to Alaska, eventually settling in all parts of the Americas.

Skill 1.3b   Demonstrate understanding of the consequences of early contacts between Europeans and Native Americans

The first documented contact between Europeans and Native Americans that has archaeological evidence to support it was the Viking settlement of eastern Canada in 1000 CE. Under the leadership of Leif Eriksson, the Norse immigrants first encountered hostile Inuit in what is now northeastern Quebec and ventured south to Inland, what is now L'ans aux Meadows, to establish a permanent settlement. Again, their encounter with the Native Americans was hostile. Eventually the incessant warfare between the Viking immigrants and the Native Americans was fought under conditions of relative parity of weapons, compelled the Vikings to abandon the Inland settlement, never to return.

The next recorded contact was in 1492 CE, when Christopher Columbus, a Genoese adventurer commanding a squadron of Spanish ships, landed in what is now believed to be the island of Hispaniola, which is now Haiti and the Dominican Republic. Although the Native American inhabitants were initially curious and welcomed the newcomers, hostilities quickly ensued as the Spaniards raided indigenous villages for gold and slaves. Unlike the Vikings of five centuries earlier, the Spaniards had an advantage in arms. They had firearms; however, many of the Native Americans perished as a result of contracting diseases for which they had no immunity. The European and African immigrants brought such diseases as smallpox, measles, shingles, cholera, and influenza. As successive Spanish expeditions established landfalls in Florida, the Gulf Coast, Mesoamerica and other locations, a similar pattern of the search for gold, the taking of native populations for slaves, and the introduction of new diseases spelled disaster for the Native Americans in their early contacts with Europeans.

Skill 1.3c   Demonstrate knowledge of colonization by various European powers

The part of North America claimed by France was called New France. It consisted of the land west of the Appalachian Mountains. This area of claim and settlement included the St. Lawrence Valley, the Great Lakes, the Mississippi Valley, and the entire region of land westward to the Rocky Mountains. They established the permanent settlements of Montreal and New Orleans, thus giving them control of the two major gateways into the heart of North America, the vast, rich interior. The St. Lawrence River, the Great Lakes, and the Mississippi River along with its tributaries made it possible for the French explorers and traders to roam at will, virtually unhindered in exploring, trapping, trading, and furthering the interests of France.

Most of the French settlements were in Canada along the St. Lawrence River. Only scattered forts and trading posts were found in the upper Mississippi Valley and Great Lakes region. The rulers of France originally intended New France to have vast estates owned by nobles and worked by peasants who would live on the estates in compact farming villages—the New World version of the Old World's medieval system of feudalism. However, it didn't work out that way. Each of the nobles wanted his estate to be on the river for ease of transportation. The peasants working the estates also wanted the prime waterfront location. The result of all this real estate squabbling was that New France's settled areas wound up mostly as a string of farmhouses stretching from Quebec to Montreal along the St. Lawrence and Richelieu Rivers.

In the non-settled areas in the interior were the French fur traders. They made friends with the friendly tribes of Indians, spending the winters with them getting the furs needed for trade. In the spring, they would return to Montreal in time to take advantage of trading their furs for the products brought from France, which usually arrived at about the same time. Most of the wealth for New France and its "Mother Country" was from the fur trade, which provided a livelihood for many, many people. Manufacturers and workmen back in France, ship-owners and merchants, as well as the fur traders and their Indian allies all benefited. However, the freedom of roaming and trapping in the interior was a strong enticement for the younger, stronger men and resulted in the French not strengthening the areas settled along the St. Lawrence.

Spanish settlement had its beginnings in the Caribbean with the establishment of colonies on Hispaniola (at Santo Domingo, which became the capital of the West Indies), Puerto Rico, and Cuba. The reasons for Spanish involvement in the Americas included the following:

- the spirit of adventure,
- the desire for land,
- expansion of Spanish power, influence, and empire,
- the desire for great wealth, and
- expansion of Roman Catholic influence and conversion of native peoples.

The first permanent settlement in what is now the United States was in 1565 at St. Augustine, Florida. A later and permanent settlement in the southwestern United States was in 1609 at Santa Fe, New Mexico. At the peak of Spanish power, the area in the United States claimed, settled, and controlled by Spain included Florida and all land west of the Mississippi River. Of course, France and England also lay claim to the same areas. Nonetheless, ranches and missions were built and the Indians who came in contact with the Spaniards were introduced to animals, plants, and seeds from the Old World that they had never seen before. These animals included horses, cattle, donkeys, pigs, sheep, goats, and poultry.

Barrels were cut in half and filled with earth to transport and transplant trees bearing the following:

Apples	Oranges	Limes	Cherries
Pears	Walnuts	Olives	Lemons
Figs	Apricots	Almonds	

Even sugar cane and flowers made it to America along with bags bringing seeds of wheat, barley, rye, flax, lentils, rice, and peas.

All Spanish colonies belonged to the King of Spain. He was considered an absolute monarch with complete or absolute power and claimed rule by divine right—the belief that God had given him the right to rule and he answered only to God for his actions. His word was final and the law. The people had no voice in government. The land, the people, the wealth all belonged to him to use as he pleased. He appointed personal representatives, or viceroys, to rule for him in his colonies. They ruled in his name with complete authority. Since the majority of them were friends and advisers, they were richly rewarded with land grants, gold and silver, privileges of trading, and the right to operate the gold and silver mines.

Spain's control over her New World colonies lasted more than 300 years, longer than that of England or France. To this day, Spanish influence remains in names of places, art, architecture, music, literature, law, and cuisine. The Spanish settlements in North America were not commercial enterprises; they were to protect and defend trading and wealth from their colonies in Mexico and South America. Russians hunting seals came down the Pacific coast, the English moved into Florida and west into and beyond the Appalachians, and the French traders and trappers were making their way from Louisiana and other parts of New France into Spanish territory. The Spanish never realized or understood that self-sustaining economic development and colonial trade was so important. Consequently, the Spanish settlements in the U.S. never really prospered.

Before 1763, when England was rapidly on the way to becoming the most powerful of the three major Western European powers, its thirteen colonies, located between the Atlantic and the Appalachians, physically occupied the least amount of land. Moreover, it is interesting that, even before the Spanish Armada was defeated, two Englishmen, Sir Humphrey Gilbert and his half-brother Sir Walter Raleigh, were unsuccessful in their attempts to build successful permanent colonies in the New World. Nonetheless, the thirteen English colonies were successful and, by the time they had gained their independence from Britain, were more than able to govern themselves. They had a rich historical heritage of law, tradition, and documents leading the way to constitutional government conducted according to laws and customs. The settlers in the British colonies highly valued individual freedom, democratic government, and getting ahead through hard work.

The English colonies, with only a few exceptions, were considered commercial ventures to make a profit for the Crown or the Company or whoever financed its beginnings. One was strictly a philanthropic enterprise and three others were primarily for religious reasons, but the other nine were started for economic reasons. Settlers in these unique colonies came for different reasons:

    a) Religious freedom
    b) Political freedom
    c) Economic prosperity
    d) Land ownership

Skill 1.3d **Demonstrate knowledge of the establishment and growth of the English colonies, including their political, economic, social, and cultural organization and institutions**

The colonies were divided generally into the three regions of **New England, Middle Atlantic, and Southern**. The culture of each was distinct and affected attitudes, ideas towards politics, religion, and economic activities. The geography of each region also contributed to its unique characteristics.

The **New England colonies** consisted of Massachusetts, Rhode Island, Connecticut, and New Hampshire. Life in these colonies was centered on the towns. What farming was done was by each family on its own plot of land; but a short summer growing season and limited amount of good soil gave rise to other economic activities such as manufacturing, fishing, shipbuilding, and trade. The vast majority of the settlers shared similar origins, coming from England and Scotland. Towns were carefully planned and laid out the same way. The form of government was the town meeting, where all adult males met to make the laws. The legislative body, the General Court, consisted of an Upper and Lower House.

The **Middle or Middle Atlantic colonies** included New York, New Jersey, Pennsylvania, Delaware, and Maryland. New York and New Jersey were at one time the Dutch colony of New Netherlands, and Delaware at one time was New Sweden. These five colonies from their beginnings were considered "melting pots," with settlers from many different nations and backgrounds. The main economic activity was farming, with settlers scattered over the countryside cultivating rather large farms. The Indians were not as much of a threat as in New England, so the settlers did not have to settle in small farming villages. The soil was very fertile, the land was gently rolling, and a milder climate provided a longer growing season.

These farms produced a large surplus of food, not only for the colonists themselves but also for sale. This colonial region became known as the "breadbasket" of the New World. The New York and Philadelphia seaports were constantly filled with ships being loaded with meat, flour, and other foodstuffs for the West Indies and England. There were other economic activities such as shipbuilding, iron mines, and factories producing paper, glass, and textiles. The legislative body in Pennsylvania was unicameral or consisted of one house. In the other four colonies, the legislative body had two houses. Also, units of local government were in counties and towns.

The **Southern colonies** were Virginia, North and South Carolina, and Georgia. Virginia was the first permanent successful English colony, and Georgia was the last. 1619 was a very important year in the history of Virginia and the United States with three very significant events. First, sixty women were sent to Virginia to marry and establish families. Second, twenty Africans, the first of thousands, arrived. Third, most importantly, the Virginia colonists were granted the right to self-government and they began by electing their own representatives to the House of Burgesses, their own legislative body.

The major economic activity in this region was farming. Here the soil was very fertile and the climate was very mild with an even longer growing season. The large plantations eventually requiring large numbers of slaves were found in the coastal or tidewater areas. Although the wealthy slave-owning planters set the pattern of life in this region, most of the people lived inland, away from coastal areas. They were small farmers; and very few, it any, owned slaves.

In the colonies, the daily life of the colonists differed greatly between the coastal settlements and the inland or interior. The Southern planters and the people living in the coastal cities and towns had a way of life similar to that in towns in England. The influence was seen and heard in how people dressed and talked. The architectural styles of houses and public buildings and the social divisions or levels of society mimicked that of England. Both the planters and city dwellers enjoyed an active social life and had strong emotional ties to England.

On the other hand, life inland on the frontier had marked differences. All facets of daily living—clothing, food, housing, economic and social activities—were connected to what was needed to sustain life and survive in the wilderness. The produced everything themselves. They were self-sufficient and extremely individualistic and independent. Little, if any, levels of society or class distinctions existed, because they considered themselves to be the equal to all others, regardless of station in life. The roots of equality, independence, individual rights and freedoms were extremely strong and well developed. People were not judged by their fancy dress, expensive houses, eloquent language, or titles following their names.

COMPETENCY 1.4   ESTABLISHING A NEW NATION (1776–1791)

Skill 1.4a   Demonstrate understanding of the American Revolution, including its causes, leaders, events, and results

One historian explained that the British were interested only in raising money to pay war debts, regulate the trade and commerce of the colonies, and look after business and financial interests between England and the rest of her empire. The establishment of overseas colonies was, first and foremost, a commercial enterprise, not a political one. The political aspect was secondary and assumed. The British took it for granted that Parliament was supreme and was recognized as such by the colonists; they were very resentful of the colonial challenge to the British Parliament's authority. They were contemptuously indifferent to politics in America and had no wish to exert any control over it. As resistance and disobedience swelled and increased in America, the British increased their efforts to punish the Americans and put them in their place.

The British had been extremely lax and totally inconsistent in enforcing the mercantile or trade laws passed in the years before 1754. The government itself was not particularly stable, so actions against the colonies occurred in anger and their attitude was one of a moral superiority, that they knew how to manage America better than the Americans did themselves. This, of course, points to a lack of sufficient knowledge of conditions and opinions in America. The colonists had been left on their own for nearly 150 years; and by the time the Revolutionary War began, they were quite adept at self-government and adequately handling the affairs of their daily lives. The Americans equated ownership of land or property with the right to vote. Property was considered the foundation of life and liberty and, in the colonial mind and tradition, these went together.

Therefore, when an indirect tax on tea was made, the British felt that since it wasn't a direct tax, there should be no objection to it. The colonists viewed any tax, direct or indirect, as an attack on their property. They felt that as a representative body, the British Parliament should protect British citizens, including the colonists, from arbitrary taxation. Since they felt they were not represented in Parliament, they had no protection. So, war began. On August 23, 1775, George III declared that the colonies were in rebellion and warned them to stop or else.

By 1776, the colonists and their representatives in the Second Continental Congress realized that things were past the point of no return. The Declaration of Independence was drafted and later declared on July 4, 1776. George Washington labored against tremendous odds to wage a victorious war. The turning point in the Americans' favor occurred in 1777 with the American victory at Saratoga. Because of this victory, the French decided to align themselves with the Americans against the British. With the aid of French warships blocking the entrance to Chesapeake Bay, British General Cornwallis trapped at Yorktown, Virginia, surrendered in 1781 and the war was over. The Treaty of Paris, officially ending the war, was signed in 1783.

During the war, and after independence was declared, the former colonies now found themselves as independent states. The Second Continental Congress was conducting a war with representation by delegates from thirteen separate states. The Congress had no power to act for the states or to require them to accept and follow its wishes. A permanent united government was desperately needed. On November 15, 1777, the Articles of Confederation were adopted, creating a league of free and independent states.

Skill 1.4b   Demonstrate knowledge of the Declaration of Independence and other revolutionary documents

The Declaration of Independence was the founding document of the United States of America. The Articles of Confederation were the first attempt that the newly independent states made to reach a new understanding among themselves with regard to self governance. The Declaration was intended to demonstrate the reasons the colonies were seeking separation from Great Britain. For the most part conceived and written by Thomas Jefferson, the Declaration is not only important for what it says, but also for how it says it. The Declaration is, in many respects, a poetic document. Instead of a simple recitation of the colonists' grievances, it set out clearly the reasons for the colonists' seeking their freedom from Great Britain. They had tried all means to resolve the dispute peacefully. It was the right of a people, when all other methods of addressing their grievances have been tried and failed, to separate themselves from that power that was keeping them from fully expressing their rights to **"life, liberty, and the pursuit of happiness."**

By 1776, the colonists and their representatives in the Second Continental Congress realized that things were past the point of no return. The Declaration of Independence was drafted and later declared on July 4, 1776. Jefferson authored the Declaration of Independence with assistance from Benjamin Franklin and John Adams. After a long string of inequities imposed by the British government without the consent of the American Colonists, taxation by Parliament, and impositions such as the quartering of British troops without recompense to the hosts, the Continental Congress resolved to address these grievances by a unanimous declaration to break away from the Crown.

American colonists in the English colonies had always considered themselves to be citizens of Great Britain and loyal subjects of the British Crown (with all the traditional rights and privileges pursuant to that status). They had lived their lives as free men and developed their own town governments and colonial legislatures based on beliefs and principles that traced back through English history to the time of Magna Carta. They had always been vocal participants in their own social, cultural and political development—unique, but considered by them to be British in its essence.

These colonists also had their own tradition of publishing the views and sentiments of individuals regarding issues of parochial interest and matters of concern that crossed colonial boundaries. In print—through newspapers and pamphlets—dialogue and debate over matters quite trivial or quite significant became common public practice in the American colonies. As strains with the mother country began to develop and increase—especially after the French and Indian War—the resulting issues became increasingly focused in print throughout the colonies. No doubt the discussions and debates published carried their sentiments over to the homes, taverns, and other places where the people met to discuss events of the day. An important result of this was a growing "Americanism" in the sentiments of those writers published, and a sense of connection among American people that transcended colonial boundaries.

From the initial Stamp Act in 1765, through the "Boston Massacre" in 1770, to the time of the Tea Act in 1773, which resulted in the "Boston Tea Party," and beyond, colonial presses were rife with discussion and debate about what they considered to be an unacceptable situation. Parliament intended to assert its right to tax and legislatively control the colonies of Great Britain in whatever manner it saw as prudent and appropriate. Most American colonists, believing themselves to be full British subjects, would deny Parliament's assertions so long as they were not provided with full and equal representation within Parliament.

One of the most notable spokesmen for the American cause was, in fact, an Englishman. Thomas Paine (1737-1809) came to America in November 1774. He was immediately taken up by the social issues and politics in the American colonies and insinuated himself into the dialogue of current issues, which was ongoing and conducted through newspapers and pamphlets. Within months of his arrival, he published his first article in America. Interestingly, his first address to the American public would presage the elaborate exposition of tyranny versus the natural rights of humans to be and act free, which would color and popularize his writings during the war years. But his topic at the time—his bold statement and unusual public stand—was African slavery.

He is best remembered for *Common Sense*. In a number of publications, spanning the war years (from 1776 through 1783), Thomas Paine wrote a series of addresses, inspiring the American people and reprimanding British authorities. One of his most famous publications, produced at a time of ill fortune for the American cause and disenchantment for many members of the fledgling American Army, began,

> THESE are the times that try men's souls. The summer soldier and the sunshine patriot will, in this crisis, shrink from the service of their country; but he that stands it now, deserves the love and thanks of man and woman. Tyranny, like hell, is not easily conquered; yet we have this consolation with us, that the harder the conflict, the more glorious the triumph.

The writings of Thomas Paine and the impact of the publication of *Common Sense* were credited with influencing Congress and the populace at large to declare independence.

Other authors, printers, publishers, and factions were also active in promoting the new American attitude toward independence. Of significant note was the **Virginia Declaration of Rights**, drafted by George Mason in May 1776 and amended by Thomas Ludwell Lee and the Virginia Convention. Thomas Jefferson was influenced by it when he drafted the Declaration of Independence only a month later. This document would also influence James Madison when drawing up the Bill of Rights (1789) and Marquis de Lafayette when he drafted the French Declaration of the Rights of Man and Citizen (1789).

The Declaration of Independence can be divided into three main parts

1. Statements of the general state of humanity and the natural rights inherent in all civil societies. Jefferson talks about "self-evident" truths, unalienable rights of people to "Life, Liberty and the pursuit of Happiness" which show considerable influence from primarily French thinkers of the Enlightenment during the 17th and 18th Centuries. He also clearly states that a government that no longer respects these inherent rights loses its legitimacy and has become despotic, and the governed have the right to throw off such a government, a call for insurrection against the sovereign.

2. An enumeration of specific and detailed grievances, which point out why the current sovereign has lost the right to govern. It also lists how the king even subverted English Common Law and legal traditions dating back to antiquity.

3. The last part of the text states that the colonists had exhausted all civil and legal means of having their grievances addressed by British government, and now had the right and duty to break with the crown and be a free and independent nation.

The final section of the Declaration contains the signatures of the representatives of the colonies to the Continental Congress in Philadelphia. Realizing that they had committed an act of treason, punishable by death by hanging, Benjamin Franklin counseled unity, lest they all hang separately. It should also be noted that, at that moment, open hostilities between British and Colonists had already been under way for more than a year. George Washington had taken command of the Continental Army, organized on June 14, 1775, at Harvard Yard, and, in the same year, the Continental Navy and the Marine Corps had been organized.

Skill 1.4c **Demonstrate knowledge of the first government of the United States under the Articles of Confederation**

Articles of Confederation—This document outlined the first political system under which the newly independent colonies tried to organize themselves. It was drafted in 1776 after the Declaration of Independence, passed by the Continental Congress on November 15, 1777, ratified by the thirteen states, and took effect on March 1, 1781. (See http://www.usconstitution.net/articles.html)

The newly independent states were unwilling to give too much power to a national government. They were already fighting Great Britain. They did not want to replace one harsh ruler with another. After many debates, the form of the Articles was accepted. Each state agreed to send delegates to the Congress, and had one vote. The Articles gave Congress the power to declare war, appoint military officers, and coin money. The Congress was also responsible for foreign affairs. The Articles of Confederation limited the powers of the Congress by giving the states final authority. Although Congress could pass laws, at least nine of the thirteen states had to approve a law before it went into effect. Congress could not pass any laws regarding taxes. To get money, Congress had to ask each state for it; no state could be forced to pay.

Thus, the Articles created a loose alliance among the thirteen states. The national government was weak, in part, because it didn't have a strong chief executive to carry out laws passed by the legislature. This weak national government might have worked if the states had been able to get along with each other. However, many different disputes arose, and they had no way to settle them. Thus, the delegates met again to try to fix the Articles; instead they scraped them and created a new Constitution that benefited from these earlier mistakes.

The central government of the new United States of America consisted of a Congress of two to seven delegates from each state with each state having just one vote. The government under the Articles solved some of the postwar problems but had serious weaknesses. Some of its powers included borrowing and coining money, directing foreign affairs, declaring war and making peace, building and equipping a navy, regulating weights and measures, and asking the states to supply men and money for an army. The delegates to Congress had no real authority as each state carefully and jealously guarded its own interests and limited powers under the Articles. Also, the delegates to Congress were paid by their states and had to vote as directed by their state legislatures. The serious weaknesses were the lack of power to regulate finances, oversee interstate and foreign trade, enforce treaties, and oversee the military. Something better and more efficient was needed.

In May of 1787, delegates from all states except Rhode Island began meeting in Philadelphia. At first, they met to revise the Articles of Confederation as instructed by Congress. However, they soon realized that much more was needed. Abandoning the instructions, they set out to write a new Constitution, the foundation of all government in the United States and a model for representative government throughout the world.

The first order of business was the agreement among all the delegates that the convention would be kept secret. No discussion of the convention outside of the meeting room would be allowed. They wanted to be able to discuss, argue, and agree among themselves before presenting the completed document to the American people.

The delegates were afraid that if the people were aware of what was taking place before it was completed, the entire country would be plunged into argument and dissension. It would be extremely difficult, if not impossible, to settle differences and come to an agreement. Between the official notes kept and the complete notes of future President James Madison, an accurate picture of the events of the Convention is part of the historical record.

The delegates went to Philadelphia representing different areas and different interests. They all agreed on a strong central government but not one with unlimited powers.

They also agreed that no one part of government could control the rest. It would be a republican form of government (sometimes referred to as representative democracy) in which the supreme power was in the hands of the voters who would elect the men who would govern for them.

One of the first serious controversies involved equal representation in Congress. Vehement disagreement arose between the small states and the large states. Virginia's Governor Edmund Randolph proposed that state population determine the number of representatives sent to Congress, also known as the Virginia Plan. New Jersey delegate William Paterson countered with what is known as the New Jersey Plan, each state having equal representation.

After much argument and debate, they devised the **Great Compromise** also known as the Connecticut Compromise, proposed by Roger Sherman. It was agreed that Congress would have two houses. A Senate would consist of two Senators from each state, giving equal representation in the Senate. The number of members elected to the House of Representatives would be based on each state's population. Both houses could draft bills to debate and vote on with the exception of bills pertaining to money, which must originate in the House of Representatives.

Another major controversy involved economic differences between North and South. One issue concerned the counting of African slaves when determining representation in the House of Representatives. The southern delegates wanted this them counted for representation, but did not want the number of slaves to determine taxes to be paid. The northern delegates argued the opposite: count the slaves for taxes but not for representation. The resulting agreement was known as the "three-fifths" compromise. Three-fifths of the slaves would be counted for both taxes and determining representation in the House.

The last major compromise, also between North and South, was the **Commerce Compromise**. The economic interests of the northern part of the country were ones of industry and business whereas the south's economic interests were primarily agricultural. The Northern merchants wanted the government to regulate and control commerce with foreign nations and with the states. Of course, Southern planters opposed this idea because they felt that any tariff laws passed would be unfavorable to them. The acceptable compromise to this dispute was that Congress was given the power to regulate commerce with other nations and the states, including levying tariffs on imports. However, Congress did not have the power to levy tariffs on any exports. This increased Southern concern about the effect it would have on the slave trade. The delegates finally agreed that the importation of slaves would continue for 20 more years with no interference from Congress. Any import tax could not exceed 10 dollars per person. After 1808, Congress would be able to decide whether to prohibit or regulate any further slave importation.

Of course, when work was completed and the document was presented, nine states had to approve it before it could go into effect. There was no little amount of discussion, arguing, debating, and haranguing. The opposition had the following three major objections:

> 1) The states seemed as if they were being asked to surrender too much power to the national government.
> 2) The voters did not have enough control and influence over the men who would be elected by them to run the government.
> 3) The document lacked a "bill of rights" guaranteeing hard-won individual freedoms and liberties.

Eleven states finally ratified the document and the new national government went into effect. It was no small feat that the delegates were able to produce a workable document that satisfied all opinions, feelings, and viewpoints. The separation of powers of the three branches of government and the built-in system of checks and balances to keep power balanced were a stroke of genius. It provided for the individuals and the states and an organized central authority to keep a new, inexperienced nation on track. They created a system of government so flexible that it has continued in its basic form to this day. In 1789, the Electoral College unanimously elected George Washington as the first President and the new nation was on its way.

Skill 1.4d   Demonstrate understanding of the process of writing and adopting the Constitution and the Bill of Rights

The central government of the new United States of America consisted of a Congress of two to seven delegates from each state, with each state having just one vote. The government under the Articles solved some of the postwar problems but had serious weaknesses.

Some of its powers included borrowing and coining money, directing foreign affairs, declaring war and making peace, building and equipping a navy, regulating weights and measures, and asking the states to supply men and money for an army. The delegates to Congress had no real authority as each state carefully and jealously guarded its own interests and limited powers under the Articles. Also, the delegates to Congress were paid by their states and had to vote as directed by their state legislatures.

The serious weaknesses were the lacks of power. They could not regulate finances, interstate trade, or foreign trade and could not enforce treaties and retain military power. Something better and more efficient was needed. In May of 1787, delegates from all states except Rhode Island began meeting in Philadelphia. At first, they met to revise the Articles of Confederation as instructed by Congress; but they soon realized that much more was needed. Abandoning the instructions, they set out to write a new Constitution, the foundation of all government in the United States and a model for representative government throughout the world.

The beginnings of civil liberties and the idea of civil rights in the United States go back to the ideas of the Greeks. The early struggles for civil rights and the very philosophies that led people to come to the New World in the first place— religious freedom, political freedom, and the right to live one's life as one sees fit—are basic to the American ideal. These ideas are embodied in the Declaration of Independence and the Constitution.

All these ideas found their final expression in the United States Constitution's first ten amendments, known as the Bill of Rights. In 1789, the first Congress passed these amendments and by December, 1791, three-fourths of the states at that time had ratified them. The Bill of Rights protects certain liberties and basic rights. James Madison, who wrote the amendments, said that the Bill of Rights does not give Americans these rights. According to Madison, people already have these rights. They are natural rights that belong to all human beings. The Bill of Rights simply prevents the government from taking away these rights.

The first amendment guarantees the basic rights of freedom of religion, freedom of speech, freedom of the press, and freedom of assembly.

Freedom of Religion: Religious freedom has not been seriously threatened in the United States historically. The policy of the government has been guided by the premise of a separation between church and state. When religious practices have been at cross-purposes with attitudes prevailing in the nation at particular times, these practices have been restricted. Some of these restrictions have been against the practice of polygamy that is supported by certain religious groups. The idea of animal sacrifice that is promoted by some religious beliefs is generally prohibited. The use of mind-altering illegal substances that some use in religious rituals has been restricted. In the United States, all recognized religious institutions are tax-exempt in following the idea of separation of church and state, and therefore, many quasi-religious groups have in the past tried to take advantage of this fact. All of these issues continue, and most likely will continue to occupy both political and legal considerations for some time to come.

Freedom of Speech, Press, and Assembly: These rights historically have been given wide latitude in their practices. However, in some instances, one or the other have been limited for various reasons. The classic limitation, for example, in regards to freedom of speech has been the famous precept that an individual is prohibited from yelling "Fire!" in a crowded theatre. This prohibition is an example of the state saying that freedom of speech does not extend to speech that might endanger other people. We also have a prohibition against slander or the knowingly stating of a deliberately falsehood against one party by another. Also many regulations exist regarding freedom of the press; the most common are the various laws against libel (or the printing of a known falsehood). In times of national emergency, various restrictions have been placed on the rights of press, speech, and sometimes assembly.

The next three amendments came out of the colonists' struggle with Great Britain. For example, the third amendment prevents Congress from forcing citizens to keep troops in their homes. Before the Revolution, Great Britain tried to coerce the colonists to house soldiers.

Amendments five through eight protect citizens who are accused of crimes and brought to trial. Every citizen has the right to due process of law (*due process*, as defined earlier, is that the government must follow the same fair rules for everyone brought to trial.) These rules include the right to a trial by an impartial jury, the right to be defended by a lawyer, and the right to a speedy trial.

The last two amendments limit the powers of the federal government to those that are expressly granted in the Constitution; any rights not expressly mentioned in the Constitution, thus, belong to the states or to the people.

The legal system in recent years has undergone a number of serious changes (some would say challenges) with the interpretation of some constitutional guarantees.

COMPETENCY 1.5   EARLY YEARS OF THE NEW NATION (1791–1829)

Skill 1.5a   Demonstrate understanding of political development, including early presidential administrations, establishment of the federal judiciary, and inception and growth of political parties

The early presidential administrations established much of the form and many of the procedures still present today, including the development of the party system. George Washington, the first U.S. President, established a cabinet form of government. In this form, individual advisors oversee the various functions of the executive branch and advise the President, who makes a final decision. Divisions within his cabinet and within Congress during his administration eventually led to the development of political parties, which Washington opposed. Washington was also instrumental in establishing the power of the federal government when he rode at the head of militia forces to put down a rebellion in Pennsylvania. He was elected to two terms and served from 1789 to 1797.

Washington's Vice President, John Adams, was elected to succeed him. Adams' administration was marked by the new nation's first entanglement in international affairs. With Britain and France at war, Adams' Federalist Party supported the British and Vice President Thomas Jefferson's Republican Party supported the French. The nation was nearly brought to the brink of war with France, but Adams managed to negotiate a treaty that avoided full conflict. In the process, however, he lost the support of his party and was defeated after one term by Thomas Jefferson.

The two parties that developed through the early 1790s were led by Jefferson as the Secretary of State and Alexander Hamilton as the Secretary of the Treasury. Jefferson and Hamilton were different in many ways — not the least of which were their views on what should be the proper form of government of the United States. This difference helped to shape the parties that formed around them.

Hamilton wanted the federal government to be stronger than the state governments. Jefferson believed that the state governments should be stronger. Hamilton supported the creation of the first Bank of the United States, while Jefferson opposed it because he felt that it gave too much power to wealthy investors who would help run it. Jefferson interpreted the Constitution strictly and argued that the Constitution does not grant the federal government the power to create a national bank. Hamilton interpreted the Constitution much more loosely. He pointed out that the Constitution gave Congress the power to make all laws "necessary and proper" to carry out its duties. He reasoned that since Congress had the right to collect taxes, then Congress had the right to create the bank. Hamilton wanted the government to encourage economic growth. He favored the growth of trade, manufacturing, and the rise of cities as the necessary parts of economic growth. He favored the business leaders and mistrusted the common people.

Jefferson believed that the common people, especially the farmers, were the backbone of the nation. He thought that the rise of big cities and manufacturing would corrupt American life.

Finally, Hamilton and Jefferson had their disagreements only in private. But when Congress began to pass many of Hamilton's ideas and programs, Jefferson and his friend James Madison decided to organize support for their own views. They moved quietly and very cautiously in the beginning. In 1791, they went to New York telling people that they were going to study its wildlife. Actually, Jefferson was more interested in meeting with several important New York politicians such as its governor, George Clinton, and Aaron Burr, a strong critic of Hamilton. Jefferson asked Clinton and Burr to help defeat Hamilton's program by getting New Yorkers to vote for Jefferson's supporters in the next election. Before long, leaders in other states began to organize support for either Jefferson or Hamilton. Jefferson's supporters called themselves Democratic-Republicans (often this was shortened just to Republicans, though in actuality it was the forerunner of today's Democratic Party). Meanwhile, Hamilton and his supporters were known as Federalists, because they favored a strong federal government. The Federalists had the support of the merchants and ship owners in the Northeast and some planters in the South. Small farmers, craft workers, and some of the wealthier landowners supported Jefferson and the Democratic-Republicans.

Article III of the US Constitution created a Supreme Court and authorized Congress to create other federal courts as it deemed necessary. In 1789, Congress passed the **Judiciary Act**, which set the number of Supreme Court justices at six, with one Chief Justice and five associates. The Judiciary Act also created 13 judicial districts, each with one district judge who was authorized to hear maritime and other types of cases. Most federal trial cases were heard by circuit courts, which were originally made up of two Supreme Court justices and the local district judge. In 1793, Congress changed the circuit court to one Supreme Court justice and the local district judge.

In 1801, the Federalist majority in Congress sought to place more power in the district courts and removed the requirement that a Supreme Court justice preside over circuit courts. The following year, however, Jeffersonian Republicans took the majority in Congress and reversed this decision. As the demands of the growing nation increased in the following decades, the federal judiciary system was expanded by adding Supreme Court justices and enlarging the district and circuit systems.

Skill 1.5b   Demonstrate understanding of foreign policy issues, including the Louisiana Purchase, the War of 1812, and the Monroe Doctrine

The next large territorial gain was under President Thomas Jefferson in 1803. In 1800, Napoleon Bonaparte of France secured the Louisiana Territory from Spain, which had held it since 1792. The vast area stretched westward from the Mississippi River to the Rocky Mountains and northward to Canada. An effort was made to keep the transaction a secret, but the news reached the U.S. State Department. The U.S. did not have a particular problem with Spanish control of the territory since Spain was weak and was not a threat to America. However, the relationship with France was different. Though not the world power that Great Britain was, France was still strong and under, Napoleon's leadership, was again acquiring an empire. President Jefferson had three major reasons for concern.

   a. With the French controlling New Orleans at the mouth of the Mississippi River and the Gulf of Mexico, westerners would lose their *right of deposit*, which would greatly affect their ability to trade. This right was very important to the Americans who were living in the area between the Mississippi and the Appalachians. They were unable to get heavy products to eastern markets but had to float them on rafts down the Ohio and Mississippi Rivers to New Orleans to ships heading to Europe or the Atlantic coast ports. If France prohibited this, it would be a financial disaster for the Americans.

   b. President Jefferson also worried that if the French possessed the Louisiana Territory, America would be extremely limited in its expansion into its interior.

   c. Under Napoleon Bonaparte, France was becoming more powerful and aggressive. This increase in power would be a constant worry and threat to the western border of the U.S. President Jefferson was very interested in the western part of the country and firmly believed that it was both necessary and desirable to strengthen western lands. So Jefferson wrote to the American Minister to France, Robert R. Livingston, to offer Napoleon up to $10 million for New Orleans and West Florida. Napoleon countered the offer with the question of how much the U.S. would be willing to pay for all of Louisiana. After some discussion, it was agreed to pay $15 million and the largest land transaction in history was negotiated in 1803, resulting in the eventual formation of 15 states.

In 1804, the United States engaged in the first of a series of armed conflicts with the Barbary pirates of North Africa. The Moslem rulers of Morocco, Algiers, Tunis, and Tripoli—the Barbary States of North Africa—had long been seizing ships of nations that were Christian and demanding ransoms for the crews. The Christian nations of Europe decided it was cheaper and easier to pay an annual tribute or bribe. The U.S. had been doing this since 1783 when trade between the Mediterranean countries and the newly independent nation begam. When the rulers in Tripoli demanded a ridiculously high bribe and chopped down the flagpole of the American consulate there, Jefferson had had enough. The first skirmish against Tripoli in 1804 and 1805 was successful. In 1815, the payment of bribes to the rulers ceased. The Americans could trade and sail freely in the Mediterranean.

The United States' unintentional and accidental involvement in the **War of 1812** came about because of the political and economic struggles between France and Great Britain. Napoleon's goal was complete conquest and control of Europe, including (and especially) Great Britain. Although British troops were temporarily driven off the mainland of Europe, the navy still controlled the seas across which France had to bring the products needed. America traded with both nations, especially with France and its colonies. The British decided to destroy the American trade with France, mainly for the following two reasons: (a) products and goods from the U.S. gave Napoleon what he needed to keep up his struggle with Britain. Napoleon and France were the enemy, and it was felt that the Americans were aiding the Mother Country's enemy. (b) Britain felt threatened by the increasing strength and success of the U.S. merchant fleet. They were becoming major competitors with the ship owners and merchants in Britain.

The British issued the Orders in Council, a series of measures prohibiting American ships from entering any French ports, not only in Europe but also in India and the West Indies. At the same time, Napoleon began efforts for a coastal blockade of the British Isles. He issued a series of Orders prohibiting all nations, including the United States, from trading with the British. And he didn't stop there. He threatened seizure of every ship entering any French ports after they stopped at any British port or British colony, even threatening to seize every ship inspected by British cruisers or that paid any duties to their government. Adding to all of this, the British were stopping American ships and seizing, or impressing, American seamen to service on British ships. Americans were outraged.

In 1807, Congress passed the **Embargo Act,** forbidding American ships from sailing to foreign ports. This embargo could not be completely enforced, and it really hurt business and trade in America, and it was repealed in 1809. Two additional acts passed by Congress after James Madison became president attempted to regulate trade with other nations and to have Britain and France remove the restrictions they had put on American shipping. The catch was that, whichever nation removed restrictions, the U.S. agreed not to trade with the other one. Napoleon was clever and the first to do this, prompting Madison to issue orders prohibiting trade with Britain, ignoring warnings from the British not to do so. Of course, this did not work either, and although Britain eventually rescinded the Orders in Council, war came in June of 1812 and ended Christmas Eve, 1814, with the signing of the Treaty of Ghent.

During the War of 1812, Americans were divided over not only whether or not it was necessary to fight, but also what territories they should fight for and take. The nation was still young and just not prepared to fight another war. The primary American objective was to conquer Canada, but it failed.

Two naval victories and one military victory stand out for the United States. Oliver Perry gained control of Lake Erie, and Thomas MacDonough fought on Lake Champlain. Both of these naval battles successfully prevented the British invasion of the United States from Canada. Nevertheless, the troops landed on the Potomac, below Washington D.C., marched into the city, and burned the public buildings, including the White House. Andrew Jackson's victory at New Orleans was a great morale boost to Americans, giving them the impression the U.S. had won the war. However, the battle actually took place after Britain and the United States had reached an agreement and it had no impact on the war's outcome. The peace treaty did little for United States' territorial expansion, but it did bring peace, release prisoners of war, restore all occupied territory, and set up a commission to settle boundary disputes with Canada. Interestingly, the war proved to be a turning point in American history. Since then, European events have profoundly shaped U.S. policies, especially foreign policies.

In President Monroe's message to Congress on December 2, 1823, he delivered the Monroe Doctrine. The United States was informing the powers of the Old World that the American continents were no longer open to European colonization and that any effort to extend European political influence into the New World would be considered by the United States "as dangerous to our peace and safety." The United States would not interfere in European wars or internal affairs and expected Europe to stay out of American affairs.

Skill 1.5c   Demonstrate understanding of economic development, including Hamilton's economic plan, tariffs, and changes in agriculture, commerce, and industry

In domestic affairs of the new nation, the first problems dealt with finances—paying for the war debts of the Revolutionary War and other financial needs. Secretary of the Treasury Alexander Hamilton wanted the government to increase tariffs and put taxes on certain products made in the U.S., for example, liquor. This money in turn would be used to pay war debts of the federal government and states. Money would be available for expenses and needed internal improvements.

To provide for this, Hamilton favored a national bank. Secretary of State Thomas Jefferson, along with southern supporters, opposed many of Hamilton's suggested plans. Later, Jefferson relented and gave support to some proposals. In return, Hamilton and his northern supporters agreed to locate the nation's capital in the South. Jefferson continued to oppose a national bank, but Congress set up the first one in 1791, chartered for the next 20 years.

Hamilton's plans and the creation of the bank had an immediate effect on the economics of the new nation. With the creation of paper securities, finance became more liquid, allowing for the creation of a stock market fueled by speculation. These securities could be used as collateral for loans to provide for expansion in industry and the creation of infrastructure such as roads, canals and bridges, which expanded the market for agricultural products. Foreign investment was also stimulated, and exports increased.

Skill 1.5d **Demonstrate understanding of social and cultural development in this period, including immigration and the frontier, family life and the role of women, religious life, and nationalism and regionalism**

During the years from 1791 to 1829, Americans were gradually becoming a new and distinct people. The heritage of European colonialism had provided the colonies with many traditions and social practices that were gradually abandoned. Some of the more common customs and traditions that blended well with the changing attitudes of the American people continued to be practiced for several decades to come. This was true of many common business practices and traditional mores regarding proper and appropriate social interactions. Concern over European intrigues and a second war against Great Britain served to help the American people distance themselves more and more from any reliance on—and old connections with—the European nations.

Immigration continued and increased during this period, especially as new territories opened for exploration and settlement. Most of the new arrivals came from the same Western European countries as the original colonists. But soon, immigrants represented a greater mix of non-English residents and an increasing membership in religious faiths other than the traditional Protestant denominations, including Roman Catholics and Jews. The major exception to the ethnicity of most immigrants to the United States through much of this period, continued to be African slaves, imported against their will to provide a chattel labor force.

Because of compromises made by the federal government with certain states, Congress was unable to act against the importation of slaves and the slave trade until January 1, 1808. At that time, a bill was unanimously passed forbidding the importation of slaves. However, since smuggling slaves was lucrative and difficult for the government to control, the illicit trade continued for more than decade. During this time, tens of thousands of additional African slaves were brought into the United States. Finally, in 1819 Congress declared this practice to be piracy. We have no record that any of the practitioners were ever condemned as pirates, but the effort by the federal government seemed to have the desired effect. Of course, the internal trade and sale of slaves continued to flourish until the Civil War, becoming far more lucrative when importation ceased.

Abigail Adams was a unique individual, but not necessarily an unusual woman for her time. Women of this period lived lives—and had attitudes about life—which might seem quite alien to American people today. The same could be said about men's lives and attitudes. Most people of the time believed there were definite distinctions regarding what it meant to be a woman and what it meant to be a man. They were aware of these distinctions in the natural world and saw them reinforced in the religious doctrine of their faiths.

Social customs, traditions, and the practices of lawmaking institutions adopted these distinctions or were adapted to conform to socially acceptable conventions. These conditions were generally accepted by women and men, alike: there were roles for men and there were roles for women—just as there were garments appropriate to each sex.

While most women were excluded from the franchise (they were not allowed to vote), many men were excluded as well. Slaves of either sex could not vote. Freedmen were often prevented from voting. And in various jurisdictions—federal, state, county, municipal elections, etc., a man could be prohibited from voting because of poverty, lack of property ownership, inability to write, or any one of many restrictions intended to limit the franchise.

Some women during this period had the right to vote and participated in the election process. These women were usually residents of new territories, which did not adhere to the restrictions of the various states. When these territories eventually became states, however, these women were excluded from this process. Women did enjoy the right to vote in one state—New Jersey. This right was granted to women in the adoption of the constitution of New Jersey in 1776, but this right was revoked in 1807.

There was very little agitation for the extension of the franchise to women during this period. The true struggle would begin several decades later, and women's suffrage would not be finally accomplished for nearly a century. But women did have their spheres of influence. Their influences were in the home and family as well as in the social, rather than political, aspects of the community. Women organized for the betterment of their community and the society in which they lived. As individuals and in groups they influenced the development and maintenance of religious and educational institutions and those establishments, that provided for the sick and indigent. Through their families and specifically the male members in their role as voters, they influenced the political life of the community as well. It would be an unwise political candidate who proposed a platform that the women of the community would not support.

But political organization and agitation for women were still far in the future. During this period, women of notable accomplishment tended to act as individuals. For example, the Troy Female Seminary was opened in New York by Emma Willard in 1821 to provide an exemplary curriculum for girls. In 1825, Frances Wright established her own Utopian community in Nashoba, Tennessee.

In this new country—this new land—there was a sense of youthful vigor and a view to new opportunities and new ideas. For many, these ideals held true as much in their spiritual life as in any other aspect of life. Many Americans seemed to be seeking something new and meaningful.

The Second Great Awakening was an evangelical Protestant revival that preached personal responsibility for one's actions both individually and socially. This movement was led by preachers, including Charles Finney, who traveled the country preaching the gospel of social responsibility. This point of view was taken up by the "mainline Protestant denominations" (Episcopal, Methodist, Presbyterian, Lutheran, Congregational, etc.). Part of the social reform movement that led to an end to child labor, to better working conditions, and to other changes in social attitudes, arose from this new recognition that the Christian faith should be expressed for the good of society.

Closely allied to the Second Great Awakening was the **temperance movement**. This movement to end the sale and consumption of alcohol arose from religious beliefs, the violence many women and children experienced from heavy drinkers, and from the effect of alcohol consumption on the work force. The Society for the Promotion of Temperance was organized in Boston in 1826.

Other social issues were also addressed. It was during this period that efforts were made to transform the prison system and its emphasis on punishment into a penitentiary system that attempted rehabilitation. It was also during this period that Dorothea Dix led a struggle in the North and the South to establish hospitals for the insane.

Utopianism is the dream of or the desire to create the perfect society. However, by the nineteenth century, few believed this was possible. One of the major "causes" of utopianism is the desire for moral clarity. Against the backdrop of the efforts of a young nation to define itself and to ensure the rights and freedoms of its citizens and within the context of the second great awakening, it becomes quite easy to see how the reform movements, the religious sentiment, and the gathering national storm would lead to the rise of expressions of desire to create the perfect society.

As the new country began to stretch its boundaries physically, new territories and opportunities were opened up to new and old Americans, alike. New concepts such as regionalism and sectionalism began to take on more meaning.

Regionalism is the political division of an area into partially autonomous regions or to loyalty to the interests of a particular region. **Sectionalism** is generally defined as excessive devotion to local interests and customs.

When the United States declared independence from England, the founding fathers created a political point of view that created national unity while respecting the uniqueness and individual rights of each of the thirteen colonies or states. The colonies had been populated and governed by England and other countries. Some came to America in search of religious freedom, others for a fresh start and others for economic opportunity. Each colony had a particular culture and identity.

As the young nation grew, territories came to be defined as states. The states began to acquire their own particular cultures and identities. In time, regional interests and cultures also began to take shape. Religious interests, economic life, and geography began to be understood as definitive of particular regions. The northeast tended toward industrial development. The south tended to rely upon agriculture. The west was an area of untamed open spaces where people settled and practiced agriculture and animal husbandry.

Each of these regions came to be defined, at least to some extent, on the basis of the way people made their living and the economic and social institutions that supported them. In the industrialized North, the factory system tended to create a division between the business and industry tycoons and the poor industrial workers. The conditions in which the labor force worked were far from ideal—long work days, poor conditions, and minimal pay.

The South was characterized by cities that were centers of social and commercial life. The agriculture that supported the region was practiced on "plantations," which were owned by the wealthy and worked by slaves or indentured servants.

The west was a vast expanse to be explored and tamed. Life on a western ranch was distinctly different from life in either the industrial North or the agricultural South. The challenges of each region were also distinctly different. For example, the roles of women and children assumed in the Northern and Southern economies were different, as was the importance of trade. Religion was called upon to support each unique regional lifestyle.

The regional differences between North and South came to a head over the issue of slavery. The rise of the abolitionist movement in the North, the publication of *Uncle Tom's Cabin*, and issues of trade and efforts by the national government to control trade for the regions coalesced around the issue of slavery in a nation that was founded on the principle of the inalienable right of every person to be free. As the South defended its lifestyle and its economy and the right of the states to be self-determining, the North became stronger in its criticism of slavery. The result was a growing sectionalism between the North and the South.

COMPETENCY 1.6   CONTINUED NATIONAL DEVELOPMENT (1829–1850S)

Skill 1.6a   **Demonstrate understanding of political development, including Jacksonian democracy, the nullification crisis , Manifest Destiny, the Mexican War and Cession, and the Oregon Territory**

The election of Andrew Jackson as President signaled a swing of the political pendulum from government influence of the wealthy, aristocratic Easterners to the interests of the Western farmers and pioneers and the era of the "common man." Jacksonian Democracy was a policy of equal political power for all. After the War of 1812, Henry Clay and supporters favored economic measures that came to be known as the American System. This involved tariffs protecting American farmers and manufacturers from having to compete with foreign products, stimulating industrial growth and employment. With more people working, more farm products would be consumed, prosperous farmers would be able to buy more manufactured goods, and the additional monies from tariffs would make it possible for the government to make the needed internal improvements. To get this going, in 1816, Congress not only passed a high tariff, but also chartered a second Bank of the United States. Upon becoming President, Jackson fought to get rid of the bank.

One of the many duties of the bank was to regulate the supply of money for the nation. The President believed that the bank was a monopoly that favored the wealthy. Congress voted in 1832 to renew the bank's charter but Jackson vetoed the bill, withdrew the government's money, and the bank finally collapsed. Jackson also faced the "null and void," or nullification issue from South Carolina. In 1828, Congress passed a law placing high tariffs on goods imported into the United States. Southerners, led by South Carolina's then Vice-President of the United States, John C. Calhoun, felt that the tariff favored the manufacturing interests of New England. Calhoun denounced it as an abomination and claimed that any state could nullify any of the federal laws it considered unconstitutional.

The tariff was lowered in 1832, but not enough to satisfy South Carolina which promptly threatened to secede from the Union. Although Jackson agreed with the rights of states, he also believed in preservation of the Union. He held firm in his stance that the federal government was sovereign over states. A year later, the tariffs were lowered and the crisis was averted.

As the nation extended its borders into the lands west of the Mississippi, thousands of settlers streamed into this part of the country bringing with them ideas and concepts adapting them to the development of the unique characteristics of the region. Equality for everyone, as stated in the Declaration of Independence, did not yet apply to minority groups, African-Americans or American-Indians. Voting rights and the right to hold public office were restricted in varying degrees in each state. All of these factors decidedly affected the political, economic, and social life of the country, and all three were focused in the attitudes of the three sections of the country on slavery.

All of this was started on an optimistic and scientific note. After the U.S. purchased the Louisiana Territory, Jefferson appointed Captains Meriwether Lewis and William Clark to explore the new territory and find out exactly what had been bought. The expedition extended out of the Louisiana Territory to the Pacific Ocean. Lewis and Clark returned two years later with maps, journals, and artifacts from their expedition. This led the way for future explorers to make more knowledge about the territory available and resulted in the Westward Movement and the later belief in the doctrine of Manifest Destiny.

It was the belief of many that the United States was destined to control all of the land between the two oceans, or as one newspaper editor coined it, "Manifest Destiny." This mass migration westward put the U.S. government on a collision course with the Native Americans, Great Britain, Spain, and Mexico. The fur traders and missionaries ran up against the Native Americans in the northwest and the claims of Great Britain for the Oregon country.

Spain had claimed the American Southwest since the 1540s and had spread northward from Mexico City and, in the 1700s, had established missions, forts, villages, towns, and very large ranches. After the purchase of the Louisiana Territory in 1803, Americans began moving into Spanish territory. A few hundred American families in what is now Texas were allowed to live there but had to agree to become loyal subjects to Spain. In 1821, Mexico successfully revolted against Spanish rule, won independence, and chose to be more tolerant towards the American settlers and traders. The Mexican government encouraged and allowed extensive trade and settlement, especially in Texas. Many of the new settlers were southerners and brought with them their slaves. Slavery was outlawed in Mexico and technically illegal in Texas, although the Mexican government looked the other way.

With the influx of so many Americans and the liberal policies of the Mexican government, concern over the possible growth and development of an American state within Mexico grew. Settlement restrictions, cancellation of land grants, the forbidding of slavery and increased military activity brought everything to a head. The order of events included the fight for Texas independence, the brief Republic of Texas, eventual annexation of Texas, statehood, and finally war with Mexico.

The Texas controversy was not the sole reason for war. Since American settlers had begun pouring into the Southwest, the cultural differences played a prominent part. Language, religion, law, customs, and government of the two groups were totally different and opposite between. A clash was bound to occur.

Friction increased between land-hungry Americans swarming into western lands and the Mexican government, which controlled these lands. The clash was not only political but also cultural and economic. The Spanish influence permeated all parts of southwestern life—law, language, architecture, and customs. By this time, the doctrine of Manifest Destiny was in the hearts and on the lips of those seeking new areas of settlement and a new life.

The impact of the entire westward movement resulted in the completion of the borders of the present-day conterminous United States. Contributing factors include the bloody war with Mexico, the ever-growing controversy over slave versus free states affecting the balance of power or influence in the U.S. Congress, especially the Senate, and finally to the Civil War itself.

Skill 1.6b   Demonstrate knowledge of geographic expansion, including the development of the transportation network and the displacement of Native Americans

The conclusion of the Civil War opened the floodgates for migration westward and settlement of new land. The availability of cheap land and the expectation of great opportunity prompted thousands, including immigrants, to travel across the Mississippi River and settle the Great Plains and California. The primary bases of the new western economy were farming, mining, and ranching. Both migration and the economy were facilitated by the expansion of the railroad, which largely replaced canal and riverway travel and transport as the preferred mode, and the completion of the transcontinental railroad in 1869. The increased efficacy of rail transport opened up new markets and enhanced existing ones. Agricultural, ranching, and other business concerns in the West boomed and flourished with this improved connection to the markets of the East and, through them, the ports of Europe and beyond. This, of course, led to increased migration of people seeking opportunity into all the territories of the West.

Migration and settlement were not easy. As the settlers moved west, they encountered Native American tribes who believed they had a natural right to the lands upon which their ancestors had lived for generations. Resentment of the new settlers was particularly strong among the tribes that had been ordered to relocate to "Indian Country" prior to 1860. Conflict was intense and frequent until 1867, when the Government established two large tracts of land called "reservations" in Oklahoma and the Dakotas to which all tribes would be confined. With the war over, troops were sent west to enforce the relocation and reservation containment policies. There were frequent wars, particularly as white settlers attempted to move onto Indian lands and as the tribes resisted this confinement.

Continuing conflict led to passage of the Dawes Act of 1887. This was recognition that confinement to reservations was not working. The law was intended to break up the Indian communities and bring about assimilation into white culture by deeding portions of the reservation lands to individual Indians who were expected to farm their land. The policy continued until 1934.

Armed resistance essentially came to an end by 1890, the same year in which the western frontier was declared by the U.S. Census Bureau to be closed. The surrender of Geronimo and the massacre at Wounded Knee led to a change of strategy by the Indians. Thereafter, the resistance strategy was to preserve their culture and traditions.

Skill 1.6c **Demonstrate knowledge of industrialization, including technological and agricultural innovations, and the early labor movement**

The **Industrial Revolution** had spread from Great Britain to the United States. Before 1800, most manufacturing activities were done in small shops or in homes. However, starting in the early 1800s, factories with contemporary machines were built, making it easier to produce goods faster. The eastern part of the country became a major industrial area, although some developed in the West. At about the same time, improvements began to be made in building roads, railroads, canals, and steamboats. The increased ease of travel facilitated the westward expansion and boosted the economy with faster and cheaper shipment of goods and products, covering larger and larger areas. An example of one of the innovations is the Erie Canal, connecting the interior and Great Lakes with the Hudson River and the coastal port of New York. Canals to facilitate travel connected many other natural waterways.

Robert Fulton's "**Clermont**," the first commercially successful steamboat, led the way as the fastest method to ship goods, making it the most important way to do so. Later, steam-powered railroads soon became the biggest rival of the steamboat as a means of shipping, eventually being the most important transportation method opening the West. With expansion into the interior of the country, the United States became the leading agricultural nation in the world. The hardy pioneer farmers produced a vast surplus and emphasis went to producing products with a high-sale value. Inventions such as the cotton gin and reaper aided in this. Travel and shipping were greatly helped in areas not yet touched by railroad and improved or new roads such as the **National Road** in the East and in the West the **Oregon and Santa Fe Trails**.

Advances in American agriculture were a direct result of the advances in technological development and the new political awareness about the power of organization and shared information and education.

Eli Whitney was born in Massachusetts during the Colonial period and as a citizen of the recently formed United States graduated from Yale College in 1792. Early in 1793, he designed and constructed the first cotton gin ("gin" for engine). This machine automated the process for separating cottonseed from the short-cotton fiber—previously, a long and laborious process. Whitney may have been a bit ahead of his time and failed to profit from his invention. However, others soon copied his cotton gin and were more successful in reaching the appropriate markets.

Once Mr. Whitney's cotton gin was accepted by the planters of the South and established on the plantations, cotton would become a king crop in Southern agriculture. The "peculiar institution" of slavery would become even more profitable and remain institutionalized for many years to come. The advent of the cotton gin and the resulting increase in the production of cotton for the world's markets meant vast increases in wealth and political power for the South.

Other agricultural areas of the country that were not part of the plantation system also experienced growth and change during these years. In the 1820s, agricultural periodicals became commonplace, providing shared information about agriculture and discussing issues of concern to farmers. From 1825 on, some schools and colleges started offering courses in agriculture or in sciences useful in agriculture.

In 1830, it took approximately 250 to 300 labor hours to produce 100 bushels (5 acres) of wheat using the walking plow, brush harrow, hand broadcast of seed, sickle, and flail. This effort would be cut dramatically as new technological advances became available for implementation on the farm. Examples of new technology were the patenting of McCormick's reaper in 1834 and John Lane's manufacture of plows faced with steel blades in the same year. Many other innovations greatly changed the means of agriculture and the lives of farmers in the United States, from the manufacturing partnership of John Deere and Leonard Andrus in 1837 to the development of the first grain elevator in Buffalo, New York, in 1842.

During this period, non-agricultural laborers in the cities and towns of the United States organized and struggled to improve their lot and the conditions under which they toiled. Women, children, and recent immigrants made up a considerable part of the workforce and often worked for the lowest wages and in the worst conditions. Some have compared the "wage slavery" of the factories and mills of the time to the chattel slavery in the plantation South.

One of the most significant issues for labor, during this period, was the struggle to achieve the ten-hour work day. Organizers and activists were able to achieve success in the legislatures of several states. But the laws always contained a loophole that allowed workers to contract for longer hours. The ability to remove any employee who was unwilling to agree to such a contract meant that these loopholes allowed employers to retain the upper hand. Some of the more notable events in labor history were the following:

1833—The Workingmen's Ticket is formed as a political party to promote labor ideology.

1834—The National Trades Union, the first attempt at a national labor federation, is formed in New York City. The Factory Girls' Association is formed in Lowell, Massachusetts and a strike is called over working conditions and wages. In Dover, New Hampshire, 800 women go out on strike over the right to organize and in opposition to wage reductions.

1836—The first national union for a specific trade, The National Cooperative Association of Cordwainers, was founded in New York City. The Equal Rights Party is formed in Utica, New York. The result was a convention of mechanics, farmers, and workingmen who wrote a Declaration of Rights in opposition to bank notes, paper money, and arbitrary power of the courts. They called for legislation to guarantee labor the right to organize. The Factory Girls' Association in Lowell goes out on strike again over working conditions and wages.

1837—The Panic of 1837 meant an end to the National Trades Union and most other unions. President Jackson declares a ten-hour work day for the Philadelphia Navy Yard to quell discontent caused by Panic of 1837.

1838—One-third of the nation's workers were unemployed because of the economic situation.

1840—The ten-hour work day without reduction in pay is proclaimed by President Van Buren for all federal employees on public works.

1842—In *Commonwealth* v. *Hunt*, the Massachusetts Supreme Court rules that labor unions are not illegal conspiracies. Legislation passes in Connecticut and Massachusetts prohibiting children from working more than ten hours per day.

1844—The New England Workingmen's Association is formed, with more than 200 delegates, to fight for the ten-hour day for non-federal workers.

1845—Female workers in five cotton mills in Allegheny, Pennsylvania, strike for the ten-hour day. They are supported by workers in Lowell, Massachusetts, and Manchester, New Hampshire. The first professional teacher's association is created in Massachusetts. The Female Labor Reform Association is formed as an auxiliary of the New England Workingmen's Association in Lowell, Massachusetts, to fight for the ten-hour day.

1847—New Hampshire is the first state to make the ten-hour day the legal workday.

1848—A new child labor law in Pennsylvania established twelve as the minimum age for workers in commercial occupations. Pennsylvania passed a ten-hour day law. When employers violated it, women mill workers rioted and attacked the factory gates with axes.

Skill 1.6d **Demonstrate understanding of social and cultural developments, such as changes in the role of women in society, and reform movements**

People were exposed to works of literature, art, newspapers, drama, live entertainment, and political rallies. With better communication and travel, more information was desired about previously unknown areas of the country, especially the West. The discovery of gold and other mineral wealth resulted in a literal surge of settlers and even more interest.

Public schools were established in many of the states with more children being educated. With more literacy and participation in literature and the arts, the young nation was developing its own unique culture and becoming less influenced by and dependent on the culture of Europe.

More industries and factories required more labor. Women, children, and at times, entire families worked the long hours and days until the 1830s. By then, the factories were getting larger and employers began hiring immigrants who were coming to America in huge numbers. Before the 1830s, efforts were made to organize a labor movement to improve working conditions and increase wages. This movement never caught on until after the Civil War, but the seed had been sown.

The following is just a partial list of well-known Americans who contributed their leadership and talents in various fields and reforms:

Lucretia Mott and **Elizabeth Cady Stanton** for women's rights.

Emma Hart Willard, Catharine Esther Beecher, and **Mary Lyon** for education for women.

Dr. Elizabeth Blackwell, the first woman doctor.

Antoinette Louisa Blackwell, the first female minister.

Dorothea Lynde Dix for reforms in prisons and insane asylums.

Elihu Burritt and **William Ladd** for peace movements.

Robert Owen for a Utopian society.

Horace Mann, Henry Barmard, Calvin E. Stowe, Caleb Mills, and **John Swett** for public education.

Benjamin Lundy, David Walker, William Lloyd Garrison, Isaac Hooper, Arthur and Lewis Tappan, Theodore Weld, Frederick Douglass, Harriet Tubman, James G. Birney, Henry Highland Garnet, James Forten, Robert Purvis, Harriet Beecher Stowe, Wendell Phillips, and John Brown for abolition of slavery and the Underground Railroad.

Louisa Mae Alcott, James Fenimore Cooper, Washington Irving, Walt Whitman, Henry David Thoreau, Ralph Waldo Emerson, Herman Melville, Richard Henry Dana, Nathaniel Hawthorne, Henry Wadsworth Longfellow, John Greenleaf Whittier, Edgar Allan Poe, Oliver Wendell Holmes, famous writers.

John C. Fremont, Zebulon Pike, Kit Carson, explorers.

Henry Clay, Daniel Webster, Stephen Douglas, John C. Calhoun, American statesmen.

Robert Fulton, Cyrus McCormick, Eli Whitney, inventors.

Noah Webster, American dictionary and spellers.

The list could go on and on, but the contributions of these and many, many others greatly enhanced the unique American culture.

COMPETENCY 1.7   CIVIL WAR ERA (1850–1870S)

Skill 1.7a   Demonstrate knowledge of the growth of sectionalism (North, South, and West), and of attempts at political compromise

The first serious clash between North and South occurred during 1819-1820 when James Monroe was in office as President, and it concerned Missouri's admittance to the Union. In 1819, the U.S. consisted of 21 states: 11 free states and 10 slave states. The Missouri Territory allowed slavery and, if admitted, would cause an imbalance in the number of U.S. Senators. Alabama had already been admitted as a slave state and that had balanced the Senate with the North and South each having 22 senators. The first Missouri Compromise resolved the conflict by approving the admission of Maine as a free state along with Missouri as a slave state.   The balance of power in the Senate continued with the same number of free and slave states.

An additional provision of this compromise was that, with the admission of Missouri, slavery would not be allowed in the rest of the Louisiana Purchase territory north of latitude 36°30'. This was acceptable to the Southern Congressmen since it was not profitable to grow cotton on land north of this latitude line anyway. It was thought that the crisis had been resolved, but, in the next year, it was discovered that in its state constitution, Missouri discriminated against free blacks. Anti-slavery supporters in Congress went into an uproar, determined to exclude Missouri from the Union. Henry Clay, known as the Great Compromiser, then proposed a second Missouri Compromise, which was acceptable to everyone. His proposal stated that the Constitution of the United States guaranteed protections and privileges to citizens of states and Missouri's proposed constitution could not deny these to any of its citizens. The acceptance in 1820 of this second compromise opened the way for Missouri's statehood—a temporary reprieve only.

Congress took up consideration of new territories between Missouri and present-day Idaho. Again, heated debate over permitting slavery in these areas flared up. Those opposed to slavery used the Missouri Compromise to prove their point showing that the land being considered for territories was part of the area the Compromise had designated as banned to slavery. On May 25, 1854, Congress passed the infamous Kansas-Nebraska Act, which nullified the provision creating the territories of Kansas and Nebraska. This provided the people of these two territories the ability to decide for themselves whether or not to permit slavery there. Feelings were so deep and divided that any further attempts to compromise would end with little, if any, success. Political and social turmoil swirled everywhere. Kansas became known as "Bleeding Kansas" because of the extreme violence and bloodshed throughout the territory because two governments existed there, one pro-slavery and the other anti-slavery.

The Supreme Court in 1857 handed down a decision guaranteed to cause explosions throughout the country. **Dred Scott** was a slave whose owner had taken him from a slave state, Missouri, then to a free state, Illinois, into the Minnesota Territory, free under the provisions of the Missouri Compromise, then finally back to slave state Missouri. Abolitionists pursued the dilemma by presenting a court case, stating that since Scott had lived in a free state and free territory, he was in actuality a free man. Two lower courts had ruled before the Supreme Court became involved, one ruling in favor and one against. The Supreme Court decided that residing in a free state and free territory did not make Scott a free man because Scott (and all other slaves) was neither a U.S. citizen nor a state citizen of Missouri. Therefore, he did not have the right to sue in state or federal courts. The Court went a step further and ruled that the old Missouri Compromise was now unconstitutional because Congress did not have the power to prohibit slavery in the Territories.

Anti-slavery supporters were stunned. They had just recently formed the new Republican Party, and one of its platforms was keeping slavery out of the Territories. Now, according to the Dred Scott decision, this basic party principle was unconstitutional. The only way to ban slavery in new areas was by a Constitutional Amendment, requiring ratification by three-fourths of all states. At this time, this was out of the question because the supporters would be unable to get a majority because of Southern opposition.

In 1858, Abraham Lincoln and Stephen A. Douglas were running for the office of U.S. Senator from Illinois. They participated in a series of debates, which directly affected the outcome of the 1860 Presidential election. Lincoln, a Republican, was not an abolitionist, but he believed that slavery was morally wrong and he firmly believed in and supported the Republican Party principle that slavery must not be allowed to extend any further.

On the other hand, Douglas, a Democrat, was up for re-election and knew that if he won this race, he had a good chance of becoming President in 1860. He coined the doctrine of "popular sovereignty" and was responsible for supporting the inflammatory **Kansas-Nebraska Act** and helped its passage through Congress. In the course of the debates, Lincoln challenged Douglas to show that popular sovereignty reconciled with the Dred Scott decision. Either way he answered Lincoln, Douglas would lose crucial support from one group or the other. If he supported the Dred Scott decision, Southerners would support him but he would lose Northern support. If he stayed with popular sovereignty, Northern support would be his but Southern support would be lost. His reply to Lincoln, stating that Territorial legislatures could exclude slavery by refusing to pass laws supporting it, gave him enough support and approval to be re-elected to the Senate. But it cost him the Democratic nomination for President in 1860.

Southerners came to the realization that Douglas supported and was devoted to popular sovereignty but not necessarily to the expansion of slavery.

On the other hand, two years later, Lincoln received the nomination of the Republican Party for President.

Skill 1.7b Demonstrate knowledge of the abolitionist movement, including the roles of African-Americans and women in the movement

While there have always been individuals opposed to slavery and the slave trade, during the colonial period in America the Society of Friends (the Quakers) were the only prominent group to denounce slave holding as incompatible with Christian moral values. Perhaps influenced by humanistic values put forth during the Age of Enlightenment and during the American War for Independence, more American communities became like-minded in disdain for slavery. As new areas were added to the country (such as the Northwest Territory in 1787) prohibition of slavery in these lands became a major issue. Some protesters were assuaged when Congress banned the transatlantic slave trade in 1808. Others were convinced that the system must exist in order to keep the Southern economy viable. Distance from the "peculiar institution" gave many Northerners cause to ignore the situation as inconsequential to their own lives. The African Colonization Society, founded in 1816, was the major channel for antislavery activity during this period. The goal of this society was to resettle former slaves back in Africa.

The **Second Great Awakening** seemed to also reawaken a moral revulsion to slavery among many Americans. Revivalist preaching created abolitionists out of congregations who were brought to believe that slave holding was the product of personal sin and emancipation of slaves was the only means of redemption. Inactivity in the cause of abolition was tantamount to compliance in the sin in the rhetoric of some activists. In the 1830s, newly founded abolitionist groups—most prominently, the American Antislavery Society, founded in 1833—lobbied to change racially discriminatory practices, recognizing that these existing sanctions, based on race, reinforced the argument for the acceptability and necessity of keeping black people in bondage.

The American Anti-Slavery Society grew very quickly and claimed a membership of tens of thousands. This alone would have been enough to draw great interest to their cause and curious listeners to their rallies. But they were activists, publishing widely and organizing petition drives to change existing laws and sanctions that supported slavery and reinforced racist attitudes. Through their lecturing agents, they provided the public with brilliant and provocative speakers. Several Northern audiences were moved by the personal testimony of runaway slaves—having had little or no contact with slavery themselves and having only the justifications of the planters and the denunciations of white abolitionists by which to draw their conclusions.

Foremost among these speakers—and a genuine celebrity in his own time—was a man who combined all of these qualities that appealed to audiences of abolitionist meetings and rallies. He was the son of a white planter and a slave mother and, under the laws of that time, he was a Negro born to a slave and therefore the slave of his father. He was a runaway slave. He was a self-made man. He was Frederick Douglass. Douglass would become the most recognized spokesman for abolition and civil rights for Negroes in his time. He would impress, confer with, and influence the thoughts and actions of such men as William Lloyd Garrison—the committed, hard-line abolition activist from Boston—and the man who would ultimately do the most to abolish slavery, President Abraham Lincoln.

Women were a large portion of the abolitionist movement from its inception. While it was common and considered acceptable for women to be concerned about and involved in issues of morality and humanity, their activism (sometimes extreme) in this cause often brought about more criticism than support from men and women who were neutral about their cause. For whatever reasons, the American Anti-Slavery Society originally banned women from their membership. But activist abolitionist women formed their own organizations which met in national conventions in 1837, 1838 and 1839. Women became an undeniable asset in their activism and fundraising for the cause underpinning the national effort. However, this caused a rift in the general movement. Many male abolitionists thought of female activism as improper and, perhaps, immoral. And many feared that the direct involvement of women might mean the addition, or redirection, of efforts intended to promote the unpopular cause of gender equality.

William Lloyd Garrison and his followers had a broader platform than many at the time were willing to support, including the extension of women's rights, temperance, and pacifism. In 1840, opponents of the election of a female officer to the American Anti-Slavery Society quit their membership allowing the Garrisonians to gain control of the Society. Thereafter, women became more prominent in the Society. And many, including Lucy Stone, Elizabeth Cady Stanton and the former slave Sojourner Truth, tolerated insult and risked physical harm to spread the doctrine in lecture halls and organize supporters. One of the most famous abolitionists of the period was Harriet Tubman, called the "Moses of Her People." She ran away from slavery and spoke and worked as an activist in the movement. She also personally returned to Maryland several times to aid other escaping slaves in their transit through the "Underground Railroad."

The "Underground Railroad" was not a conveyance, but rather an apparatus for the escape of slaves, ultimately to Canada. The railroad consisted of information, resources (money, food, clothing, etc,) guides and "safe" houses to aid the runaways in escaping their masters and eluding the law, which was bound to return them to the slave holders.

Because of the great risks involved, it was impossible to provide for the aid of slaves consistently, in the same manner and through the same channels, but the process know as the "Underground Railroad" was instrumental in helping thousands upon thousands of escaped slaves achieve freedom.

Many radical and militant abolitionists philosophically opposed the Garrisonians. Mostly, they acted as individuals, apparently impatient with the methods of the larger organizations. But certain conditions and events would bring these militants to act as a group. "Bleeding Kansas," a situation which brought bloodshed to the contest of whether the state would be "slave" or "free," was just such an event. Some have described it as a prelude to the Civil War. And the most impatient militant to emerge from that fracas was John Brown.

Skill 1.7c   Demonstrate understanding of the failure of political institutions in the 1850s

During the 1850s, the issue of slavery in newly admitted states once again surfaced. The state of California was admitted as a "free" state. Texas, a slave state, agreed to alter its border and was compensated for its loss of territory. In the New Mexico Territory, which included the area that is now New Mexico, Arizona and Utah, no specific prohibition on slavery was implemented. In addition, the Fugitive Slave law was passed, which required all citizens to assist in the return of runaway slaves to their owners. Faced with two opposite choices, Congress opted to compromise. This group of acts is called the **Compromise of 1850**. It was aimed at balancing the competing claims of the slave-owning southern states and the free northern states.

Congress had made a similar compromise in 1820, called the **Missouri Compromise**, which had allowed the new state of Missouri to allow slavery but restricted slavery in any new territories to below latitude 36°30'. However, both of these compromises were repealed in 1854 by the Kansas-Nebraska act. This act divided the western territory that had been purchased from France along the 40th parallel with the Kansas Territory to the south and the Nebraska Territory to the north. Furthermore, it was decided that each territory would decide for itself whether or not to allow slavery. This had the potential to both tip the formerly equal balance between slave and free states to the side of slavery and to allow slavery north of 36°30' should the new territories opt for it.

Rather than creating a quiet balance, this series of compromises actually increased political tension. The **Kansas-Nebraska Act** was one of the primary campaign issues in the famous Lincoln-Douglas debates, as Stephen Douglas had been the architect of the Act. Congress' intention to balance the interests of the nation's states only served to accentuate them and draw them into the politcal arena, contributing directly to the secession of the Confederate States and the Civil War.

In 1859, **Abolitionist John Brown** and his followers seized the federal arsenal at Harper's Ferry in what is now West Virginia. His purpose was to take the guns stored in the arsenal, give them to slaves nearby, and lead them in a widespread rebellion. He and his men were captured by Colonel Robert E. Lee of the United States Army and after a trial with a guilty verdict, he was hanged. Most Southerners felt that the majority of Northerners approved of Brown's actions but in actuality, most of them were stunned and shocked. Southern newspapers took great pains to quote a small but well-known minority of abolitionists who applauded and supported Brown's actions, which merely served to widen the gap between the two sections.

The final straw came with the election of Lincoln to the Presidency the next year. Because of a split in the Democratic Party, there were four candidates from four political parties. Lincoln received a minority of the popular vote and a majority of electoral votes. In response, the Southern states, one by one, voted to secede from the Union, as they had promised they would do if Lincoln and the Republicans were victorious.

In the decade leading up to the Civil War, tensions between the northern and southern states intensified over the issue of slavery. The United States had acquired new territories in the southwest as a result of the Mexican-American War in the late 1840's. In 1850, as the nation was poised to expand, Congress took up the question of whether slavery would be allowed in the new territories.

Skill 1.7d   Demonstrate knowledge of the Civil War (1861–1865), including its causes, leaders, and major events

South Carolina was the first state to secede from the Union and the first shots of the war were fired on Fort Sumter in Charleston Harbor. Both sides quickly prepared for war. The North had more in its favor—a larger population; superiority in finances and transportation facilities; and more manufacturing, agricultural, and natural resources. The North possessed most of the nation's gold, had about 92 percent of all industries, and almost all known supplies of copper, coal, iron, and various other minerals. Most of the nation's railroads were in the North and mid-West, men and supplies could be moved wherever needed; food could be transported from the farms of the mid-West to workers in the East and to soldiers on the battlefields. Trade with nations overseas could go on as usual because of control of the navy and the merchant fleet. The 24 northern states included western (California and Oregon) and border (Maryland, Delaware, Kentucky, Missouri, and West Virginia) states.

The 11 southern states, including South Carolina, Georgia, Florida, Alabama, Mississippi, Louisiana, Texas, Virginia, North Carolina, Tennessee, and Arkansas, made up the Confederacy. Although outnumbered in population, the South was completely confident of victory. They knew that all they had to do was fight a defensive war and protect their own territory. The North had to invade and defeat an area almost the size of Western Europe. They figured the North would get tired of the struggle and give up. Another advantage of the South was that a number of its best officers had graduated from the U.S. Military Academy at West Point and had had long years of army experience. Many had exercised varying degrees of command in the Indian Wars and the war with Mexico. Men from the South were conditioned to living outdoors and were more familiar with horses and firearms than men from northeastern cities. Since cotton was such an important crop, Southerners felt that British and French textile mills were so dependent on raw cotton that they would be forced to help the Confederacy in the war.

The South had specific reasons and goals for fighting the war, more so than the North. The major aim of the Confederacy never wavered: to win independence, the right to govern themselves as they wished, and to preserve slavery. The Northerners were not as clear in their reasons for conducting war. In the beginning, most believed, along with Lincoln, that preservation of the Union was paramount. Only a few extremely fanatical abolitionists looked on the war as a way to end slavery. However, by war's end, more and more northerners had come to believe that freeing the slaves was just as important as restoring the Union.

The war strategies for both sides were relatively clear and simple. The South planned a defensive war, wearing down the North until it agreed to peace on Southern terms. The only exception was to gain control of Washington, D.C., go north through the Shenandoah Valley into Maryland and Pennsylvania in order to drive a wedge between the Northeast and mid-West, interrupt the lines of communication, and end the war quickly. The North had three basic strategies:

1. Blockade the Confederate coastline in order to cripple the South;
2. Seize control of the Mississippi River and interior railroad lines to split the Confederacy in two; and
3. Seize the Confederate capital of Richmond, Virginia, driving southward joining up with Union forces coming east from the Mississippi Valley.

The South won decisively until the Battle of Gettysburg, July 1 - 3, 1863. Until Gettysburg, Lincoln's commanders, McDowell and McClellan, were less than desirable. Burnside and Hooker were not what was needed. General Robert E. Lee, on the other hand, depended heavily on many able officers, such as "Stonewall" Jackson and J.E.B. Stuart. Jackson died at Chancellorsville and was replaced by Longstreet. Lee decided to invade the North and depended on Stuart and his cavalry to keep him informed of the location of Union troops and their strengths.

The following four events worked against Lee at Gettysburg:

1) The Union troops gained the best positions and the best ground first, making it easier to make a stand.

2) Lee's move into Northern territory put him and his army a long way from food and supply lines. They were more or less on their own.

3) Lee thought that his Army of Northern Virginia was invincible and could fight and win under any conditions or circumstances.

4) Stuart and his men did not arrive at Gettysburg until the end of the second day of fighting, and, by then, it was too little too late. He and the men had had to detour around Union soldiers, and he was delayed getting the information Lee needed.

Consequently, he made the mistake of failing to listen to Longstreet and following the strategy of regrouping back into Southern territory to the supply lines. Lee felt that regrouping was retreating and almost an admission of defeat.

He was convinced the army would be victorious. Longstreet was concerned about the Union troops occupying the best positions and felt that regrouping to a better position would be an advantage. He was also very concerned about the distance from supply lines.

Neither side intended to fight there, but the fighting began when a Confederate brigade, looking for shoes, stumbled into a Union cavalry unit. On the third and last day, Lee launched the final attempt to break Union lines. General George Pickett sent his division of three brigades under Generals Garnet, Kemper, and Armistead against Union troops on Cemetery Ridge under command of General Winfield Scott Hancock. Union lines held, and Lee and the defeated Army of Northern Virginia made their way back to Virginia. Although Lincoln's commander George Meade successfully turned back a Confederate charge, he and the Union troops failed to pursue Lee and the Confederates. This battle was the turning point for the North. After this, Lee never again had the troop strength to launch a major offensive.

The day after Gettysburg, on July 4, Vicksburg, Mississippi surrendered to Union General Ulysses Grant, thus severing the western Confederacy from the eastern part. In September 1863, the Confederacy won its last important victory at Chickamauga. In November, the Union victory at Chattanooga made it possible for Union troops to go into Alabama and Georgia and split the eastern Confederacy in two. Lincoln gave Grant command of all Northern armies in March of 1864. Grant led his armies into battles in Virginia while Phil Sheridan and his cavalry did as much damage as possible. In a skirmish at a place called Yellow Tavern, Virginia, Sheridan's and Stuart's forces met. Stuart was fatally wounded.

The Union won the Battle of Mobile Bay, and in May 1864, William Tecumseh Sherman began his march to successfully demolish Atlanta, then on to Savannah. He and his troops turned northward through the Carolinas to meet Grant in Virginia. On April 9, 1865, Lee formally surrendered to Grant at the Appomattox Courthouse in Virginia.

The Civil War took more American lives than any other war in history. The South lost one-third of its soldiers in battle, whereas the North lost about one-sixth. More than half of the total deaths were caused by disease and the horrendous conditions of field hospitals. Both sides paid a tremendous economic price, but the South suffered more severely from direct damages. Destruction was pervasive with towns, farms, trade, and industry. Lives and homes of men, women, children were destroyed, and an entire Southern way of life was lost. The South had no voice in the political, social, and cultural affairs of the nation, lessening to a great degree the influence of the more traditional Southern ideals. The Northern Yankee Protestant ideals of hard work, education, and economic freedom became the standard of the United States and helped influence the development of the nation into a modem, industrial power.

The effects of the Civil War were tremendous. It changed the methods of waging war and has been called the first modern war. It introduced weapons and tactics that, when improved later, were used extensively in wars of the late 1800s and early1900s. Civil War soldiers were the first to fight in trenches, under a unified command, wage defenses called "major cordon defenses" (a strategy of advance on all fronts). They were also the first to use repeat and breech loading weapons. Observation balloons were first used during the war along with submarines, ironclad ships, and mines. Telegraphy and railroads were put to use first in the Civil War. It was considered a modern war because of the vast destruction and was "total war," involving the use of all resources of the opposing sides. There was no *way* it could have ended other than total defeat and unconditional surrender of one side or the other.

Skill 1.7e **Demonstrate knowledge of the Reconstruction period, including the various plans for Reconstruction, the new amendments to the Constitution, and the Compromise of 1877**

Following the Civil War, the nation was faced with repairing the torn Union and readmitting the Confederate states. **Reconstruction** refers to this period between 1865 and 1877 when the federal and state governments debated and implemented plans to provide civil rights to freed slaves and to set the terms under which the former Confederate states might once again join the Union.

Planning for Reconstruction began early in the war in 1861. Abraham Lincoln's Republican Party in Washington favored the extension of voting rights to black men but was divided as to how far to extend the right. Moderates, such as Lincoln, wanted only literate blacks and those who had fought for the Union to be allowed to vote. Radical Republicans wanted to extend the vote to all black men. Conservative Democrats did not want to give black men the vote at all. In the case of former Confederate soldiers, moderates wanted to allow all but former leaders to vote, while the radicals wanted to require an oath from all eligible voters that they had never borne arms against the US, which would have excluded all former rebels. On the issue of readmission into the Union, moderates favored a much lower standard, with the radicals demanding nearly impossible conditions for rebel states to return.

Lincoln's moderate plan for Reconstruction was actually part of his effort to win the war. Lincoln and the moderates felt that if it remained easy for states to return to the Union and if moderate proposals on black suffrage were made, then Confederate states involved in the hostilities might be swayed to re-join the Union rather than continue fighting. The radical plan was to ensure that Reconstruction did not actually start until after the war was over.

By executive proclamation and constitutional amendment, slavery was officially unconstitutional. However, deep prejudice and racism still remained in the South. At the end of the war, the Union was preserved and the states were finally truly united. **Sectionalism**, especially in the area of politics, remained strong for another 100 years but not to the degree and with the violence as existed before 1861. It has been noted that the Civil War may have been American democracy's greatest failure. From 1861 to 1865, the basic democratic ideals fell to human passion. Nevertheless, democracy survived. The victory of the North established that no state has the right to leave the Union. Because of this unity the U.S. started to become a major global power. Lincoln never proposed to punish the South. Instead, he was most concerned with restoring the South to the Union in a program that was flexible and practical rather than rigid and unbending. In fact he never really felt that the states had succeeded in leaving the Union but that they had left the 'family circle" for a short time. His plans consisted of two major steps.

- All Southerners taking an oath of allegiance to the Union who promised to accept all federal laws and proclamations dealing with slavery would receive a full pardon. The only ones excluded from this were men who had resigned from civil and military positions in the federal government to serve in the Confederacy, those who were part of the Confederate government, in the Confederate army above the rank of lieutenant, and Confederates who were guilty of mistreating prisoners of war and blacks.

- Each state would be able to write a new constitution, elect new officials, and return to the Union fully equal to all other states on certain conditions: a minimum number of persons (at least 10 percent of those who were qualified voters in their states before secession from the Union who had voted in the 1860 election) must take an oath of allegiance.

Lincoln's Emancipation Proclamation in 1863 and the 13th Amendment to the U.S. Constitution in 1865 ended slavery in the United States. But, these measures did not erase the centuries of racial prejudices hat held blacks to be second class citizens. These prejudices, along with fear of economic competition from newly freed slaves, led to a series of state laws that permitted or required businesses, landlords, school boards, and others to physically segregate blacks and whites in their everyday lives.

In 1865, Abraham Lincoln was assassinated, leaving Vice President Andrew Johnson to oversee the actual implementation of Reconstruction. Johnson took a moderate stance and was willing to allow former confederates to keep control of their state governments. These governments quickly enacted Black Codes that denied the vote to blacks and granted them only limited civil rights.

The economic and social chaos in the South after the war was unbelievable. Starvation and disease were rampant, especially in the cities. The U.S. Army provided some relief with food and clothing for both white and blacks, but the major responsibility fell to the **Freedmen's Bureau**. Though the bureau agents to a certain extent helped southern whites, their main responsibility was to the freed slaves. They were to help the freedmen others. Northerners looked on it as a real, honest effort to help the South out of the chaos it was in. Most white Southerners charged the bureau with causing racial friction, deliberately encouraging the freedmen to consider former owners as enemies.

In 1866, radical Republicans won control of Congress and passed the Reconstruction Acts, which placed the governments of the southern states under the control of the federal military. With this backing, the Republicans began to implement such radical policies as granting all black men the vote and denying the vote to former confederate soldiers. Congress had passed the 13th, 14th and 15th Amendments, granting citizenship and civil rights to blacks, and made ratification of these amendments a condition of readmission into the Union by the rebel states. The Republicans found support in the south among Freedmen (freed slaves), Scalawags (white southerners who did not support the Confederacy), and Carpetbaggers (northerners who had moved to the South).

Military control of the South continued throughout Grant's administration, despite growing conflict both inside and outside the Republican Party. Conservatives in Congress and in the states opposed the liberal policies of the Republicans. Some Republicans became concerned over corruption issues among Grant's appointees and dropped support for him.

Segregation laws were foreshadowed in the Black Codes. These strict laws proposed by some southern states during Reconstruction sought to recreate the conditions of pre-war servitude. Under these codes, blacks were to remain subservient to their white employers and were subject to fines and beatings if they failed to work. Freedmen were afforded some civil rights protection during the Reconstruction period, but beginning around 1876, so called Redeemer governments began to take office in southern states after the removal of Federal troops that had supported Reconstruction. The Redeemer-state legislatures began passing segregation laws that came to be known as Jim Crow laws.

Jim Crow laws varied from state to state, but the most significant required separate school systems and libraries for blacks and whites and separate ticket windows, waiting rooms and seating areas on trains and, later, other public transportation. Restaurant owners were permitted or sometimes required to provide separate entrances, tables, and counters for blacks and whites, so that the two races could not see one another while dining. Public parks and playgrounds were constructed for each race. Landlords were not allowed to mix black and white tenants in apartment houses in some states. Jim Crow laws were given credibility in 1896 when the Supreme Court handed down its decision in the case *Plessy* v. *Ferguson*. In 1890, Louisiana had passed a law requiring separate train cars for blacks and whites. In 1892, to challenge this law, Homer Plessy, a man who had a black great grandparent and so was considered legally "black" in that state, purchased a ticket in the white section and took his seat. Upon informing the conductor that he was black, he was told to move to the black car. He refused and was arrested. His case was eventually elevated to the Supreme Court.

The Court ruled against Plessy, thereby ensuring that the Jim Crow laws would continue to proliferate and be enforced. The Court held that segregating races was not unconstitutional as long as the facilities for each were identical. This became known as the "separate but equal" principle. In practice, facilities were seldom equal. Black schools were not funded at the same level, for instance. Streets and parks in black neighborhoods were not maintained.

Paralleling the development of segregation legislation in the mid-nineteenth century was the appearance of organized groups opposed to any integration of blacks into white society. The most notable of these was the Ku Klux Klan.

First organized in the South during Reconstruction, the KKK was a loose group made up mainly of former Confederate soldiers who opposed the Reconstruction government and espoused a doctrine of white supremacy. KKK members intimidated and sometimes killed their enemies. The first KKK was never completely organized, despite having nominal leadership. In 1871, President Grant took action to use federal troops to halt the activities of the KKK, and actively prosecuted them in federal court. Klan activity waned, and the organization disappeared.

The **13th Amendment** abolished slavery and involuntary servitude, except as punishment for a crime. The amendment was proposed on January 31, 1865. It was declared ratified by the necessary number of states on December 18, 1865. The Emancipation Proclamation, 1863, had freed slaves held in states that were considered to be in rebellion. This amendment freed slaves in states and territories controlled by the Union. The Supreme Court has ruled that this amendment does not bar mandatory military service.

The **14th Amendment** provides for due process and equal protection under the law. It was proposed on June 13, 1866 and ratified on July 28, 1868. The drafters of the Amendment took a broad view of national citizenship. The law requires that states provide equal protection under the law to all persons (not just all citizens). This amendment also came to be interpreted as overturning the Dred Scott case (which said that blacks were not and could not become citizens of the U.S.). The full potential of interpretation of this amendment was not realized until the 1950s and 1960s, when it became the basis of ending segregation in the Supreme Court case *Brown* v. *Board of Education*. This amendment includes the stipulation that all children born on American soil, with very few exceptions, are U.S. citizens. There have been recommendations that this guarantee of citizenship be limited to exclude the children of illegal immigrants and tourists, but this has not yet occurred. There is no provision in this amendment for loss of citizenship.

The second section of the amendment establishes the "one man, one vote" apportionment of congressional representation. This ended the counting of blacks as 3/5 of a person. Section 3 prohibits electing anyone who has engaged in insurrection, rebellion or treason to Congress or the Electoral College. Section 4 stipulates that the government will not pay "damages" for the loss of slaves or for debts incurred by the Confederate government (e.g., with English or French banks).

After the Civil War, many Southern states passed laws that attempted to restrict the movements of blacks and prevent them from bringing lawsuits or testifying in court. In the *Slaughterhouse Cases* (1871), the Supreme Court ruled that the 14th Amendment applies only to rights granted by the federal government. In the *Civil Rights Cases*, the Court held that the guarantee of rights did not outlaw racial discrimination by individuals and organizations. In the next few decades the Court overturned several laws barring blacks from serving on juries or discriminating against the Chinese immigrants in regulating the laundry businesses.

The **15th Amendment** grants voting rights regardless of race, color, or previous condition of servitude. It was ratified on February 3, 1870.

All three of these Constitutional Amendments were part of the Reconstruction effort to create stability and rule of law to provide, protect, and enforce the rights of former slaves throughout the nation.

COMPETENCY 1.8 EMERGENCE OF THE MODERN UNITED STATES (1877–1900)

Skill 1.8a **Demonstrate understanding of United States expansion and imperialism, including the displacement of Native Americans, the development of the West, and international involvement**

The post-Reconstruction era represents a period of great transformation and expansion for the United States, both economically and geographically. These changes were particular for the South, which was still recovering from the devastation of the Civil War and migration west of the Mississippi River. Great numbers of freedmen moved west, away from their former masters and were lured by the promise of land. White migration was also spurred by similar desires for land and resources, leading to boom economies of cotton, cattle, and grain starting in Kansas and spreading westward. During this period, industrial production grew fastest in the South. However, the South was still predominantly agricultural, which featured land tenancy and sharecropping. This did not really advance the remaining freed slaves economically since most of the land was still owned by the large plantation landowners who retained their holdings from before the Civil War. The economic chasm dividing white landowners and black freedmen only widened as the tenants sank further into debt to their landlords.

Westward movement of significant populations from the eastern United States originated with the discovery of gold in the West in the 1840s and picked up greater momentum after the Civil War. Settlers were lured by what they perceived as unpopulated places with land for the taking. However, when they arrived, they found that the lands were populated by earlier settlers of Spanish descent and Native Americans, who did not particularly welcome the newcomers. The Spanish and Native American inhabitants frequently clashed with those who were moving west. Despite having signed treaties with the United States government years earlier, virtually all were ignored and broken as westward settlement accelerated and the government was called upon to protect settlers en route and those that had reached their destinations. This led to a series of wars between the United States and the various Native American nations that were deemed hostile. Although the bloodshed during these wars was great, it paled in comparison to the number of Native Americans who died from epidemics of deadly diseases for which they had no resistance. Eventually, the government sought to relocate Native Americans to Indian reservations and to Oklahoma, which lacked necessary resources and was geographically remote from their home range. The justification for this westward expansion, at the expense of the previous inhabitants, was America's "Manifest Destiny" to tame and settle the continent from coast-to-coast.

Another major factor affecting the opening of the West to migration of Americans and displacement of native peoples was the expansion of the railroad. The transcontinental railroad was completed in 1869, joining the west coast with the existing rail infrastructure terminating at Omaha, Nebraska, its westernmost point. This not only enabled unprecedented movement of people and goods, it also hastened the near extinction of bison, which the Indians of the Great Plains depended on for their survival.

Once the American West was subdued and firmly under United States control, the United States started looking beyond its shores. Overseas markets were becoming important as American industry produced goods more efficiently and manufacturing capacity grew. Out of concern for the protection of shipping, the United States modernized and built up its Navy, which by 1900 ranked third in the world and gave it the means to become an imperial power.

The first overseas possessions were Midway Island and Alaska, purchased back in 1867 as championed by William Henry Seward. By the 1880s, Secretary of State James G. Blaine pushed for expanding U.S. trade and influence to Central and South America. In the 1890s, President Grover Cleveland invoked the Monroe Doctrine to intercede in Latin American affairs when it looked like Great Britain was going to exert its influence and power in the Western Hemisphere. In the Pacific, the United States lent its support to American sugar planters who overthrew the Kingdom of Hawaii and eventually annexed it as U.S. territory.

The turning point in American international affairs was the Spanish-American War in 1898. The U.S. used the explosion of the USS Maine as a pretext to invade Cuba when the underlying reason was the ambition for empire and economic gain. The war with Spain also triggered the dispatch of the fleet under Admiral George Dewey to the Philippines, followed up by sending Army troops. Victory over the Spanish proved fruitful for American territorial ambitions. Although, in a rare moment of idealism, Congress passed legislation renouncing claims to annex Cuba, the United States did gain control of the island of Puerto Rico; a permanent deep-water naval harbor at Guantanamo Bay, Cuba; the Philippines; and various other Pacific islands formerly possessed by Spain. The occupation of the Philippines led to a guerrilla war, the "Philippines Insurrection," which lasted until 1902. U.S. rule over the Philippines lasted until 1942, but unlike the guerrilla war years, American rule was relatively benign.

Skill 1.8b **Understand the process of industrialization and the political, economic, and social changes associated with industrialization in this period**

There was a marked degree of industrialization before and during the Civil War, but at war's end, industry in America was small. After the war, dramatic changes took place. Machines replaced hand labor and extensive nationwide railroad service made possible the wider distribution of goods, New products were invented and made available in large quantities, and large amounts of money from bankers and investors were available for expansion of business operations. American life was certainly affected by this phenomenal industrial growth. Cities became the centers of new business activity resulting in mass population movements and tremendous growth. This new boom in business resulted in huge fortunes for some Americans and extreme poverty for many others. The discontent this caused resulted in a number of new reform movements from which came measures controlling the power and size of big business and helping the poor.

Industry before, during, and after the Civil War was centered mainly in the North, especially the tremendous industrial growth after. The late 1800s and early 1900s saw the increasing buildup of military strength and the U.S. becoming a world power.

The use of machines in industry enabled workers to produce larger quantities of goods much faster than by hand. With the increase in business, hundreds of workers were hired and assigned to perform a certain job in the production process. This method of organization was called "division of labor." Because of the increasing rate of production, businesses could lower prices for their products and make them affordable for more people. As a result, sales and businesses were increasingly successful and profitable.

A great variety of new products or inventions became available such as the typewriter, the telephone, barbed wire, the electric light, and the phonograph. One invention that that had the greatest effect on America's economy was the automobile.

The increase in business and industry was greatly affected by the many rich natural resources found throughout the nation. The industrial machines were powered by the abundant water supply. The construction industry as well as products made from wood depended heavily on lumber from the forests. An abundance of coal and iron ore were needed for the steel industry, which profited and increased from the use of steel in such things as skyscrapers, automobiles, bridges, railroad tracks, and machines. Other minerals such as silver, copper, and petroleum played a large role in industrial growth, especially petroleum, from which gasoline was refined as fuel for the increasingly popular automobile.

Skill 1.8c Understand the causes and consequences of urban development in this period

Between 1870 and 1916, more than 25 million immigrants came into the United States, adding to the phenomenal population growth taking place. This tremendous growth aided business and industry in two ways:

> (1) The number of consumers increased creating a greater demand for products, thus enlarging the markets for the products.
> (2) With increased production and expanding business, more workers were available for newly created jobs.

The completion of the nation's transcontinental railroad in 1868 contributed greatly to the nation's economic and industrial growth. Some benefits of using the railroads include fast shipping of raw materials by the mining companies and wide dispersion of products to all parts of the country. Many wealthy industrialists and railroad owners saw tremendous profits steadily increasing because of this improved method of transportation. Another impact of interstate railroad expansion was the standardization of time zones in order to maintain the reliability and accuracy of train schedules across vast east-west routes.

Innovations in new industrial processes and technology grew at a pace unmatched at any other time in American history. Thomas Edison was the most prolific inventor of that time. He used a systematic and efficient method to invent and improve on current technology in a profitable manner. The abundance of resources, together with growth of industry and the pace of capital investments led to the growth of cities. Populations were shifting from rural agricultural areas to urban industrial areas, and, by the early 1900s, a third of the nation's population lived in cities. Industry needed workers in its factories, mills, and plants, and rural workers were being displaced by advances in farm machinery and their increasing use and other forms of automation. The dramatic growth of population in cities was fueled by growing industries, more efficient transportation of goods and resources, and the people who migrated to those new industrial jobs, either from rural areas of the United States or from foreign lands. Increased urban populations, often packed into dense tenements, often without adequate sanitation or clean water, led to public health challenges that required cities to establish sanitation, water and public health departments to cope with and prevent epidemics. Political organizations also saw the advantage of mobilizing the new industrial working class and created vast patronage programs that sometimes became notorious for corruption in big-city machine politics such as Tammany Hall in New York City.

As business grew, methods of sales and promotion were developed. Salespersons went to all parts of the country promoting the various products, opening large department stores in the growing cities, offering the varied products at reasonable affordable prices. People who lived too far from the cities had the advantage of using a mail order service, buying what they needed from catalogs furnished by the companies.

The developments in communication, such as the telephone and telegraph, increased the efficiency and prosperity of big business.

Skill 1.8d   Understand political, cultural, and social movements

The late 1800s and early 1900s were a period of the efforts of many to make significant reforms and changes in the areas of politics, society, and the economy. There was a need to reduce the levels of poverty and to improve the living conditions of those affected by it. Regulating big business, ridding government of corruption, and making it more responsive to the needs of the people were also on the list of reforms to be accomplished. Until 1890, there was very little success, but from then on the reformers gained increasing public support and were able to achieve some influence in government. Since some of these individuals referred to themselves as "progressives," the period of 1890 to 1917 is referred to by historians as the **Progressive Era**.

Skilled laborers organized into a labor union, the **American Federation of Labor (AFL),** in an effort to gain better working conditions and wages for its members. Farmers joined organizations such as the National Grange and Farmers Alliances. Farmers were producing more food than people could afford to buy because of (1) new farmlands rapidly sprouting on the plains and prairies and (2) development and availability of new farm machinery and newer and better methods of farming. They tried selling their surplus abroad but faced stiff competition from other nations selling the same farm products. Other problems contributed significantly to their situation. Items they needed for daily life were priced exorbitantly high. Having to borrow money to carry on farming activities kept them constantly in debt. Higher interest rates, shortage of money, falling farm prices, dealing with the so-called middlemen, and the increasingly high charges by the railroads to haul farm products to large markets all contributed to the desperate need for reform to relieve the plight of American farmers.

American women began actively campaigning for the right to vote. In 1869, Elizabeth Cady Stanton and Susan B. Anthony founded the organization called **National Women Suffrage Association**, the same year the Wyoming Territory gave women the right to vote. Soon after, a few states followed by giving women the right to vote in local elections only.

Governmental reform began with the passage of the **Civil Service Act**, also known as the Pendleton Act. It provided for the Civil Service Commission, a federal agency responsible for giving jobs based on merit rather than as political rewards or favors. Another successful reform was the adoption of the secret ballot in voting, as were such measures as the direct primary, referendum, recall, and the passage of the 17th Amendment to the Constitution—direct election of U.S. Senators by the people rather than by their state legislatures. Following the success of reforms made at the national level, the progressives were successful in gaining reforms in government at state and local levels.

After 1890, more and more attention was called to needs and problems through the efforts of social workers and clergy and the writings of people such as Lincoln Steffans, Ida M. Tarbell, and Upton Sinclair.

A number of presidents supported progressive legislation. In 1884, President Grover Cleveland did much to see that the Civil Service Act was enforced. After 1880, a number of political or "third" parties were formed and, although they were unsuccessful in getting their Presidential candidates elected, Congress passed into law significant reform legislation, including Constitutional amendments, because of their efforts. Presidents Theodore Roosevelt, William Howard Taft, and Woodrow Wilson supported many of the reform laws after 1890. Some of this legislation was aimed at unfair business practices of large corporations. Such legislation included the **Sherman Antitrust Act of 1890**, the Clayton Antitrust Act of 1914, the Underwood Tariff of 1913, and the establishment of the Federal Trade Commission in 1914.

By the late 1890s and early 1900s, the United States had become a world power and began a leading role in international affairs. War loomed on the horizon again, and the stage was set for increased activity in world affairs, which had been avoided since the end of the Civil War.

COMPETENCY 1.9   PROGRESSIVE ERA THROUGH THE NEW DEAL (1900–1939)

Skill 1.9a   Demonstrate knowledge of political, economic, and social developments

During the period of 1823 to the 1890s, the major interests and efforts of the American people were concentrated on expansion, settlement, and development of the continental United States. The Civil War, 1861-1865, preserved the Union and eliminated the system of slavery. From 1865 onward, the focus was on taming the West and developing industry. During this period, travel and trade between the United States and Europe were continuous. By the 1890s, American interests turned to areas outside the boundaries of the United States. The West was developing into a major industrial area, and people in the United States became very interested in selling their factory and farm surplus to overseas markets. In fact, some Americans desired getting and controlling land outside the U.S. boundaries. Before the 1890s, the U.S. had little, if anything to do with foreign affairs, was not a strong militarily nation, and had inconsequential influence on international political affairs. In fact, the Europeans looked on the American diplomats as inept and bungling in their diplomatic efforts and activities. However, all of this changed, and the Spanish-American War of 1898 saw the entry of the United States as a world power.

During the 1890s, Spain controlled such overseas possessions as Puerto Rico, the Philippines, and Cuba. Cubans rebelled against Spanish rule, and the U.S. government found itself besieged by demands from Americans to assist the Cubans in their revolt. When the U.S. battleship Maine blew up off the coast of Havana, Cuba, Americans blamed the Spaniards for it and demanded American action against Spain. Two months later, Congress declared war on Spain and the U.S. quickly defeated them. The peace treaty gave the U.S. possession of Puerto Rico, the Philippines, Guam and Hawaii, which was annexed during the war. This success enlarged and expanded the U.S. role in foreign affairs.

Skill 1.9b **Understand the causes of United States participation in the First World War and the consequences at home and abroad**

Causes for the United States' participation in World War I included the surge of nationalism, the increasing strength of military capabilities, massive colonization for raw materials needed for industrialization and manufacturing, and military and diplomatic alliances.

In Europe, Italy and Germany each united into one nation from many smaller states. There were revolutions in Austria and Hungary, the Franco-Prussian War, the dividing of Africa among the strong European nations, interference and intervention of Western nations in Asia, and the breakup of Turkish dominance in the Balkans.

France, Great Britain, Italy, Portugal, Spain, Germany, and Belgium controlled the entire continent of Africa except Liberia and Ethiopia. In Asia and the Pacific Islands, only China, Japan, and Siam (present-day Thailand) kept their independence. The others were controlled by the strong European nations.

This success enlarged and expanded the U.S. role in foreign affairs. Under the administration of Theodore Roosevelt, the strength of U.S. armed forces was greatly increased. Roosevelt's foreign policy was summed up in the slogan of "Speak softly and carry a big stick," backing up the efforts in diplomacy with a strong military. During the years before the outbreak of World War I, evidence of U.S. emergence as a world power could be seen in a number of actions. In the spirit of the Monroe Doctrine of non-involvement of Europe in the affairs of the Western Hemisphere, President Roosevelt forced Italy, Germany, and Great Britain to remove their blockade of Venezuela. In addition he gained the rights to construct the Panama Canal by threatening force and assumed the finances of the Dominican Republic to stabilize it and prevent any intervention by Europeans. In 1916, President Woodrow Wilson ordered U.S. troops to the Dominican Republic.

In Europe, World War I started in 1914, eventually involving nearly 30 nations, and ended in 1918. One of the major causes of the war was the tremendous surge of nationalism during the 1800s and early 1900s. People of the same nationality or ethnic group sharing a common history, language or culture began uniting or demanding the right of unification. This was especially true in the empires of Eastern Europe, such as Russian Ottoman and Austrian-Hungarian Empires. Getting stronger and more intense were the beliefs of these peoples that loyalty to common political, social, and economic goals took priority any loyalty to the controlling nation or empire.

Emotions ran high and minor disputes magnified into major ones and sometimes quickly led to threats of war. Especially sensitive to these conditions was the area of the states on the Balkan Peninsula. Along with the imperialistic colonization for industrial raw materials, military build-up (especially by Germany) and diplomatic and military alliances, the conditions for one tiny spark to set off the explosion were in place. In July 1914, a Serbian national assassinated the Austrian heir to the throne, Archduke Franz Ferdinand, and his wife. Within a few weeks, war began. The few attempts to keep war from starting were futile.

At the same time, Great Britain intercepted and decoded a secret message from Germany to Mexico. This message urged Mexico to go to war against the U.S. The publishing of the Zimmerman Telegram, along with continued German destruction of American ships resulted in the eventual entry of the U.S. into the conflict. Though the U.S. was unprepared for war, governmental efforts and activities resulted in massive defense mobilization with America's economy directed to the war effort. Though America made important contributions of war materials, its greatest contribution to the war was manpower, soldiers desperately needed by the Allies.

Some ten months before the war ended, President Wilson proposed a program called the Fourteen Points as a method of bringing the war to an end with an equitable peace settlement. In these points, five set out general ideals, eight pertained to immediately working on resolving territorial and political problems, and the fourteenth counseled establishing The League of Nations, an organization of nations to help keep world peace.

When Germany agreed in 1918 to an armistice, it assumed that the peace settlement would be drawn up on the basis of these Fourteen Points. However, the peace conference in Versailles ignored these points, and Wilson had to be content with efforts at establishing the League of Nations. Italy, France, and Great Britain, having suffered and sacrificed far more in the war than America, wanted retribution. The Versailles Treaty severely punished the Central Powers, taking away arms and territories and requiring payment of reparations. Germany received a harsher punishment than the others and, according to one clause in the treaty, was forced to assume the responsibility for causing the war.

Pre-war empires lost tremendous amounts of territories as well as the wealth of natural resources in them. New, independent nations were formed, and some predominately ethnic areas came under control of nations of different cultural backgrounds. Some national boundary changes overlapped and created tensions and hard feelings as well as political and economic confusion. The wishes and desires of every national or cultural group could not possibly be realized and satisfied, resulting in disappointments for both—those who were victorious and those who were defeated. Germany received harsher terms than expected from the treaty, which weakened its post-war government.

Along with the worldwide depression of the 1930s, the stage was set for the rise of Adolf Hitler and his Nationalist Socialist Party and, eventually. World War II.

World War I saw the introduction of new types of warfare. Tanks, airplanes, machine guns, submarines, poisonous gas, and flame throwers got their first use in World War I. Fighting on the Western front was characterized by a series of trenches that were used throughout the war until 1918. U.S. involvement in the war did not occur until 1917. When it began in 1914, President Woodrow Wilson declared U.S. neutrality, and, anyway, most Americans were opposed to any involvement.

In 1916, Wilson was re-elected to a second term based on the slogan proclaiming his efforts at keeping America out of the war. For a few months after, he put forth most of his efforts to stopping the war, but German submarines began unlimited warfare against American merchant shipping.

President Wilson lost in his efforts to get the U.S. Senate to approve the Peace Treaty of Versailles. The Senate at the time reflected American public opinion, and its rejection of the treaty was a rejection of Wilson. The approval of the treaty would have made the U.S. a member of the League of Nations but Americans had just come off a bloody war to ensure that democracy would exist throughout the world. Americans did not want to accept any responsibility that resulted from its new position of power and were afraid that membership in the League of Nations would embroil the U.S. in future disputes in Europe.

Skill 1.9c   Demonstrate knowledge of political, economic, social, and cultural life in the "Roaring Twenties"

The end of World War I and the decade of the 1920s saw tremendous changes in the United States, signifying the beginning of its development into today's modern society. The shift from farm to city life was occurring in tremendous numbers. Social changes and problems were occurring at such a fast pace that it was extremely difficult and perplexing for many Americans to adjust to them. Politically the **18th Amendment** to the Constitution, the Prohibition Amendment, prohibited selling alcoholic beverages throughout the U.S., resulting in problems affecting all aspects of society. The passage of the **19th Amendment** gave women the right to vote in all elections. The decade of the 1920s also showed a marked change in roles and opportunities for women with more and more of them seeking and finding careers outside the home. They began to think of themselves as the equal of men and not as housewives and mothers.

The influence of the automobile, the entertainment industry, and the rejection of the morals and values of pre-World War I life, resulted in the fast-paced "**Roaring Twenties.**" There were significant effects on events leading to the Depression of the 1930s and the Second World War. Many Americans greatly desired the pre-war life and supported political policies and candidates in favor of the return to what was considered normal. They wanted to end government's strong role and adopt a policy of isolating the country from world affairs, a result of the war.

Prohibition of the sale of alcohol caused the increased activities of bootlegging and the rise of underworld gangs, illegal speakeasies, jazz music, and dances it promoted. The customers of these clubs were considered "modern," reflected by extremes in clothing, hairstyles, and attitudes towards authority and life. Movies and, to a certain degree, other types of entertainment, influenced Americans to admire, emulate, and support individual accomplishments. For example, the increased interest in sports figures and the accomplishments of national heroes, such as Lindbergh were reflections of this admiration.

As wild and uninhibited modern behavior became, this decade witnessed an increase in a religious tradition known as "revivalism" or emotional preaching. Although many Americans demanded law and order, the administration of President Warren G. Harding was marked by widespread corruption and scandal, not unlike the administration of Ulysses S. Grant. Grant, however, was honest and innocent. The decade of the '20s also saw the resurgence of such racist organizations as the Ku Klux Klan.

The U.S. economy experienced a tremendous period of boom. Restrictions on business no longer existed because of war and because conservatives in control adopted policies that helped and encouraged big business. To keep foreign goods from competing with American goods, tariffs were raised to the highest level.

American manufacturers developed many new products, and many different items, including refrigerators, radios, washing machines, and, most importantly, the automobile, became readily available to the people. These included.

Skill 1.9d   Demonstrate knowledge of political, economic, and social developments during the Great Depression and the New Deal

The 1929 Stock Market Crash was the powerful event that is generally interpreted as the beginning of the Great Depression in America. Although the crash of the Stock Market was unexpected, it was not without identifiable causes. The 1920s had been a decade of social and economic growth and hope. But the attitudes and actions of the 1920s regarding wealth, production, and investment created several trends that quietly set the stage for the 1929 disaster.

The legislative and executive branches of the Coolidge administration tended to favor businesses and the wealthy. The Revenue Act of 1926 significantly reduced income taxes for the wealthy. This bill lowered taxes so that a person with a million-dollar income saw his or her taxes reduced from $600,000 to $200,000. Despite the rise of labor unions, even the Supreme Court ruled in ways that further widened the gap between the rich and the middle and lower classes. In the case of Adkins v. Children's Hospital (1923), the Court ruled that minimum wage legislation was unconstitutional.

The majority of the population did not have enough money to buy what was necessary to meet their needs. The concept of buying on credit caught on very quickly. Buying on credit, however, creates artificial demand for products people cannot ordinarily afford. This has two effects: first, at some point there is less need to purchase products (because they have already been bought), and second, at some point paying for previous purchases makes it impossible to purchase new products. This effects exacerbated the problem of a surplus of goods.

The economy also relied on investment and luxury spending by the rich in the 1920s. Luxury spending, however, only occurs when people are confident with the economy and the future. Should these people lose confidence, that luxury spending comes to an abrupt halt, which is precisely what happened when the stock market crashed in 1929. Business investments produces returns for the investor. During the 1920s, while investing was very healthy, investors began to expect greater returns on their investments. This led many to make speculative investments in risky opportunities.

Two industries, automotive and radio, drove the economy in the 1920s. During this decade, the government tended to support new industries rather than agriculture. During WWI, the government had subsidized farms and paid ridiculously high prices for grains. Farmers had been encouraged to buy and farm more land and to use new technology to increase production. The nation was feeding much of Europe during and in the aftermath of the war. But when the war ended, these farm policies were cut off. Prices plummeted, farmers fell into debt, and farm prices declined. The agriculture industry was on the brink of ruin before the stock market crash.

The concentration of production and economic stability in the automotive industry and the production and sale of radios was expected to last forever. But there comes a point when the growth of an industry slows because of market saturation. When these two industries declined, because of decreased demand, they caused the collapse of other industries upon which they were dependent (e.g., rubber tires, glass, fuel, construction, etc.).

The other factor contributing to the Great Depression was the economic condition of Europe. The U.S. was lending money to European nations to rebuild after World War I. Many of these countries used this money to purchase U.S. food and manufactured goods, but they were not able to pay off their debts. While the U.S. was providing money, food, and goods to Europe, Americans were not willing to buy European goods. Trade barriers were enacted to maintain a favorable trade balance.

Risky speculative investments in the stock market were the second major factor contributing to the stock market crash of 1929 and the ensuing depression. Stock market speculation was spectacular throughout the 1920s. In 1929, shares traded on the New York Stock Exchange reached 1,124,800,410. In 1928 and 1929 stock prices doubled and tripled (RCA stock prices rose from 85 to 420 within one year). The opportunity to achieve such profits was irresistible. In much the same way that buying goods on credit became popular, buying stock on margin allowed people to invest a very small amount of money in the hope of receiving an exceptional profit. This created an investing craze that drove the market higher and higher. But brokers were also charging higher interest rates on their margin loans (nearly 20 percent). If, however, the price of the stock dropped, the investor owed the broker the amount borrowed plus interest.

Some scholars cite several other factors as contributing to the Great Depression. First, in 1929, the Federal Reserve increased interest rates. Second, some believe that, as interest rates rose and the stock market began to decline, people began to hoard money. This hoarding certainly took place after the crash. However, whether or not it was a cause of the crash is questionable.

In September 1929, stock prices began to slip somewhat, yet people remained optimistic. On Monday, October 21, prices began to fall quickly. The volume traded was so high that the tickers were unable to keep up. Investors were frightened, and they started selling very quickly, causing further collapse. For the next two days prices stabilized somewhat. On **Black Thursday**, October 24, prices plummeted again. By this time investors had lost confidence. On Friday and Saturday, some leading bankers tried to stop the crash But on Monday the 28th, prices began to fall again, declining by 13 percent in one day. The next day, **Black Tuesday, October 29**, saw 16.4 million shares traded. Stock prices fell so far that often no one was willing to buy at any price.

Unemployment quickly reached 25 percent nation-wide. People thrown out of their homes created makeshift domiciles of cardboard, scraps of wood, and tents. With unmasked reference to President Hoover, who was quite obviously overwhelmed by the situation and incompetent to deal with it, these communities were called "**Hoovervilles**." Families stood in bread lines, rural workers left the dust bowl of the plains to search for work in California, and banks failed. More than 100,000 businesses failed between 1929 and 1932. The despair that swept the nation left an indelible scar on all who endured the Depression.

When the stock market crashed, businesses collapsed. Without demand for products other businesses and industries collapsed. This set in motion a domino effect, bringing down the businesses and industries that provided raw materials or components to these industries. Hundreds of thousands became jobless. Then the jobless often became homeless. Desperation prevailed. Little has been done to assess the toll hunger, inadequate nutrition, or starvation took on the health of those who were children during this time. Indeed, food was cheap, relatively speaking, but there was little money to buy it.

Everyone who lived through the Great Depression was permanently affected in some way. Many never trusted banks again. Many people of this generation later hoarded cash so they would not risk losing everything again. Some permanently rejected the use of credit.

In the immediate aftermath of the stock market crash, many urged President Herbert Hoover to provide government relief. Hoover responded by urging the nation to be patient. By the time he signed relief bills in 1932, it was too late.

In several parts of the country, economic disaster was exacerbated by natural disaster. The Florida Keys were hit by the "**Labor Day Hurricane**" in 1935. This was one of only three hurricanes in history to make landfall as a Category 5 storm. More than 400 died in the storm, including 200 WWI veterans who were building bridges for a public works project. In the Northeast, the **Great Hurricane of 1938** struck Long Island, New York, causing more than 600 fatalities, decimating Long Island, and resulting in millions of dollars in damage to the coast from New York City to Boston.

By far the worst natural disaster of the decade came to be known as the **Dust Bowl.** Because of severe and prolonged drought in the Great Plains and previous reliance on inappropriate farming techniques, a series of devastating dust storms occurred in the 1930s that resulted in destruction, economic ruin for many, and dramatic ecological change.

Plowing the plains for agriculture removed the grass and exposed the soil. When the drought occurred, the soil dried out and became dust. Wind blew away the dust. Between 1934 and 1939 winds blew the soil to the east, all the way to the Atlantic Ocean. The dust storms, called "black blizzards," created huge clouds of dust that were visible all the way to Chicago. Topsoil was stripped from millions of acres. In Texas, Arkansas, Oklahoma, New Mexico, Kansas and Colorado more than half a million people were homeless. Many of these people journeyed west in the hope of making a new life in California.

Crops were ruined, the land was destroyed, and people either lost or abandoned homes and farms. Fifteen percent of Oklahoma's population left. Because so many of the migrants were from Oklahoma, the migrants came to be called **"Okies"** no matter where they came from. Estimates of the number of people displaced by this disaster range from 300,000 or 400,000 to 2.5 million.

Hoover's bid for re-election in 1932 failed. The new president, Franklin D. Roosevelt, won the White House on his promise to the American people of a "new deal." Upon assuming the office, Roosevelt and his advisers immediately launched a massive program of innovation and experimentation to try to bring the Depression to an end and get the nation back on track. Congress gave the President unprecedented power to act to save the nation. During the next eight years, the most extensive and broadly based legislation in the nation's history was enacted. The legislation was intended to accomplish three goals—relief, recovery, and reform.

The first step in the Roosevelt's **"New Deal"** was to relieve suffering. This was accomplished through a number of job-creation projects. The second step, the recovery aspect, was to stimulate the economy. The third step was to create social and economic change through innovative legislation.

The National Recovery Administration attempted to accomplish the following goals:
- Restore employment,
- Increase general purchasing power,
- Provide character-building activity for unemployed youth,
- Encourage decentralization of industry and thus divert population from crowded cities to rural or semi-rural communities,
- Develop river resources in the interest of navigation and cheap power and light,
- Complete flood control on a permanent basis,

- Enlarge the national program of forest protection and develop forest resources,
- Control farm production and improve farm prices,
- Assist home builders and home owners,
- Restore public faith in banking and trust operations, and
- Recapture the value of physical assets, whether in real property, securities, or other investments.

These objectives and their accomplishments implied a restoration of public confidence and courage.

Among the "alphabet organizations" set up to work out the details of the recovery plan, the most prominent were:

- **Agricultural Adjustment Administration** (AAA), designed to readjust agricultural production and prices, thereby, boosting farm income.
- **Civilian Conservation Corps** (CCC), designed to give wholesome, useful activity in the forestry service to unemployed young men.
- **Civil Works Administration** (CWA) and the **Public Works Administration** (PWA) were designed to provide employment in the construction and repair of public buildings, parks, and highways.
- **Works Progress Administration** (WPA) sought to move individuals from relief rolls to work projects or private employment.

The **Tennessee Valley Authority** (TVA) was of a more permanent nature. Designed to improve the navigability of the Tennessee River and increase productivity of the timber and farm lands in its valley, this program built 16 dams that provided water control and hydroelectric generation.

The **Public Works Administration** employed Americans on more than 34,000 public works projects at a cost of more than $4 billion. Among these projects were the construction of a highway that linked the Florida Keys and Miami, the Boulder Dam (now the Hoover Dam), and numerous highway projects.

To provide economic stability and prevent another crash, Congress passed the **Glass-Steagall Act**, which separated banking and investing. The Securities and Exchange Commission was created to regulate dangerous speculative practices on Wall Street. The **Wagner Act** guaranteed a number of rights to workers and unions, including the right to collectively bargain, in an effort to improve worker-employer relations. The **Social Security Act of 1935** established pensions for the aged and infirm as well as a system of unemployment insurance.

While much of the New Deal aimed to resolve the Depression immediately, certain permanent national policies emerged. The public, through its government, wanted to supervise and, to an extent, regulate business operations, from corporation activities to labor problems. These included protecting bank depositors and the credit system of the country, employing gold resources and currency adjustments to aid permanent restoration of normal living, and, if possible, establishing a line of subsistence below which no useful citizen would be permitted to sink.

Many of the steps taken by the Roosevelt administration have had far-reaching effects. They alleviated the economic disaster of the Great Depression, they enacted controls that would mitigate the risk of another stock market crash, and they provided greater security for workers. The nation's economy, however, did not fully recover until America entered World War II.

During the first 100 days in office, the Roosevelt administration responded to this crisis with programs designed to restore the ecological balance. One action was the formation of the **Soil Conservation Service** (now the Natural Resources Conservation Service). The story of this natural disaster and its toll in human suffering is poignantly preserved in the photographs of Dorothea Lange.

There were negative reactions to some of the measures taken to pull the country out of the Depression. There was a major reaction to the deaths of the WWI veterans in the Labor Day Hurricane, ultimately resulting in a Congressional investigation into possible negligence. The Central Valley Project ruffled feathers of farmers who lost tillable land and some water supply to the construction of the aqueduct and the Hoover Dam. Tennesseans were initially unhappy with the changes in river flow and navigation when the Tennessee Valley Authority began its construction of dams and the directing of water to form reservoirs and power hydroelectric plants. Some businesses and business leaders were not happy with the introduction of minimum wage laws and restrictions and controls on working conditions and limitations of work hours for laborers. The numerous import and export tariffs of the period were the subject of controversy.

In the long view, however, much that was accomplished under the New Deal had positive long-term effects on economic, ecological, social, and political issues for the next several decades. The Tennessee Valley Authority and the Central Valley Project in California provided reliable sources and supplies of water to major cities and electrical power to meet the needs of an increasingly electricity-dependent society. For the middle class and the poor, the labor regulations, the establishment of the Social Security Administration, and the separation of investment and banking have served the nation admirably for more than six decades.

The charter of the National Recovery Administration included a statement defending the right of labor unions to exist and to negotiate with employers. This was interpreted by thousands as support for unions. But the Supreme Court declared this unconstitutional.

The following major events and actions are particularly important to the history of organized labor during this decade:

- The Supreme Court upheld the Railway Labor Act, including its prohibition of employer interference or coercion in the choice of bargaining representatives (1930).
- The Davis-Bacon Act provided that employers of contractors and subcontractors on public construction should be paid the prevailing wages (1931).
- The Anti-Injunction Act prohibited Federal injunctions in most labor disputes (1932).
- Wisconsin created the first unemployment insurance act in the country (1932).
- The Wagner-Peyser Act created the United States Employment Service within the Department of Labor (1933).
- Half a million Southern mill workers walked off the job in the Great Uprising of 1934.
- The Secretary of Labor called the first National Labor Legislation Conference to get better cooperation between the Federal Government and the States in defining a national labor legislation program (1934).
- The U.S. joined the International Labor Organization (1934).
- The Wagner Act (The National Labor Relations Act) established a legal basis for unions, set collective bargaining as a matter of national policy required by the law, provided for secret ballot elections for choosing unions, and protected union members from employer intimidation and coercion. This law was later amended by the Taft-Hartley Act (1947) and by the Landrum Griffin Act (1959).
- The Guffey Act stabilized the coal industry and improved labor conditions (1935). It was later declared unconstitutional in 1936.
- The Social Security Act was approved in1935.
- The Committee for Industrial Organization (CIO) was formed within the AFL to carry unionism to the industrial sector in 1935.
- The United Rubber Workers staged the first sit-down strike (1936).
- The United Auto Workers used the sit-down strike against General Motors (1936).
- The Anti-Strikebreaker Act (the Byrnes Act) made it illegal to transport or aid strikebreakers in interstate or foreign trade (1936).
- The Public Contracts Act (the Walsh-Healey Act) of 1936 established labor standards, including minimum wages, overtime pay, child and convict labor provisions and safety standards on federal contracts.

- General Motors recognized the United Auto Workers in 1937.
- US Steel recognized the Steel Workers Organizing Committee in 1937.
- The Wagner Act was upheld by the Supreme Court (1937).
- During a strike of the Steel Workers Organizing Committee against Republic Steel, police attacked a crowd gathered in support of the strike, killing ten and injuring eighty. This came to be called **The Memorial Day Massacre** (1937).
- The CIO was expelled from the AFL over charges of dual unionism or competition (1937).
- The National Apprenticeship Act established the Bureau of Apprenticeship within the Department of Labor (1937).
- The Merchant Marine Act created a Federal Maritime Labor Board (1938).
- The Fair Labor Standards Act created a $0.25 minimum wage, stipulated time-and-a-half pay for hours over 40 per week.
- The CIO becomes the Congress of Industrial Organizations.

COMPETENCY 1.10   THE SECOND WORLD WAR AND THE POSTWAR PERIOD (1939-1963)

Skill 1.10a   Understand the causes of United States participation in the Second World War and the consequences at home and abroad

The U.S. had opposed Japan's invasion of Southeast Asia, an effort to gain Japanese control of that region's rich resources. Consequently, the U.S. stopped all important exports to Japan, whose industries depended heavily on petroleum, scrap metal, and other raw materials. Later Roosevelt blocked the Japanese withdrawal of its funds from American banks. General Tojo became the Japanese premier in October, 1941, and quickly realized that the U.S. Navy was powerful enough to block Japanese expansion into Asia. Deciding to cripple the U.S. Pacific Fleet, the Japanese air force, without warning, bombed the Fleet December 7, 1941, while it was at anchor in Pearl Harbor in Hawaii. Temporarily it was a success. It destroyed many aircraft and disabled much of the U.S. Pacific Fleet. In the end, it was a costly mistake because it quickly motivated the Americans to prepare for and wage war.

Military strategy in the war as developed by Roosevelt, Churchill, and Stalin was to concentrate on Germany's defeat first, then Japan's. The start was made in North Africa, pushing Germans and Italians off the continent, beginning in the summer of 1942 and ending successfully in May, 1943. Before the war, Hitler and Stalin had signed a non-aggression pact in 1939, which Hitler violated in 1941 by invading the Soviet Union. The German defeat at Stalingrad, marking a turning point in the war, was caused by a combination of entrapment by Soviet troops and death of German troops by starvation and freezing because of the horrendous winter conditions. All this occurred at the same time the Allies were driving the Germans and Italians out of North Africa.

The liberation of Italy began in July 1943 and ended May 2, 1945. The third part of the strategy was D-Day, June 6, 1944, an Allied invasion of France at Normandy. At the same time, starting in January 1943, the Soviets began pushing the German troops back into Europe, and they were greatly assisted by supplies from Britain and the United States. By April 1945, Allies occupied positions beyond the Rhine and the Soviets moved on to Berlin, surrounding it by April 25. Germany surrendered May 7 and the war in Europe was finally over.

Meanwhile, in the Pacific, in the six months after the attack on Pearl Harbor, Japanese forces moved across Southeast Asia and the western Pacific Ocean. By August 1942, the Japanese Empire was at its largest and stretched northeast to Alaska's Aleutian Islands, west to Burma, south to what is now Indonesia. Invaded and controlled areas included Hong Kong, Guam, Wake Island, Thailand, part of Malaysia, Singapore, the Philippines; and they bombed Darwin on the north coast of Australia.

The raid of General Doolittle's bombers on Japanese cities and the American naval victory at Midway along with the fighting in the Battle of the Coral Sea helped turn the tide against Japan. Island-hopping by U.S. Seabees and Marines and the grueling bloody battles fought resulted in gradually pushing the Japanese back towards Japan.

After victory was attained in Europe, concentrated efforts were made to secure Japan's surrender, but it took dropping two atomic bombs on the cities of Hiroshima and Nagasaki to end the war in the Pacific. Japan formally surrendered on September 2, 1945, aboard the U.S. battleship Missouri, anchored in Tokyo Bay. The war had finally ended.

Before war in Europe ended, the Allies had agreed on a military occupation of Germany. It was divided into four zones each one occupied by one of four powers: Great Britain, France, the Soviet Union, and the United States. Each nation would jointly administer Berlin. After the war, the Allies agreed that Germany's armed forces would be abolished, the Nazi Party outlawed, and the territory east of the Oder and Neisse Rivers taken away. Nazi leaders were accused of war crimes and brought to trial.

After Japan's defeat, the Allies began a military occupation directed by American General Douglas MacArthur, who introduced a number of reforms, eventually ridding Japan of its military institutions and transforming it into a democratic nation. A constitution was drawn up in 1947, transferring all political rights from the emperor to the people, granting women the right to vote, and denying Japan the right to declare war. War crimes trials of 25 war leaders and government officials were also conducted. The U.S. did not sign a peace treaty until 1951. The treaty permitted Japan to rearm but took away its overseas empire.

Again, after a major world war came efforts to prevent war from occurring again throughout the world. Preliminary work began in 1943 when the U.S., Great Britain, the Soviet Union, and China sent representatives to Moscow where they agreed to set up an international organization that would work to promote peace around the earth. In 1944, the four Allied powers met again and made the decision to name the organization the United Nations. In 1945, a charter for the U. N. was drawn up and signed, taking effect in October of that year.

Major consequences of the war included horrendous death and destruction, millions of displaced persons, the gaining of strength and spread of Communism, and Cold War tensions as a result of the beginning of the nuclear age. The death toll and casualties of World War II were more than any other war in history.

Besides the losses of millions of military personnel, the devastation and destruction directly affected civilians, reducing cities, houses, and factories to ruin and rubble and totally wrecking communication and transportation systems.

Millions of civilian deaths, especially in China and the Soviet Union, were the results of famine.

More than 12 million people were uprooted by war's end, having no place to live. Those included were prisoners of war, those that survived Nazi concentration camps and slave labor camps, orphans, and people who escaped war-torn areas and invading armies. Changing national boundary lines also caused the mass movement of displaced persons.

Germany and Japan were completely defeated; Great Britain and France were seriously weakened; and the Soviet Union and the United States became the world's leading powers. Although they were allied during the war, the alliance fell apart as the Soviets pushed Communism and the U.S. strove to combat it in Europe and Asia. In spite of the tremendous destruction it suffered, the Soviet Union was stronger than ever. During the war, it took control of Lithuania, Estonia, and Latvia and by mid-1945 parts of Poland, Czechoslovakia, Finland, and Romania. It helped Communist governments gain power in Bulgaria, Romania, Hungary, Czechoslovakia, Poland, and North Korea. China fell to Mao Tse-Tsung's Communist forces in 1949.

Until the fall of the Berlin Wall in 1989 and the dissolution of Communist governments in Eastern Europe and the Soviet Union, the United States and the Soviet Union faced off in what was called a Cold War. The possibility of the terrifying destruction by nuclear weapons loomed over both nations.

Skill 1.10b   Understand domestic and foreign developments during the Cold War

The major thrust of U.S. foreign policy from the end of World War II to 1991 was the post-war struggle between non-Communist nations, led by the United States, and the Soviet Union and the Communist nations who were its allies. It was referred to as a "Cold War" because its conflicts did not lead to a major war of fighting, or a "hot war." Both the Soviet Union and the United States embarked on an arsenal buildup of atomic and hydrogen bombs as well as other nuclear weapons. Both nations could destroy each other but, because of the continuous threat of nuclear war and accidents, extreme caution was practiced on both sides. The efforts of both sides to serve and protect their political philosophies and to support and assist their allies resulted in a number of events during this 46-year period.

In 1946, Josef Stalin stated publicly that the presence of capitalism and its development of the world's economy made international peace impossible. As a result, an American diplomat in Moscow, George F. Kennan, in response to Stalin, proposed a statement of U.S. foreign policy. The idea and goal of the U.S. was to contain or limit the extension or expansion of Soviet Communist policies and activities. After Soviet efforts to make trouble in Iran, Greece, and Turkey, U.S. President Harry Truman stated what is known as the **Truman Doctrine,** which committed the U.S. to a policy of intervention in order to contain or stop the spread of communism throughout the world.

After 1945, social and economic chaos continued in Western Europe, especially in Germany. Secretary of State George C. Marshall came to realize that the U.S. had serious problems. To assist the recovery, he proposed a program known as the European Recovery Program, or the **Marshall Plan**. Although the Soviet Union withdrew from any participation, the U.S. continued helping Europe regain economic stability. In Germany, the situation was critical with the American Army shouldering the staggering burden of relieving the serious problems of the German economy. In February, 1948, Britain and the U.S. combined their two zones, and France joined in June.

The Soviets were opposed to German unification, and, in April 1948, took serious action to either stop it or to force the Allies to give up control of West Berlin to the Soviets. The Soviets blocked all road traffic access to West Berlin from West Germany. To avoid any armed conflict, it was decided to airlift needed food and supplies into West Berlin. From June 1948 to mid-May 1949 Allied air forces flew in all that was needed for the West Berliners, forcing the Soviets to lift the blockade and permit vehicular traffic access to the city.

The first "hot war" in the post-World War II era was the Korean War, which began on June 25, 1950, and ended July 27, 1953. Troops from communist North Korea invaded democratic South Korea in an effort to unite both sections under communist control. The United Nations organization asked its member nations to furnish troops to help restore peace. Many nations responded, and President Truman sent American troops to help the South Koreans. The war dragged on for three years and ended with a truce, not a peace treaty. Like Germany then, Korea remained divided and remains divided to this day.

In 1954, the French were forced to give up their colonial claims in Indochina, the present-day countries of Vietnam, Laos, and Cambodia. Afterwards, the communist northern part of Vietnam began battling with the democratic southern part over control of the entire country. In the late 1950s and early 1960s, U.S. Presidents Eisenhower and Kennedy sent a number of military advisers to Vietnam. They also sent military aid to assist and support South Vietnam's non-communist government. During Lyndon Johnson's presidency, the war escalated with thousands of American troops being sent to participate in combat with the South Vietnamese. The war was extremely unpopular in America and caused such serious divisiveness among its citizens that Johnson decided not to seek reelection in 1968. It was during President Richard Nixon's second term in office that the U.S. signed an agreement ending the Vietnam War and restoring peace. This was done January 27, 1973, and by March 29, the last American combat troops and American prisoners of war left Vietnam for home. After the last Americans left Vietnam, the North Vietnamese moved into South Vietnam uniting both sides in communist Vietnam. It was the longest war in U.S. history and to this day carries the perception that it was a "lost war."

In 1962, during President John F. Kennedy's administration, Premier Khrushchev and the Soviets decided to install nuclear missiles on Cuba as a protective measure against American invasion. In October, American U-2 spy planes photographed over Cuba what were identified as missile bases under construction. The decision in the White House was how to handle the situation without starting a war. The only recourse was removal of the missile sites and preventing more being set up. Kennedy announced that the U.S. had set up a "quarantine" of Soviet ships heading to Cuba. It was in reality a blockade but the word itself could not be used publicly as a blockade was actually considered an act of war.

Thirteen days of incredible tension and anxiety gripped the entire world until Khrushchev capitulated. Soviet ships carrying missiles for the Cuban bases turned back and the crisis eased. What precipitated the crisis was Khrushchev's underestimation of Kennedy. The President made no effort to prevent the erection of the Berlin Wall and was reluctant to commit American troops to invade Cuba and overthrow Fidel Castro. The Soviets assumed this was a weakness and decided they could install the missiles without any interference.

The Soviets were concerned about American missiles installed in Turkey aimed at the Soviet Union and about a possible invasion of Cuba. If successful, Khrushchev would demonstrate to the Russian and Chinese critics of his policy of peaceful coexistence that he was tough and not to be intimidated. At the same time, the Americans feared that if Russian missiles were put in place and launched from Cuba to the U.S., the short distance of 90 miles would not allow enough time for adequate warning. Furthermore, it would originate from a direction that radar systems could not detect. It was felt that if America gave in and allowed a Soviet presence practically at the back door that the effect on American security and morale would be devastating.

As tensions eased in the aftermath of the crisis, several agreements were made. The missiles in Turkey were removed, as they were obsolete. A telephone "hot line" was set up between Moscow and Washington to make it possible for the two heads of government to have instant contact with each other. The U.S. agreed to sell its surplus wheat to the Soviets.

Probably the highlight of the foreign policy of President Richard Nixon, after the end of the Vietnam War and withdrawal of troops, was his 1972 trip to China. When the Communists gained control of China in 1949, the policy of the U.S. government was refusal to recognize the Communist government. It regarded as the legitimate government of China to be that of Chiang Kai-Shek, exiled on the island of Taiwan.

In 1971, Nixon sent Henry Kissinger on a secret trip to Peking to investigate whether or not America could recognize China. In February 1972, the President and his wife spent a number of days in China visiting well-known landmarks and dining with the two leaders, Mao Tse-Tung and Chou En-Lai. Agreements were made for cultural and scientific exchanges, eventual resumption of trade, and future unification of the mainland with Taiwan. In 1979, formal diplomatic recognition was achieved. With this one visit, the structure of the Cold War shifted.

During the administration of President Jimmy Carter, Egyptian President Anwar el Sadat and Israeli Prime Minister Menachem Begin met at presidential retreat Camp David. For years before this, negotiations were taking place between the two nations, including a historic visit to Jerusalem by Sadat. After a series of meetings, the two countries agreed to sign a formal peace treaty. In 1979, the Soviet invasion of Afghanistan was perceived by Carter and his advisers as a threat to the rich oil fields in the Persian Gulf. At the time, U.S. military capability to prevent further Soviet aggression in the Middle East was weak. The last year of Carter's presidential term was taken up with the 53 American hostages held in Iran. The Shah of Iran had been deposed and control of the government and the country was in the hands of fundamentalist Muslim leader Ayatollah Ruhollah Khomeini.

Khomeini's extreme hatred for the U.S. was the result of the 1953 overthrow of Iran's Mossadegh government, sponsored by the CIA. To make matters worse, the CIA proceeded to train the Shah's ruthless secret police force. So, when the terminally-ill, exiled shah was allowed into the U.S. for medical treatment, a fanatical mob, supported and encouraged by Khomeini, stormed into the American embassy, taking the 53 Americans as prisoners.

President Carter froze all Iranian assets in the U.S., set up trade restrictions, and approved a risky rescue attempt, which failed. He had appealed to the UN for aid in gaining release for the hostages and to European allies to join the trade embargo on Iran. Khomeini ignored U.N. requests for releasing the Americans and Europeans refused to support the embargo. They did not want to risk losing access to Iran's oil. American prestige was damaged, and Carter's chances for re-election were doomed. The hostages were released on the day of Ronald Reagan's inauguration as President when Carter released Iranian assets as ransom.

President Reagan's foreign policy was, in his first term, focused primarily on the Western Hemisphere, particularly in Central America and the West Indies. U.S. involvement in the domestic revolutions of El Salvador and Nicaragua continued into Reagan's second term when Congress held televised hearings on what came to be known as the Iran-Contra Affair. A cover-up was exposed showing that profits from secretly selling military hardware to Iran had been used to give support to rebels, called Contras, who were fighting in Nicaragua. In 1983 in Lebanon, 241 American Marines were killed when an Islamic suicide bomber drove an explosive-laden truck into U.S. Marines headquarters located at the airport in Beirut.

This tragic event came as part of the unrest and violence between the Israelis and the Palestine Liberation Organization (PLO) forces in southern Lebanon. In October, 1983, 1,900 U.S. Marines landed on the island of Grenada to rescue a small group of American medical students at the medical school and depose the leftist government. Perhaps the most intriguing and far-reaching event towards the end of Reagan's second term was the arms-reduction agreement Reagan reached with Soviet General Secretary Mikhail Gorbachev. Gorbachev began easing East-West tensions by stressing the importance of cooperation with the West and easing the harsh and restrictive life of the people in the Soviet Union. In retrospect, it was clearly a prelude to the events occurring during the administration of President George Bush.

After Bush took office, it appeared for a brief period that democracy would gain a hold and influence in China, but the brief movement was quickly and decisively crushed. The biggest surprise was the fall of the Berlin Wall, resulting in the unification of all of Germany. The loss of the communists' power in other Eastern European countries and the fall of communism in the Soviet Union and the breakup of its republics into independent nations were no less surprising. The countries of Poland, Hungary, Romania, Czechoslovakia, Albania, and Bulgaria replaced communist rule with a democratic system.

The former Yugoslavia broke apart into individual ethnic enclaves, with the republics of Serbia, Croatia, and Bosnia-Herzegovina embarking on wars of ethnic cleansing between Catholics, Orthodox, and Muslims. In Russia, as in the other former republics and satellites, democratic governments were put into operation and the difficult task of changing communist economies into ones of capitalistic free enterprise began. For all practical purposes, it appeared that the tensions and dangers of the post-World War II "Cold War" between the U.S. and Soviet-led Communism were over.

Skill 1.10c   Demonstrate knowledge of political, economic, social, and cultural life in the 1950s

President Harry Truman's administration entered the 1950s with a daunting task. A former ally, the Soviet Union under Josef Stalin, was now a rival for geopolitical influence, and the Cold War had been underway with East Germany and Eastern Europe well into the Soviet sphere of control. China had recently ended a decades-long civil war that put the Communist Party under the chairmanship of Mao Tse-Tung and exiled the Guomindang (Nationalist Party) under Chiang Kai-shek to Taiwan. In Indochina (Vietnam, Laos and Cambodia), the Viet Minh, under Ho Chi-Minh and forces under Vo Nguyen Giap's command had mounted a resistance to French colonial rule. In the minds of right-wing American politicians, these events were evidence for the "Red Menace" and a conspiracy for international domination by the communist bloc. Truman, a Democrat, was confronted at home by a Congress controlled by the Republican Party, which carried on a series of hearings and investigation to ferret out "Reds" and communist sympathizers, starting with government agencies. It soon spread to labor organizations, the arts and entertainment industry, and eventually to the infamous "Blacklist" of individuals suspected of Communist Party affiliations that prevented the listed individuals from pursuing their chosen professions.

Economically, the post-World War II economic boom continued into the 1950s. The Korean War era, 1950-1953 did not see the kind of general mobilization that World War II had. Most Americans were not directly affected by the war in Korea and the expansion of the economy continued. The growing middle class was spurred by the GI Bill of Rights, which gave educational, occupational, and mortgage assistance to veterans who could enjoy a middle class lifestyle on an unprecedented scale.

The population boom of the babies born to veterans led to another social and cultural phenomenon, the "Baby Boomers." The election of Dwight D. Eisenhower as President in 1952 marked a continuation of economic progress and a burgeoning suburban population, fueled by low-interest Veterans Administration mortgage loans and new wealth.

After World War II and the Korean War, efforts to relieve the problems of millions of African-Americans, including ending discrimination in education, housing, and jobs and the grinding widespread poverty increased. Although President Truman ordered the Armed Forces to integrate in 1947, the same year Jackie Robinson broke the "color barrier" of Major League Baseball, the military services were slow to integrate until the Korean War when African-American soldiers were assigned to front-line Army units without regard to race. The other services followed suit, but only begrudgingly and out of necessity to replace personnel as casualties reduced their ranks. The efforts of civil rights leaders found success in a number of Supreme Court decisions, the best-known case, *Brown* v. *Board of Education of Topeka* (1954)" ending compulsory segregation in public schools.

COMPETENCY 1.11 RECENT DEVELOPMENTS (1960S–PRESENT)

Skill 1.11a Understand political developments, including the war in Vietnam, the "imperial presidency," and the new conservatism

Poverty remained a serious problem in the central sections of large cities and resulted in riots and soaring crime rates, which ultimately found their way to the suburbs. The American entry into, and the escalation of, the war in Vietnam, caused a social conflict and upheaval between supporters of the war and those opposed to U.S. involvement. This conflict eventually led to many antiwar demonstrations. Increased drug abuse; the weakening of the family unit; homelessness; poverty; mental illness; and increasing social, mental, and physical problems experienced by the Vietnam veterans returning to families and marriages contributed to a country divided and torn apart across generational lines.

The 1960 election of President John F. Kennedy signaled a new era in American politics and culture. Kennedy was the first president born in the twentieth century and the second youngest to hold that office, after Theodore Roosevelt. As president, he called for Americans to serve society and the world, to improve it through voluntary service at home and abroad. The Peace Corps was one of the better-known programs that he created as part of his "New Frontiers" platform during the presidential campaign. His mettle as a world leader was tested early in his administration. The Bay of Pigs invasion to unseat Fidel Castro from power in Cuba ended in disaster for the United States and gave Cuba a propaganda coup. The Cuban Missile Crisis nearly brought the United States to the brink of nuclear war with the Soviet Union. He also ordered military advisors to the Republic of Vietnam to support the Republic against the communist National Liberation Front (Viet Cong) who were South Vietnamese proxies for North Vietnam, thus commencing what later turned out to be a political and military quagmire for the United States. When Kennedy was assassinated in 1963, the country faced an internal period of grief and lost a considerable amount of prestige among world leaders. Vice President Lyndon B. Johnson was sworn in as President after Kennedy's death in accordance with constitutional rules of succession. As President, Johnson retained Kennedy's cabinet pretty much intact with few leaving and appointed Senator Hubert H. Humphrey of Minnesota as Vice President.

U.S. involvement was the second phase of three in Vietnam's twentieth century history. The first phase began in 1946 when the Vietnamese fought French troops for control of the country. Before 1946, Vietnam was part of the French colony of Indochina (since 1861 along with Laos and Kampuchea or Cambodia). In 1954, the defeated French left and the country became divided into communist north and democratic south. United States' aid and influence continued as part of the U.S. "Cold War" foreign policy to help any nation threatened by Communism.

The second phase involved the U.S. commitment. The communist Vietnamese considered the war one of national liberation, a struggle to avoid the continual dominance and influence of a foreign power. A cease-fire was arranged in January 1973 and by March U.S. troops left for good. The third and final phase consisted of fighting between the Vietnamese but ended April 30, 1975, with the surrender of South Vietnam, the entire country being united under Communist rule.

Participants were the United States of America, Australia, New Zealand, South and North Vietnam, South Korea, Thailand, and the Philippines. With active U.S. involvement from 1957 to 1973, it was the longest war participated in by the U.S.; it was tremendously destructive and completely divided the American public in their opinions and feelings about the war. Many were frustrated and angered by the fact that it was the first war fought on foreign soil in which U.S. combat forces were totally unable to achieve their goals and objectives.

Returning veterans faced not only a hard readjustment to normal civilian life but also bitterness, anger, rejection, and no heroes' welcome. Many suffered severe physical and deep psychological problems. The war set a precedent with Congress and the American people actively challenging U.S. military and foreign policy. The conflict, though tempered markedly by time, still exists and still has a definite effect on people.

The Vietnam War also divided the Democratic Party, and the 1968 Democratic National Convention in Chicago turned out to be a highly contentious and bitterly fought, both on the floor of the convention and outside, where thousands had gathered to protest the Vietnam War. Vice President Hubert H. Humphrey became the party's nominee, but he led a divided party. 1968 was a bad year for the United States and especially the Democratic Party. In Vietnam, the forces of the Viet Cong and the North Vietnamese Army (NVA) launched a coordinated and devastating offensive on January 30, on the eve of Tet, the Lunar New Year, disproving the Johnson Administration officials who claimed that the Vietnamese Communists were no longer a viable military force. Although the Tet Offensive was a tactical defeat for the Viet Cong because it no longer could field a large enough military force to match American firepower in a set-piece engagement, it was a strategic defeat for the Americans in public relations and the political will to continue in a seemingly endless conflict. Also, the Reverend Martin Luther King, Jr., an influential leader of the Civil Rights Movement and its most eloquent spokesman, was assassinated in Memphis, Tennessee, sparking racial riots in many American cities. Senator Robert F. Kennedy of New York, the late President John F. Kennedy's younger brother, was also assassinated in Los Angeles after winning the California Democratic Primary. Before he died, it looked very possible that he would have won the party's nomination, running on an anti-war platform.

The Presidential Election campaign of 1964 pitted President Johnson against the Republican nominee, Senator Barry Goldwater of Arizona. Goldwater represented the "New Conservative" wing of his party, which advocated scaling back government from Roosevelt's New Deal and the liberal social policies of the Kennedy and Johnson administrations. The Goldwater campaign also advocated a strong military to counter the "Red Menace" of the Soviet Union, the People's Republic of China, and the Communist bloc nations of the Warsaw Pact. Lyndon Johnson successfully won re-election, based partly on depicting Goldwater as a warmonger who would plunge the United States into a mutually destructive thermonuclear war with the Soviet Union. President Johnson won a landslide victory.

Unfortunately for Johnson, the war in Vietnam overshadowed his domestic programs and indelibly marked his legacy. It became known as "Johnson's War." The Gulf of Tonkin Resolution was enacted in late 1964 after an incident off the coast of Vietnam involving U.S. Naval ships and North Vietnamese coastal patrol boats and effectively gave the President the power to prosecute a war without Congress declaring it, as clearly stated in the Constitution. Soon afterward, in 1965, Johnson authorized the commitment of conventional military forces to Vietnam. The war proved to be a drain on the nation's economy and a growing burden for the President. Anti-war sentiment divided the nation as it hadn't since the Civil War. Eventually, the Vietnam quagmire became such a hindrance to his administration that Johnson declared, in a nationally televised address, that he would halt the bombing of North Vietnam and not be a candidate for the Democratic Party's nominee for the 1968 Presidential Election.

Former Vice President Richard M. Nixon defeated the current Vice President Hubert Humphrey, who had been closely identified with Johnson's Vietnam policy. One of Nixon's campaign promises included a "secret plan" to end American involvement in Vietnam. Ironically, the war dragged on for the length of his first term, and he ordered a widening of the war by ordering troops to invade previously neutral Cambodia in 1970. This action led to even more dissent against the war and the killing of four students at Kent State University in Ohio during a protest over the invasion of Cambodia.

In other international dealings, with a major role played by his National Security Advisor and later Secretary of State Henry Kissinger, Nixon undertook a bold international policy of détente with the Soviet Union and the unexpected step of opening official relations with the People's Republic of China. Given Nixon's political reputation as a staunch anti-Communist, this undertaking was surprising because China gave both political and material support to North Vietnam.

The Nixon administration was characterized as an "**Imperial Presidency**" because of his aggrandizement of presidential power—usurping powers that have been the purview of Congress and carrying on activities without the express consent of the Congress. The **Watergate** scandal resulted in the first-ever resignation of a sitting American president. The population of the U.S. had continued to increase along with the nation's industries and the resulting harmful pollution of the environment. Factory smoke, automobile exhaust, waste from factories and other sources all combined to create hazardous air, water, and ground pollution which, if not brought under control and significantly diminished, would severely endanger all life on earth. The 1980s was the decade of the horrible Exxon Valdez oil spill off the Alaskan coast and the nuclear accident and melt-down at the Ukrainian nuclear power plant at Chernobyl. The U.S. had a narrow escape with the near disaster at Three Mile Island Nuclear Plant in Pennsylvania.

Skill 1.11b　Understand economic developments, including changes in industrial structure, the growth of the budget deficit, the impact of deregulation, and energy and environmental issues

Economic problems emerged in the late1960s as a result of the high costs of waging war in Vietnam, the arms race with the Soviet Union and the increasing costs of growing social programs that quickly outstripped military spending as a share of the federal budget, exacerbated by an aversion for raising federal tax rates. The boom times for the economy of the 1950s slowed down by the mid- and late-60s, but America's appetite for non-renewable petroleum to power cars, utilities, and industrial production grew unchecked, making the country more reliant on imports as demand outstripped domestic reserves' capacity to keep up. Persian Gulf nations provided the bulk of the imported oil, mainly from Saudi Arabia and Iran. The United States was, therefore, dependent on a critical resource from an increasingly unstable part of the world. It was further complicated by American support for Israel in the 1967 Six Day War against Egypt, Syria, and Jordan, who were receiving aid from a number of other Arab nations; and the 1973 Yom Kippur War against Egypt and Syria, who were receiving aid from at least nine other Arab nations.

In order to support the unprecedented levels of spending, President Nixon instituted deficit spending, where government spending exceeded collected revenues. This led to a dramatic increase in the national debt, as measured by the outstanding obligations in U.S. Treasury securities (bills, notes and bonds) that were issued to cover the costs of government. The 1970s witnessed a period of high unemployment, the result of a severe recession. This was also accompanied by high inflation and wage increases, and the Nixon Administration imposed wage and price controls in August, 1971, in order to lift the economy out of recession and offset the effects of "stagflation," a stagnant economy in a period of high inflation.

Angered by the United States support of Israel in the Yom Kippur War, the Arab oil-producing nations of OPEC (Organization of Petroleum Exporting Countries) cut back on oil production and boycotted exports to the United States, thus raising the price of a barrel of oil and creating a fuel shortage. Clearly, energy and fuel conservation were necessary in the American economy, especially since fuel shortages created two energy crises during the decade of the 1970s. Americans experienced shortages of fuel oil for heating and gasoline for cars and other vehicles.

A great awakening to environmental concerns was evident by the mid and late-1960s as smog, polluted waterways, effects of poisons on the environment and dwindling nonrenewable resources caught the attention of the public. Major oil spills such as the Torrey Canyon spill into the English Channel in 1967 and the gigantic 1969 oil spill off the coast of Santa Barbara, California, signaled alarming trends to come. President Nixon signed bills banning DDT, the Environmental Protection Act of 1969 which established the Environmental Protection Agency (EPA), the Occupational Safety and Health Act of 1970 (OSHA), and he supported enactment of Clean Air and Clean Water acts.

In 1980, Ronald Reagan, former Governor of California and former movie actor, was elected President, defeating President Jimmy Carter. President Reagan was an advocate of "trickle-down" economics, which espoused cutting social programs to save money and decrease the tax burden on the wealthy and corporations, believing that largesse for the top tier of the population would eventually trickle down to the lower income strata of workers. Ronald Reagan was a strong supporter of deregulation, insisting that private sector corporations could do oversight and self-policing better, an idea that was contradicted by the high level of corporate abuse for safety, health, and environmental concerns. Although the Reagan Era was a period of great wealth and financial boom times, the unprecedented level of military spending increased the national debt to its highest levels to date during peacetime.

Fiscal restraint returned during the two terms that President Bill Clinton served. He managed to balance the federal budget, the first since the Nixon Administration, and left office with a $10 trillion budget surplus and a record of high economic growth. Toward the end of Clinton's presidency, the economy started to slow. Coupling this with the economic hardships following September 11, 2001, the budget surplus was replaced by a budget deficit during George W. Bush's first term as president.

Skill 1.11c   Understand major social movements and social policy initiatives in this period

President Lyndon B. Johnson continued many of the programs that John F. Kennedy started, notably passage of the **Civil Rights Act of 1964** for African-Americans, the "War on Poverty," and sustained support for the Republic of Vietnam. President Johnson pushed for the enactment of the **Voting Rights Act of 1965** to enfranchise Black voters, particularly in states of the former Confederacy, where they were actively discouraged from voting by multiple obstacles to registering to vote and, if registered, from voting, including intimidation and lynching. The Voting Rights Act also filled in some of the holes left in the Civil Rights Act.

In the 1960s, the civil rights movement under the leadership of Dr. Martin Luther King, Jr. really gained momentum. Under President Lyndon B. Johnson the Civil Rights Acts of 1964 and 1968 prohibited discrimination in housing sales and rentals, employment, public accommodations, and voter registration. President Johnson's "Great Society" programs exceeded Roosevelt's New Deal. As a former public school teacher, Johnson made education a cornerstone of his policy, creating the Head Start Program. He was also responsible for getting legislation enacted to create Medicare, Job Corps, VISTA (Volunteers in Service to America, a domestic counterpart to the Peace Corps), and other programs to help the historically disadvantaged.

Skill 1.11d   Understand the social and cultural effects of changes in the American family and in the ethnic composition of the United States population in this period

The first children of the Baby Boom generation born after World War II grew up to maturity in this period. The Vietnam War and the Selective Service loomed large as young men who were born in 1946 became eligible for the draft in 1964 and 1965, just as the United States started deploying conventional military forces to Vietnam. Unlike in previous wars, draft-age men could be granted deferments or exemptions for educational and family reasons. Thus the upper class, wealthier and mainly white men, could avoid military service, leaving the working class and economically disadvantaged who couldn't afford college to serve in combat.

Youth activism in political and social activities started as part of the Civil Rights Movement during the voter registration drives in the South for the 1964 elections in which college students participated. These students became leaders of social reform activism in later years of the decade. Such organizations as the Students for a Democratic Society (SDS) and the Youth International Party ("Yippies") also sprang up. During this growing countercultural trend, youth resisted traditional culture and society, taking up artists, rock stars and other cultural icons of the era as models for emulation, including the use of such hallucinogenic drugs as LSD and euphoria-inducing marijuana. In 1971, the Constitution was amended to lower the voting age to eighteen.

During this period, exhibiting a new found pride as a growing trend among the nation's ethnic minorities. The African-American community found its voice in a number of Civil Rights organizations. Examples include the non-violent coalition led by Rev. Martin Luther King, Jr.; the militant Black Panther Party led by Eldridge Cleaver, Huey Newton and others; the Black Muslims led by Elijah Muhammad and Malcolm X (who later broke away from the Nation of Islam). The Nation of Islam counted among its converts, Cassius Clay, the charismatic heavyweight boxing champion later known as Muhammad Ali who also resisted the war in Vietnam by refusing induction. Latino activism also started to come to fruition. Cesar Chavez organized Mexican-American farm workers in California, reflecting the importance and numbers of Latino workers in the American economy and society. Cultural awareness among Native Americans was heightened after a takeover of Alcatraz in 1969 and the occupation of Wounded Knee in 1973 by the American Indian Movement (AIM).

Gender politics became an issue as feminism and women's liberation became prominent, advocating equality for women in society and the workplace. Challenging many long-held notions of family led to the organization of the National Organization for Women (NOW), which supported an Equal Rights Amendment (ERA) to the Constitution and applauded the Supreme Court's decision in the 1973 case, *Roe v. Wade.* In this decision, the Court struck down restrictions against abortion, strengthening women's reproductive rights. The Gay Rights' movement's defining moment came with the Stonewall incident in 1969 which led to greater prominence of gay, lesbian and transgender issues, including the American Psychiatric Association removing homosexuality as a mental disorder in 1974.

Skill 1.11e   Demonstrate understanding of international relations, including United States relations with the Soviet Union and its successor states and the changing role of the United States in world political and economic affairs

The decade of the '60s started with foreign policy challenges for the new administration of President John F. Kennedy. Tensions between the United States and the Soviet Union grew, as both nations used proxies in the global rivalry between East and West. Continuing with the Eisenhower administration policy of containing communism, Kennedy authorized the Bay of Pigs invasion to unseat Fidel Castro from power in Cuba, which ended in disaster. In 1962, Premier Khrushchev and the Soviets decided, as a protective measure for Cuba against an American invasion, to install nuclear missiles on the island. In October, incredible tension and anxiety gripped the entire world until Khrushchev ordered Soviet ships carrying missiles for the Cuban bases to turn back and the crisis eased. What precipitated the crisis was Khrushchev's underestimation of Kennedy, since the President made no effort to prevent the erection of the Berlin Wall and was reluctant to commit American troops to invade Cuba and overthrow Fidel Castro. A telephone "hot line" was set up between Moscow and Washington so that the two heads of government could have instant contact with each other.

The involvement in the Vietnam War was the other major foreign policy challenge of the 1960s and 1970s. For Lyndon B. Johnson, the war in Vietnam overshadowed nearly all foreign policy concerns and led to widespread international disapproval. The next president, Nixon, promised a "secret plan" to end American involvement in Vietnam. However, the war escalated during his first term, and he ordered an escalation of the war by sending troops to invade previously neutral Cambodia in 1970. Eventually, the combatant sides agreed to the Paris Peace Talks and the end of U.S. involvement in Vietnam.

One of the highlights of the détente foreign policy of President Richard Nixon was his 1972 trip to China. In 1971, Nixon sent Henry Kissinger on a secret trip to Peking to investigate whether or not it would be possible for America to give recognition to China. In February 1972, Nixon spent a number of days in the country visiting well-known Chinese landmarks and dining with the two leaders, Chairman Mao Zedong and Premier Zhou Enlai. Agreements were made for cultural and scientific exchanges and the eventual resumption of trade. In 1979, formal diplomatic recognition was achieved.

During the administration of President Jimmy Carter, Egyptian President Anwar el-Sadat and Israeli Prime Minister Menachem Begin met at presidential retreat Camp David and agreed, after a series of meetings, to sign a formal treaty of peace between the two countries. In 1979, the Soviet invasion of Afghanistan was perceived by Carter and his advisers as a threat to the rich oil fields in the Persian Gulf, but at the time U.S. military capability to prevent further Soviet aggression in the Middle East was weak.

The last year of Carter's presidential term was taken up with the 53 American hostages held in Iran. The shah had been deposed and control of the government and the country was in the hands of Muslim leader, Ayatollah Ruhollah Khomeini, whose extreme hatred for the U.S. was fueled by the 1953 CIA-orchestrated overthrow of Iran's democratically elected Mossadegh government. Also, the CIA trained the Savak, the ruthless secret police. When the terminally-ill, exiled shah was allowed into the U.S. for medical treatment, a mob, supported and encouraged by Khomeini, stormed the American embassy taking the 53 Americans as hostages,.

The foreign policy of President Ronald Reagan was, in his first term, focused primarily on the Western Hemisphere, particularly in Central America and the West Indies. U.S. involvement in the domestic revolutions of El Salvador and Nicaragua continued into Reagan's second term when Congress held televised hearings on what came to be known as the Iran-Contra Affair. A cover-up was exposed showing that profits from secretly selling military hardware to Iran had been used to give support to rebels, called Contras, who were fighting in Nicaragua. In 1983 in Lebanon, 241 American Marines were killed when an Islamic suicide bomber drove an explosive-laden truck into U.S. Marines headquarters located at the airport in Beirut.

Toward the end of Reagan's second term, an arms-reduction agreement was reached with Soviet General Secretary Mikhail Gorbachev. Gorbachev began easing East-West tensions by stressing the importance of cooperation with the West and easing the harsh and restrictive life of the people in the Soviet Union. In retrospect, it was clearly a prelude to the events occurring during the administration of President George H. W. Bush. The Berlin Wall fell, reuniting Germany. The Union of Soviet Socialist Republics (U.S.S.R.) disintegrated, leading to the independence of the Baltic nations of Estonia, Latvia and Lithuania, other former Soviet republics of Ukraine, Armenia, Azerbaijan, Georgia, and other Central Asian countries. Concurrent was the dissolution of the Warsaw Pact of Eastern European nations, who were considered for eventual membership in the European Union and the North Atlantic Treaty Organization (NATO), which was originally formed to be a defensive alliance against the Soviet Union and the Warsaw Pact nations.

The United States, dependent on a critical resource from an increasingly unstable part of the world, supported Israel in the 1967 Six Day War against Egypt, Syria and Jordan and in the 1973 Yom Kippur War against Egypt, which pitted the Jewish state against its Arab and predominantly Muslim neighbors, whom the Saudi government supported. In retaliation for the United States' support of Israel in the Yom Kippur War, the Arabic leading oil-producing nations of OPEC (Organization of Petroleum Exporting Countries) cut back on oil production and boycotted exports to the United States, thus raising the price of a barrel of oil and creating a fuel shortage.

DOMAIN II.   WORLD HISTORY

COMPETENCY 2.0   PREHISTORY TO 1400 CE

Skill 2.1.a   Demonstrate knowledge of human society before approximately 3000 BCE

Prehistory is defined as the period of human achievements before the development of writing. The Stone Age cultures had three different periods. The **Lower Paleolithic Period** is illustrated with the use of crude tools. The **Upper Paleolithic Period** exhibited a greater variety of better-made tools and implements, the wearing of clothing, highly organized group life, and skills in art. And the **Neolithic Period** featured domesticated animals; food production; the arts of knitting, spinning, and weaving cloth; fires started through friction; house building rather than living in caves; the development of institutions including the family, religion; and a form of government or the origin of the state.

Hunting and gathering societies are the earliest and most primitive form of human social groups, dating back to the **Paleolithic Age**. They are small bands composed of closely related individuals who established temporary camps as they roamed the land. They subsisted on gathering naturally occurring edibles and hunting for larger game and used simple tools and instruments. Their only possessions consisted of what they could carry with them from place to place. Generally, the women, children, and the elderly remained in their temporary camps, tending to camp chores and foraging for edible plants, insects, eggs, small mammals, and birds. The men and older adolescent males organized themselves into hunting parties that cooperatively stalked or trapped larger game. There is evidence that dogs were tamed for use in hunting. Typically, they consumed freshly killed game immediately and preserved with the remainder by smoking and drying so it could be carried easily. Some hunting and gathering societies fished if they were close to a sea or large body of water. When competing bands encountered each other, hostility resulted unless kinship ties existed to inhibit it. They were competing for limited resources in a given area, and one band's usual territory may not support another competing band.

The Neolithic Age marked several major changes in how people lived. Herd animals such as goats and sheep were domesticated along with pigs. So, it was no longer necessary to hunt animals for meat and hides. Just as significant was the domestication of cereal crops—wheat and barley in Mesopotamia and rice in Asia. Also, pottery makes its appearance during this period. With food now available from a single location, people no longer had to move around to hunt game and forage for their sustenance and started to live in permanent settlements. They also had a more clearly delineated division of labor with people specializing in occupations that were not necessarily directly tied to the acquisition of food. Rudimentary metallurgy, in the form of copper smelting, was beginning to lead the societies who had it away from the Stone Age entirely.

Skill 2.1b   Understand the development of city civilizations 3000–1500 BCE

Mesopotamia, part of the "Fertile Crescent," extended from the Persian Gulf at the estuary of the Tigris and Euphrates Rivers. Following the rivers in a northwesterly direction is the "Cradle of Western Civilization." The Sumerians had established walled city-states, notably at Lagash, Uruk, and Ur. The Sumerians developed a writing system that used ideographs and phonetic symbols called cuneiform. Much of what is known about Sumer comes from the tens of thousands of clay tablets that the Sumerian scribes left. Most of the information concerned commercial, economic, and administrative activities. However, thousands of tables containing literary texts were uncovered, implying that Sumerians engaged in extensive trade and centralized urban planning. They also created an irrigation system of canals and dikes to take advantage of the water from the Tigris and Euphrates Rivers in order to cultivate large areas of arid desert and control the unpredictable and devastating flooding of the rivers. In Sumerian cities, the lives of the inhabitants were highly diversified; the division of labor that first appeared in Neolithic settlements became even more specialized and, in some cases, codified and imposed on the populace by the ruling and religious elite. The Sumerians were conquered by the Akkadian-speaking Babylonian invaders under the leadership of Sargon the Great. The Babylonians were awed by the cultural sophistication of the Sumerians and retained Sumerian as the language of government and religion. Hammurabi, another notable Babylonian king, had his code of law set in stone pillars and erected throughout the territory of the empire. The Babylonians, in turn, were conquered by the Assyrians, who also adopted Sumerian language and culture for the court and religious ritual.

The Nile River gave rise to another ancient valley civilization, the Egyptians, The annual summer floods of the Nile supported a rich agricultural society that enjoyed surpluses that could be stored for leaner times. Two rival kingdoms emerged on the banks of the Nile. Lower Egypt was the Nile Delta in the north where it joins the Mediterranean Sea, and Upper Egypt occupied the land south of the delta, along the banks of the Nile River approximately 800 miles to the First Cataract. Although both kingdoms were sporadically united into one during the Old Kingdom period (3000-2200 BCE), they represented two distinct cultural and political entities during that time. The Egyptians were well known for their monumental stone structures and statuary and for a highly centralized bureaucracy. The kings were considered gods and worshipped by their subjects.

After more than a century of intervening disorder, the Middle Kingdom period (2100-1800 BCE) saw a united kingdom, which established its capital at Thebes in the south and later moved north to Memphis for better central control. The Middle Kingdom period ended in 1800 BCE with the invasion of the Hyksos, who introduced the chariot and bow to Egypt. Eventually, the Egyptians drove out the conquerors in 1550 BCE, and the New Kingdom period was ushered in.

In the **Indian subcontinent**, the Indus River Valley was first settled by a Dravidian civilization that built elaborate cities at Mohenjo Daro and Harappa (modern place names) that were centrally planned, with streets and structures arranged in uniform grids, sophisticated water and sewage systems and numerous public buildings and facilities. Archaeological evidence shows that the Indus River cities met a sudden and violent end. Most human skeletal remains that have been found show evidence of sword cuts and severe trauma. The invaders, known as Aryans, swept into the Indian subcontinent from the northwest via what is modern-day Iran and Afghanistan, from the Central Asian steppes.

China is considered by some historians to be the oldest, uninterrupted civilization in the world and was in existence around the same time as the ancient civilizations founded in **Egypt**, **Mesopotamia**, and the **Indus Valley**. Early Chinese civilization originally developed in the Huang He (Yellow River) Valley. It is shrouded in mystery, since accounts of the first era of Sage-Emperors (Di) indicate unnaturally long reigns (in excess of 500 years for one emperor).

They are credited with the invention of writing, irrigation, flood control, pottery, spinning and weaving silk, jade working, divination by scapulomancy (reading portents from patterns produced by heating livestock shoulder bones and turtle plastrons), and domestication of pigs, dogs, oxen, sheep, fowl and goats. The Chinese studied nature, astronomy and weather, stressed the importance of family, and a strong monarch who also acted on behalf of populace as a medium to the sky spirit, worshipped spirits that controlled natural and man-made phenomena, including ancestor worship. The Xia Dynasty followed, but its existence has not been proven with physical evidence. It only exists in legends and in the Confucian classics "Classic of Records (History)" and some of the poems contained in the "Classic of Odes (Songs)." It is considered the first Chinese dynasty because it established the pattern of rule being passed from father to eldest son. The Xia Dynasty was overthrown by the next dynasty, the Shang Dynasty, which was also considered legendary and existed only in literature, until archeological evidence was unearthed in the early twentieth century, where the ancient records said it would be. This set the precedent that dynasties rule because they earned that right by the Mandate of Heaven, and had proven that the ruling family was worthy. The notable features of Shang culture are a fully developed writing system (Shang Dynasty writing can still be read by modern readers of Chinese), highly sophisticated and intricate bronze casting and engraving, polished jade pieces of a luster indicating use of micro-abrasives (unmatched until the late twentieth century), and a formal system of social hierarchy.

The civilization in **Japan** appeared during this time, having borrowed much of their culture from China and Korea. It was the last of these classical civilizations to develop. The native religion was a form of nature worship, Shintoism, which worshipped Ame (translation: "The sky above") as its principal deity. The Japanese foundation mythology recounts that the first emperor was a child of the sun goddess and that all Japanese emperors descended from him.

Japan's imperial family has the longest line of continuous rule by the same family of any monarchy still in existence today.

The civilizations in **Africa** south of the Sahara were developing the refining and use of iron, especially for farm implements and later for weapons. Trading was overland using camels and at important seaports. The Arab influence was extremely important, as was their later contact with Indians, Christian Nubians, and Persians. In fact, their trading activities were probably the most important factor in the spread of and assimilation of different ideas and stimulation of cultural growth.

Skill 2.1c   Demonstrate knowledge of ancient empires and civilizations 1700 BCE – 500 CE

Egypt made numerous significant contributions including construction of the great pyramids; development of hieroglyphic writing; preservation of bodies after death; making paper from papyrus; contributing to developments in arithmetic and geometry; the invention of the method of counting in groups of one to ten (the decimal system); completion of a solar calendar; and laying the foundation for science and astronomy.

The earliest historical record of **Kush** is in Egyptian sources. They describe a region upstream from the first cataract of the Nile as "wretched." This civilization was characterized by a settled way of life in fortified mud-brick villages. They subsisted on hunting and fishing, herding cattle, and gathering grain. Skeletal remains suggest that the people were a blend of Negroid and Mediterranean peoples. This civilization appears to be the second oldest in Africa (after Egyptian).

Either the people were Egyptian or they were heavily influenced by Egyptians at a very early period in the development of the society. They appear to have spoken Nilo-Saharan languages. The area in which they lived is called Nubia. The capital city was Kerma, a major trading center between the northern and southern parts of Africa.

During the period of Egypt's Old Kingdom (ca. 2700-2180 BCE), this civilization was essentially a diffused version of Egyptian culture and religion. When Egypt came under the domination of the Hyksos, Kush reached its greatest power and cultural energy (1700-1500 BCE). When the Hyksos were eventually expelled from Egypt, the New Kingdom brought Kush back under Egyptian colonial control.

The collapse of the New Kingdom in Egypt (ca. 1000 BCE) provided the second opportunity for Kush to develop independently of Egyptian control and to conquer the entire Nubian region. The capital was then moved to Napata.

For the most part, the Kushites apparently considered themselves Egyptian and inheritors of the pharaonic tradition. Their society was organized on the Egyptian model, adopting Egyptian royal titles, etc. Even their art and architecture was based on Egyptian models. But their pyramids were smaller and steeper.

In what has been called "a magnificent irony of history," the Kushites conquered Egypt in the eigth century, creating the 25th dynasty. The dynasty ended in the seventh century when the Assyrians defeated Egypt.

The Kushites were gradually pushed farther south by the Assyrians and later by the Persians. This essentially cut off contact with Egypt, the Middle East and Europe. They moved their capital to Meroe in about 591 BC, when Napata was conquered. Their attention then turned to sub-Saharan Africa. Free of Egyptian dominance, they developed innovations in government and other areas.

In government, the king ruled through a law of custom that was interpreted by priests. The king was elected from the royal family. Descent was determined through the mother's line (as in Egypt). But in *an unparalleled innovation*, the Kushites were ruled by a series of female monarchs.

The Kushite religion was polytheistic, including all of the primary Egyptian gods. There were, however, regional gods that were the principal gods in their regions. Derived from other African cultures, there was also a lion warrior god.

This civilization was vital through the last half of the first millennium BC, but it suffered about 300 years of gradual decline until the Nuba people eventually conquered it.

The ancient civilization of the **Sumerians** invented the wheel; developed irrigation through use of canals, dikes, and devices for raising water; devised the system of cuneiform writing; learned to divide time; and built large boats for trade. The Babylonians devised the famous **Code of Hammurabi**, a code of laws.

The ancient **Assyrians** were warlike and aggressive empire-builders, who possessed a highly organized and disciplined army that featured specialized units of horse drawn chariots, cavalry, elaborate siege engines and other specialized troops to augment well-armed foot soldiers who attacked in massed formations.

The **Hebrews**, also known as the ancient Israelites instituted "monotheism," which is the worship of one God, Yahweh. They compiled a collection of sacred writings containing worship texts, historical accounts, prophecy, instructive writings and law, including the Ten Commandments. Their Bible consists of the Old Testament.

The **Minoans** had a system of writing using symbols to represent syllables in words. They built palaces with multiple levels containing many rooms, water and sewage systems with flush toilets, bathtubs, hot and cold running water, and bright paintings on the walls.

The **Mycenaeans** changed the Minoan writing system to aid their own language and used symbols to represent syllables.

The **Phoenicians** were sea traders well known for their manufacturing skills in glass and metals and the development of their famous purple dye. They became so very proficient in the skill of navigation that they were able to sail by the stars at night. Further, they devised an alphabet using symbols to represent single sounds, which was an improved extension of the Egyptian principle and writing system.

In **India**, the Aryan invaders from the northwest introduced the caste system, which restricted what a person could or could not do as a profession. The principle of zero in mathematics was invented. **Vedic Hinduism,** as practiced by the Aryans, evolved into its now recognizable form, as Dravidian states, south of the Indus River, were conquered and local deities and heroes (such as Krishna, Naga and Hanuman) were incorporated into the Hindu belief system of multiple aspects of a single godhead. Industry and commerce developed along with extensive trading with the Near East. Outstanding advances in the fields of science and medicine were made along with being one of the first to be active in navigation and maritime enterprises during this time.

Buddhism is an offshoot of Brahmanical Hindu thought, which arose during the fifth century BCE. However, unlike traditional Hinduism, Buddhism was founded by Gautama Siddartha Shakyamuni, a crown prince who renounced the material world after observing suffering in the form of illness, old age and death, much to the dismay of his father, the maharajah, and to seek enlightenment. After years of asceticism and austerities, the prince achieved enlightenment after meditating under a tree for 49 days. He was called the "Buddha" (a Sanskrit word meaning "Awakened One") after his enlightenment. He told his followers that life was suffering, suffering was caused by desire, desire was caused by delusion of the mind, which leads to death and rebirth, which leads to another cycle of suffering. To avoid suffering, one must get rid of the delusions that cause desire and break the cycle of life, death and rebirth, called "samsara" a concept from Hindu theology. Other concepts adapted from Hindu theology are "karma," which is the balance of action versus later effect, which will trigger samsara and "dharma," which can mean "fate," "destiny," or "unbreakable rules that govern all phenomena," depending on its context. Escape from the cycles of samsara was called "nirvana," or "extinguishment." Buddhism later split off into two main schools: Theravada ("Older Way") or Southern Buddhism and Mahayana ("Great Vehicle").

Theravada Buddhism teaches that individuals can gain enough merit over countless cycles of rebirth and eventually attain enlightenment. This branch of Buddhism is the original one as practiced shortly after the Buddha's death. It is the form that spread south to Sri Lanka and Southeast Asia.

Mahayana Buddhism is a later school that revises the Theravada and teaches that individuals who had achieved enlightenment, decline and stay behind to assist other, less enlightened individuals attain enlightenment rather than passing into Nirvana. This is the form that spread to Tibet and eastward to China, Korea and Japan.

China began building the Great Wall to prevent outsiders from invading; practiced irrigation, flood control, crop rotation and terrace farming; increased the importance of the silk industry, and developed caravan routes across Central Asia for extensive trade. After the fall of the Zhou Dynasty and during the ensuing Warring States period, Confucius edited the Confucian Classics and a collection of his teachings, The Analects was compiled. Daoism emerged as the teachings of Lao Zi were being written down and espoused by Daoist scholars They also increased proficiency in rice cultivation.

During the waning years of the Shang Dynasty, the "Yi Jing" (Classic of Change), the divination manual was first compiled, based on 64 hexagrams, which is still consulted today. Continuing the dynastic cycle, the Shang Dynasty was overthrown by the Zhou Dynasty , in turn earned the Mandate of Heaven to rule. The early Zhou Dynasty was later considered by Confucius, several centuries later, to be the "Golden Age" of rule by enlightened men of ability and moral rectitude. During fifth century BCE the Zhou Dynasty began to disintegrate, eventually falling. China split up into several independent kingdoms that were in near constant state of war with each kingdom vying for supremacy over the others in a myriad combination of alliances, which often changed. It was in this period, known as the Warring States period, one of chaos and disarray. Two of the best known figures of the period, Confucius (Kong Zi) and Lao Zi appeared (there are questions regarding whether or not Lao Zi was a real person).

Eventually, after nearly 200 years of fighting, the Qin Dynasty, under Qin Shi Huang Di ("Exalted First Emperor") gained the advantage and conquered the other kingdoms to unite China into a single empire. The Qin emperor commissioned his ministers to standardize weights and measures, and reduced the number of Chinese characters to 3,000 from tens of thousands, by eliminating redundant and superfluous characters. The Qin dynasty was known for its harsh authoritarian rule, with an emphasis on severe punishment for even minor infractions. Within twenty years, there was a successful revolt that overthrew the Qin in 206 BCE and replaced it with the Han Dynasty.

The **Han Dynasty** lasted four centuries, longer than any other dynasty in China's history.

Paper and the writing brush, in its present form, were invented during this period and Chinese characters took the form that is familiar to today's readers. Through the Han, under Emperor Wu Di ("Martial Emperor", reigned 141-87 BCE), China expanded its boundaries to their greatest extent through military conquest, including an embarkation on a campaign to rid the northern borders of the Huns. This set off a chain of events and westward migrations of Huns and other nomadic pastoralists into Europe. In the aftermath of the fall of Qin,

Confucianism became the official political philosophy of the Han. Scholarship and the criterion for appointment to the imperial bureaucracy were based on the Five Classics: Odes, History, Rites (Etiquette), Change (Yi Jing), and the Spring and Autumn Annals (a history of a portion of the Zhou Dynasty edited by Confucius).

Additionally, scholars were expected to have a thorough knowledge of the Analects of Confucius (a collection of his teachings) and Mencius (Meng Zi was a Confucian scholar who expanded on the themes espoused by Confucius and his most esteemed students). The accomplishments of the Han Dynasty were so unprecedented and profound, that later Chinese refer to themselves as "People of the Han" and Chinese characters have been called "Han Words" (literal translation of the two characters that make up the word for "Chinese characters").

Daoism was one of many schools of thought that sprang up in ancient China, and, like **Confucianism**, has endured to modern times. Its main tenet is that all phenomena are governed by natural forces that cannot be comprehended by ordinary people's minds and that resisting it or trying to make it act in a contrary manner only leads to frustration and just makes things worse than they already are. The two major literary works that influenced Daoism the most were "Dao De Jing" ("Discourse on the Way and Virtue") and Zhuang Zi's eponymous work "The Zhuang Zi" (most Classical Chinese books were named after their primary contributors or the first words in the body of the text). In order to understand how these cosmic forces work, Lao Zi and Zhuang Zi said that one should not seek anything, since the only way to truly know something, one must not think about it and let the Way of nature run its course without interference by not doing anything contrary to the Way.

The ancient **Persians** developed an alphabet; contributed the religions/philosophies of **Zoroastrianism**, **Mithraism**, and **Gnosticism**; and allowed conquered peoples to retain their own customs, laws, and religions.

The classical civilization of **Greece** reached the highest levels in man's achievements based on the foundations already laid by such ancient groups as the Egyptians, Phoenicians, Minoans, and Mycenaeans.

Among the more important contributions of Greece were the Greek alphabet derived from the Phoenician letters that formed the basis for the Roman alphabet and our present-day alphabet. Extensive trading and colonization resulted in the spread of the Greek civilization. The love of sports, with an emphasis on a sound body, led to the tradition of the Olympic Games. Greece was responsible for the rise of independent, strong city-states. Note the complete contrast between independent, freedom-loving Athens with its practice of pure democracy i.e. direct, personal, active participation in government by qualified citizens and the rigid, totalitarian, militaristic Sparta.

Other important areas that the Greeks are credited with influencing include drama, epic and lyric poetry, fables, myths centered on the many gods and goddesses, science, astronomy, medicine, mathematics, philosophy, art, architecture, and recording historical events. The conquests of Alexander the Great spread Greek ideas to the areas he conquered and brought to the Greek world many ideas from Asia. Above all, Alexander the Great sought the value of ideas, wisdom, curiosity and the desire to learn as much about the world as possible.

The ancient civilization of **Rome** lasted approximately 1,000 years including the periods of republic and empire, although its lasting influence on Europe and its history was for a much longer period. A very sharp contrast existed between the curious, imaginative, inquisitive Greeks and the practical, simple, down-to-earth, no-nonsense Romans, who spread and preserved the ideas of ancient Greece and other culture groups. The contributions and accomplishments of the Romans are numerous, but their greatest included language, engineering, building, law, government, roads, trade, and the "**Pax Romana,**" the long period of peace enabling free travel and trade and spreading people, cultures, goods, and ideas all over a vast area of the known world.

A most interesting and significant characteristic of the Greek, Hellenic, and Roman civilizations was "secularism," where emphasis shifted away from religion to the state. Men were not absorbed in or dominated by religion as had been the case in Egypt and the nations located in Mesopotamia. Religion and its leaders did not dominate the state and its authority was greatly diminished.

Skill 2.1d **Understand the decline of classical civilizations and changes 500–1400 CE**

The **Western Roman Empire** fell when Germanic tribes migrated to and controlled most of central and Western Europe. The five major tribes were the Visigoths, Ostrogoths, Vandals, Saxons, and Franks. In later years, the Franks successfully stopped the invasion of southern Europe by Muslims by defeating them under the leadership of Charles Martel at the Battle of Tours in 732 AD. Thirty-six years later in 768 AD, the grandson of Charles Martel became King of the Franks and is known throughout history as Charlemagne. Charlemagne was a man of war but was unique in his respect for and encouragement of learning. He made great efforts to rule fairly and ensure just treatment for his people.

The **Vikings** were Scandinavian Norse seafarers who quickly gained a reputation for ruthlessness and surprise as they raided any settlement or monastery that they could reach on their swift and seaworthy long boats The Vikings had a lot of influence at this time with spreading their ideas and knowledge of trade routes and sailing, accomplished first through their conquests and later through trade. The two main groups of Vikings were the West Vikings, from Norway and Denmark, and the East Vikings, from Sweden. The West Vikings raided and traded with coastal areas of Britain and Ireland, Europe's Atlantic coast and as far as Sicily in the Mediterranean Sea, setting up trading outposts, permanent settlements and in some cases setting themselves up as rulers. They also ventured beyond the North Sea to settle in Iceland, Greenland, and North America, although Iceland was the only North Atlantic settlement that was a lasting permanent success. The East Vikings voyaged east and south, through the Baltic nations and via the rivers of Eastern Europe to Kiev in what is now Ukraine where they ruled as royalty and were called the "Rus." They further voyaged south to Constantinople, where they also served as mercenaries and functionaries to the Byzantine Roman Emperor.

The **Huns** were a horse-riding pastoral people who originated in Asia, north of the Great Wall of China, and had finally been displaced by the Chinese emperors after centuries of border skirmishes and all-out military campaigns to rid them from the lands bordering China. They were led as far west as the eastern edges of the Roman Empire by Attila, their leader, attacking swiftly on horseback, spreading terror and havoc among their victims. After Attila suddenly and unexpectedly died after a night of celebrating his marriage to another wife, the Huns stopped their advance on Europe and either returned to Central Asia or became assimilated into the local populations where they settled.

After the fall of the Han Dynasty, China was once again split into different kingdoms and entered a long period of war and chaos with ever-shifting alliances and counter-alliances and a brief period of unity. At one point China divided into 17 separate kingdoms.

The **Sui** (pronounced "Sway") Dynasty, although lasting less than twenty years, heralded the beginning of a long period of national and cultural unity starting in 589 CE, giving way to the Tang Dynasty in 618 CE.

The **Tang Dynasty** consolidated imperial authority and is considered by many historians to be the renaissance and flowering of Chinese culture, helped by the fact that long-term stability had returned to China. The population grew to its historic high during this period, and the arts, particularly poetry, found its most creative and aesthetically pleasing levels. The Sui and Tang introduced wide-scale government examinations for recruiting new talent into the imperial bureaucracy from the highest court ministers, all the way to local county and township officials. Also, Buddhism, which was introduced earlier, became the official state religion under the Tang, and the emperors endowed monasteries and temples lavishly. Printing was invented during the Ninth Century (several centuries before Gutenberg) and was spurred by the need to produce and distribute Buddhist literature on a wide scale.

The **Song Dynasty** was a transitional period, which went from late classic China, to early modern China. Buddhism was rejected, and a return to Confucianism emerged and is called Neo-Confucianism. Also, an aristocratic society, which held sway until the Tang Dynasty, virtually disappeared as a political force, ceding that authority to the landowning class and the blossoming meritocracy that came up through the government examination system, which emphasized Confucian learning. Although mercantile activities were traditionally shunned by the traditional elite of China, a commercial revolution and a great expansion of the economy coincided with an unprecedented rise in population and a similar growth in agricultural production. The Chinese were using the magnetic compass by the Twelfth Century, and they made great advances in shipbuilding, which allowed them to trade with people as far away as India and the Persian Gulf. The invention of gunpowder was also a significant development in military technology, although the use of gunpowder for use in pyrotechnic displays also became a more important use as a form of celebration and entertainment. One drawback to the Song Dynasty's developments in commercial and artistic pursuits was the weakening of military power and greater vulnerability along the northern frontier.

The **Mongols** were but one of many "barbarian" pastoral peoples who rode horses, used Bactrian camels for transport of cargo, and herded flocks of sheep and goats. They were a collection of loosely affiliated tribes and clans that competed with each other for pasturage, horses, and livestock. They were united by Chinggis (also spelled "Genghis") Khan in the thirteenth century CE. As the Mongols under Chinggis conquered other neighboring territories, they gained a reputation as formidable horsemen as their cavalry attacked in swift, disciplined formations that took advantage of maneuver, surprise, and skillful and deadly use of archery while riding, overwhelming their foes.

The Mongol Empire was highly adaptable at incorporating absorbed people's expertise, including Chinggis' leading commander, Subotai, who was Tuvan, a distinct Central Asian ethnic group with its own language. Eventually, during Chinggis' lifetime, the empire encompassed nearly all of the north-central Asia and the northwest of China. After his death, his son Ogatei assumed the title "Great Khan." followed by Mongke, one of Chinngis' grandsons.

To the west and south, under the rule of Chinggis' grandsons, the Mongols conquered what is now Russia, South Asia, and Southwest Asia, which includes what is now Iraq, Turkey, Iran, and Afghanistan, where they acquired a ferocious reputation for wanton destruction and aggression. The most well known of Chinngis' grandsons was Khubilai, who founded the Yuan Dynasty in China and assumed the title of Emperor, whom Marco Polo wrote about when he was a guest of the Mongol court. Khubilai adopted Chinese dress and customs, left government bureaucracy and institutions fairly intact, expanded the empire into Korea, made incursions into what is now Vietnam. His attempt to invade Japan was thwarted by a typhoon (called the "Kamikaze" in Japanese or "Divine Wind"), which demolished the Mongol fleet. After the passing of Chinggis' grandsons, the Mongol Empire quickly lost control over its far-flung domain and was forced to cede political and military power. The Yuan Dynasty in China fell in 1368 CE, succeeded by an ethnically Han-Chinese dynasty.

The **Ming Dynasty** lasted from 1368 to 1644 CE and marked one of the longest eras of order and stability in government and society in world history. It was also a period of great artistic and creative achievements. However, the stability of Chinese government and society was such that it stayed relatively unaltered until the early twentieth century CE, when Imperial China ended with the 1911 Chinese Revolution. As with the Dynastic Cycle, which started with the end of the legendary Xia Dynasty, the Ming came to power as the result of a rebellion that overthrew the Mongols and expelled them from China proper. The Ming revived the purely Chinese mode of rule over China that existed during the Tang and Song Dynasties. Confucianism and its classics were put into the forefront as the basis of all knowledge that was important for an enlightened official to possess. Ming scholarship in Confucian studies flourished and produced a myriad of texts on all subjects from commentaries on materialist philosophy to scientific texts to creative prose and poetic literature. Although Chinese elites were traditionally anti-commercial in their worldview, the Chinese economy and commercial infrastructure expanded dynamically during the Ming Dynasty, including the migration of Chinese merchants to overseas markets. The Ming Dynasty, like all previous ones, in the end, eventually suffered from internal decay and official corruption that led to rebellion and weakening central authority and made it susceptible to external takeover.

The purpose of the **Crusades** was to rid Jerusalem of Muslim control and replace it with Christian rule. This series of violent, bloody conflicts did affect trade and stimulated later explorations seeking the new, exotic products such as silks and spices.

The Crusaders came into contact with other religions and cultures and learned and spread many new ideas.

During this time, the system of **feudalism** became the dominant feature of domestic life. It was a system of loyalty and protection. The strong protected the weak, which returned the service with farm labor, military service, and loyalty. Life was lived out on a vast estate, owned by a nobleman and his family, called a "manor." It was a complete village supporting a few hundred people, mostly peasants. Improved tools and farming methods made life more bearable although most never left the manor or traveled from their village during their lifetime.

Also coming into importance at this time was the era of knighthood and its code of chivalry the tremendous influence of the Roman Catholic Church. Until the period of the Renaissance, the Church was the only place where people could be educated. The Bible and other books were hand-copied by monks in the monasteries. Cathedrals were built and were decorated with art depicting religious subjects.

With the increase in trade and travel, cities sprang up and began to grow. Craft workers in the cities developed their skills to a high degree, eventually organizing guilds to protect the quality of the work and to regulate the buying and selling of their products. City government developed and flourished centered on strong town councils. Active in city government and the town councils were the wealthy businessmen who made up the rising middle class.

The feudal manorial system ended with the outbreak and spread of the infamous **Black Death**. This plague killed more than one-third of the total population of Europe. Those who survived and were skilled in any job or occupation were in demand, and many serfs or peasants found freedom and, for that time, a decidedly improved standard of living. Strong nation-states became powerful, and people developed a renewed interest in life and learning.

The **Byzantines** (Christians) made important contributions in art and the preservation of Greek and Roman achievements including architecture (especially in Eastern Europe and Russia), the Code of Justinian and Roman law. Bordering the east of Europe was the **Byzantine Empire**, which was the Eastern Roman Empire, after it was split into two by Emperor Diocletian. Diocletian's successor, Emperor Constantine, renamed the capital Byzantium to Constantinople, after himself. When Western Rome fell in 476 CE, the Byzantine emperors, starting with Justinian, attempted to regain the lost western territories.

Because of ineffective rulers between the seventh and ninth centuries CE, any gains were completely lost, and territorial limits reverted back to the eastern Balkans of Ancient Greece and Asia Minor. The late ninth through eleventh centuries were considered the Golden Age of Byzantium.

Although Constantine had earlier made Christianity the official state religion of Rome, it left an unresolved conflict between Christian and Classical (Greek and Roman) ideals for the Byzantines. There were points of contention between the Pope in Rome and the Patriarch of Constantinople including celibacy of priests, language of the Liturgy (Latin in the west, Greek in the east), religious doctrine, and other unreconciled issues that led to the Great Schism, which permanently split the church into the Roman Catholic and the Eastern Orthodox Churches.

In secular matters, Emperor Justinian codified Roman law, summarizing a millennia of Roman legal developments into the Justinian Code. This codification laid the basis for modern western legal systems, which are still studied and used in European and American legal circles. The Byzantines combined the styles of Greco-Roman and Asia Minor to create monumental domed structures such as the Hagia Sophia church (later converted into a Muslim mosque), elaborate mosaics and a distinctive style of painting, richly embellished icons depicting religious figures.

Islamic (or Saracenic) civilization, grew out of religious fervor shortly after the founding of Islam (Arabic for "Surrender to God") by Muhammad in the seventh century CE. Islam is a monotheistic faith that traces its traditions to the Hebrew Patriarch Abraham and considers the Jewish patriarchs and prophets (especially Moses and King Solomon) and the Christian prophet Jesus Christ as earlier "Prophets of God" and venerates them accordingly. The Arabic word "Allah" and its root "'Lh" means "The Almighty" or "God" and is not a name, like Zeus. Muhammad preached jihad ("holy war") in two forms; Lesser Jihad was the call to arms to spread Islam by military force and Greater Jihad, the more important of the two, was the battle that an individual undertakes for the salvation of the soul and surrender to the will of God. The Quran was dictated to Muhammad as the Word of God, composed in verse in sections called "sura," each of which begins with the invocation, "In the Name of God, the Compassionate, the Merciful."

The Islamic armies spread their faith by conquering the Arabian Peninsula, conquering Mesopotamia, Egypt, Syria and Persia by 650 CE and expanding to North Africa and most of the Iberian Peninsula by 750 CE. During this period of expansion, the Muslim conquerors established great centers of learning, universities, at Baghdad in Mesopotamia, Damascus in Syria, Alexandria in Egypt and Cordoba in Spain. They preserved Classical knowledge of the Greeks and Romans, while Europe was in the depths of the Dark Ages after the fall of the Western Roman Empire. Muslim scholars are credited with great progress in the areas of science and philosophy and were responsible for accomplishments in astronomy, mathematics, physics, chemistry, medicine, literature, art, trade and manufacturing, agriculture, and a marked influence on later European scholarship and intellectual development.

The civilizations in **Africa** south of the Sahara were developing the refining and use of iron, especially for farm implements and later for weapons. Trading was overland using camels and at important seaports. The Arab influence was extremely important, as was their later contact with Indians, Christian Nubians, and Persians. In fact, their trading activities were probably the most important factor in the spread of and assimilation of different ideas and stimulation of cultural growth.

The people who lived in the Americas before Columbus arrived had a thriving, connected society. The civilizations in North America tended to spread out more and were in occasional conflict but maintained their sovereignty, for the most part. The South American civilizations, however, tended to migrate into empires, with the strongest city or tribe assuming control of the lives and resources of the rest of the nearby peoples.

Native Americans in North America had a spiritual and personal relationship with the various Spirits of Nature and a keen appreciation of the ways of woodworking and metalworking. Various tribes dotted the landscape of what is now the U.S. They struggled against one another for control of resources such as food and water but had no concept of ownership of land, since they believed that they were living on the land with the permission of the Spirits. The North Americans mastered the art of growing many crops and, to their credit, were willing to share that knowledge with the various Europeans who eventually showed up. Artwork made of hides, beads, and jewels was popular at this time.

The most well known empires of South America were the **Aztec, Inca, and Maya**. Each of these empires had a central capital where the emperor lived who controlled all aspects of the lives of his subjects. The empires traded with other peoples; and if the relations soured, the results were usually absorption of the trading partners into the empire. These empires, especially the Aztecs, had access to large numbers of metals and jewels, and they created weapons and artwork that continue to impress historians today. The Inca Empire stretched across a vast period of territory down the western coast of South America and was connected by a series of roads. A series of messengers ran along these roads, carrying news and instructions from the capital, Cusco. The Incas, however, did not have the wheel. The Mayas are most well known for their famous pyramids and calendars, as well as their language, which still stumps archaeologists.

COMPETENCY 2.2   WORLD HISTORY: 1400 TO 1914

Skill 2.2a   Understand emerging global-wide interactions 1400–1800 CE

At the beginning of this period, most of the economies were based on subsistence agriculture. The farmers produced enough to feed themselves with a little extra to sell to the cities. The slave-based economies eventually gave way to tenant farms in the institution of **feudalism**. Even under feudalism, the tenant farmer was trying to attain greater freedom and rights. The serfs were heavily taxed under feudalism. Many of the owners and lords absented themselves from rural areas and stayed in the cities. This was the later period of feudal society as the medieval society has all but collapsed. These were the last days of the Holy Roman Empire, and the Hapsburg Empire was strong in Europe. The Byzantine Empire was also coming to an end in the 1400s. Russia at this time was ruled by the Golden Horde. In South America, the Inca and Aztec Empires were centralized states, with all income going to the state coffers and all trade going through the emperor as well.

The centralized states basically came into being as a result of the feudal lords and the Church. As a result of so much fighting, the stronger of the surviving lords took on the functions of kings and other members of royalty, many due to the support of the Church. Loyalty shifts from the feudal lord to the ruler. As the cities grew, so did commerce as market economies became more developed and trade became more important. The growth of trade resulted in greater reliance on markets. The Renaissance was now taking place in Europe.

The word "Renaissance" literally means "rebirth," and signaled the rekindling of interest in the glory of ancient classical Greek and Roman civilizations. It was the period in human history marking the start of many ideas and innovations leading to our modern age.

Between the fourth and ninth centuries, Asia was a story of religions and empires, of kings and wars and of increasing and decreasing contact with the West.

India began this period recovering from the invasion of Alexander the Great. One strong man who met the great Alexander was **Chandragupta Maurya**, began one of India's most successful dynasties. Chandragupta conquered most of what we now call India. His grandson, **Asoka**, was more of a peaceful ruler but powerful nonetheless. He was also a great believer in the practices and power of Buddhism, sending missionaries throughout Asia to preach the ways of the Buddha. Succeeding the Mauryas were the Guptas, who ruled India for a longer period of time and brought prosperity and international recognition to their people.

The Guptas were great believers in science and mathematics, especially their uses in production of goods. They invented the decimal system the concept of zero, two things that put them ahead of the rest of the world on the mathematics timeline. They were the first to make cotton and calico, and their medical practices were much more advanced than those in Europe and elsewhere in Asia at the time. These inventions and innovations made Indian goods in high demand throughout Asia and Europe.

The idea of a united India continued after the Gupta Dynasty ended. It was especially favorable to the invading Muslims, who took over in the eleventh century, ruling the country for hundreds of years through a series of sultanates. The most famous Muslim leader of India was Tamerlane, who founded the Mogul Dynasty and began a series of conquests that expanded the borders of India. Tamerlane's grandson **Akbar** is considered the greatest Mogul. He believed in freedom of religion and is perhaps most well-known for the series of buildings that he had built, including mosques, palaces, forts and tombs, some of which are still standing today. During the years of Muslim rule, Hinduism continued to be respected, although it was a minority religion; Buddhism, however, died out almost entirely from the country that begot its founder.

The imposing mountains to the north of India served as a deterrent to Chinese expansion. India was more vulnerable to invaders who came from the west or by sea from the south. The Indian people were also vulnerable to the powerful monsoons, which came driving up from the south a few times every year, bringing howling winds and devastation in their wake.

During this time, Chinese dynasties controlled various parts of what are now China and Tibet. The **Tang Dynasty** was one of the longest lasting and the most proficient dynasty. The Tangs invented the idea of civil service and the practice of block printing. Succeeding the Tang was the Sung Dynasty, which produced some of the world's greatest paintings and porcelain pottery but failed to unify China in a meaningful way. This would prove instrumental in the takeover of China by the Mongols, led by Genghis Khan and his most famous grandson, Kublai. (See Skill 2.1d)

Genghis Khan was known as a conqueror, and Kublai was known as a uniter. They both extended the borders of their empire, however; and at its height, the Mongol Empire was the largest the world has ever seen, encompassing all of China, Russia, Persia, and central Asia. Following the Mongols were the Ming and Manchu Dynasties, both of which focused on isolation. As a result, China at the end of the eighteenth century knew very little of the outside world, and vice versa. Ming artists created beautiful porcelain pottery, but not much of it saw its way into the outside world until much later. The Manchus were known for their focus on farming and road building, two practices that were instituted in greater numbers in order to try to keep up with expanding population.

Confucianism, Taoism, and ancestor worship—the staples of Chinese society for hundreds of years—continued to flourish during all this time.

The other major power in Asia was **Japan**, which developed independently and tried to keep itself that way for hundreds of years. Early Japanese society focused on the emperor and the farm, in that order. Japan was early and often influenced by China, from which it borrowed many things, including Buddhism, a system of writing, calendar, and even fashion. The Sea of Japan protected Japan from more than Chinese invasion, including the famous Mongol one that was blown back by the "divine wind." The power of the emperor declined as it was usurped by the era of the Daimyo and his loyal soldiers, the **Samurai**. Japan flourished economically and culturally during many of these years, although the policy of isolation the country developed kept the rest of the world from knowing such things. Buddhism and local religions were joined by Christianity in the sixteenth century, but it wasn't until the mid-nineteenth century that Japan rejoined the world community.

African civilizations during these centuries were few and far between. By this time, Moslem armies had conquered most of northern coastal Africa. The preponderance of deserts and other inhospitable lands restricted African settlements to a few select areas. The city of Zimbabwe became a trading center in south central Africa in the fifth century but didn't last long. More successful was Ghana, a Muslim-influenced kingdom that arose in the ninth century and lasted for nearly 300 years. Ghanaians had large farming areas and also raised cattle and elephants. They traded with people from Europe and the Middle East. Eventually overrunning Ghana was Mali, whose trade center Timbuktu survived its own empire's demise and blossomed into one of the world's caravan destinations.

Iron, tin, and leather came out of Mali with a vengeance. The succeeding civilization of the Songhai had relative success in maintaining the success of their predecessors. Religion in all of these places was definitely Muslim; and even after extended contact with other cultures, technological advancements were few and far between.

The word "Renaissance" literally means "rebirth," and signaled the rekindling of interest in the glory of ancient classical Greek and Roman civilizations. It was the period in human history marking the start of many ideas and innovations leading to our modern age. The **Renaissance** began in Italy with many of its ideas starting in Florence, controlled by the famous Medici family. Education, especially for some of the merchants, required reading, writing, math, studying law, and the writings of classical Greek and Roman writers. A combination of a renewed fascination with the classical world and new infusion of money into the hands of those so fascinated brought on the Renaissance. In the areas of art, literature, music, and science, the world changed for the better.

Most famous are the Renaissance artists, first and foremost the more important artists were **Giotto** and his development of perspective in paintings; **Leonardo da Vinci** was not only an artist but also a scientist and inventor. Other artists included Michelangelo, Raphael, Titian, Donatello, and Rembrandt. All of these men pioneered a new method of painting and sculpture—that of portraying real events and real people as they really looked, not as the artists imagined them to be. One needs to look no further than Michelangelo's *David* to illustrate this.

Literature was a focus as well during the Renaissance. Humanists such as Petrarch, Boccaccio, Erasmus, and Sir Thomas More advanced the idea of being interested in life here on earth and the opportunities it can bring, rather than constantly focusing on heaven and its rewards. The monumental works of Shakespeare, Dante, and Cervantes found their origins in these ideas as well as the ones that drove the painters and sculptors. All of these works, of course, owe much of their existence to the invention of the printing press, which occurred during the Renaissance. In the area of political philosophy the writings of **Machiavelli** were considered influential.

The Renaissance changed music as well. It was no longer just a religious experience, and it could be fun and composed for its own sake, to be enjoyed in fuller and more humanistic ways than during the Middle Ages. Musicians worked for themselves, rather than for the churches, as before, and so could command good money for their work, increasing their prestige.

Science advanced considerably during the Renaissance, especially in the area of physics and astronomy. Copernicus, Kepler, and Galileo led a Scientific Revolution in proving that the earth was round and certainly not perfect, an earth-shattering revelation to those who clung to medieval ideals of a geocentric, church-centered existence. In **medicine** the work of Brussels-born **Andrea Vesalius** earned him the title of "father of anatomy" and had a profound influence on the Spaniard **Michael Servetus** and the Englishman **William Harvey.**

In Germany, Gutenberg's invention of the **printing press** with movable type facilitated the rapid spread of Renaissance ideas, writings and innovations, thus ensuring the enlightenment of most of Western Europe. Contributions were also made by Durer and Holbein in art and by Paracelsus in science and medicine.

The effects of the Renaissance in the Low Countries can be seen in the literature and philosophy of Erasmus and the art of van Eyck and Breughel the Elder. Rabelais and de Montaigne in France also contributed to literature and philosophy. In Spain, the art of El Greco and de Morales flourished, as did the writings of Cervantes and de Vega. In England, Sir Thomas More and Sir Francis Bacon wrote and taught philosophy and inspired by Vesalius. The greatest talent was found in literature and drama and given to mankind by Chaucer, Spenser, Marlowe, Johnson, and the incomparable Shakespeare.

The **Reformation** period consisted of two phases: the **Protestant Revolution** and the **Catholic Reformation**. The Protestant Revolution came about because of religious, political, and economic reasons. The religious reasons stemmed from abuses in the Catholic Church including fraudulent clergy with their scandalous immoral lifestyles; the sale of religious offices, indulgences, and dispensations; different theologies within the Church; and frauds involving sacred relics.

The political reasons for the Protestant Revolution involved the increase in the power of rulers who were considered "absolute monarchs," who desired all power and control, especially over the Church. The growth of "nationalism" or patriotic pride in one's own country was another contributing factor.

Economic reasons included the greed of ruling monarchs to possess and control all lands and wealth of the Church, the deep animosity against the burdensome papal taxation, the rise of the affluent middle class and its clash with medieval Church ideals, and the increase of an active system of "intense" capitalism.

The **Protestant Revolution** began in Germany with the revolt of Martin Luther against Church abuses. It spread to Switzerland where it was led by Calvin. It began in England with the efforts of King Henry VIII to have his marriage to Catherine of Aragon annulled so he could wed another and have a male heir. The results were the increasing support given not only by the people but also by nobles and some rulers, and of course, the attempts of the Church to stop it.

The **Catholic Reformation** was undertaken by the Church to "clean up its act" and to slow or stop the Protestant Revolution. The Council of Trent and the Jesuits supplied the major efforts to this end. Six major results of the Reformation included:

• Religious freedom,
• Religious tolerance,
• More opportunities for education,
• Power and control of rulers limited,
• Increase in religious wars, and
• An increase in fanaticism and persecution.

The Scientific Revolution and the Enlightenment were two of the most important movements in the history of civilization, resulting in a new sense of self-examination and a wider view of the world than ever before. The Scientific Revolution was, above all, a shift in focus from **belief to evidence**. Scientists and philosophers wanted to see the proof, not just believe what other people told them. It was an exciting time, if you were a forward-looking thinker.

A Polish astronomer, **Nicolaus Copernicus**, began the Scientific Revolution. He crystallized a lifetime of observations into a book that was published about the time of his death; in this book, Copernicus argued that the Sun, not the Earth, was the center of a solar system and that other planets revolved around the Sun, not the Earth. This flew in the face of established (Church-mandated) doctrine. The Church still wielded tremendous power at this time, including the power to banish people or sentence them to prison or even death.

The Danish astronomer **Tycho Brahe** was the first to catalog his observations of the night sky, of which he made thousands. Building on Brahe's data, German scientist Johannes Kepler instituted his theory of planetary movement, embodied in his famous Laws of Planetary Movement. Using Brahe's data, Kepler also confirmed Copernicus's observations and argument that the Earth revolved around the Sun.

The most famous defender of this idea was **Galileo Galilei**, an Italian scientist who conducted many famous experiments in the pursuit of science. He is most well known for his defense of the heliocentric (sun-centered) idea. He wrote a book comparing the two theories, but most readers could tell easily that he favored the new one. He was convinced of this mainly because of what he had seen with his own eyes. He had used the relatively new invention of the telescope to see four moons of Jupiter. They certainly did not revolve around the Earth, so why should everything else? His ideas were not at all favored with the Church, which continued to assert its authority in this and many other matters. The Church was still powerful enough at this time, especially in Italy, to order Galileo to be placed under house arrest.

Galileo died under house arrest, but his ideas didn't die with him. Picking up the baton was an English scientist named **Isaac Newton**, who became perhaps the most famous scientist of all. He is known as the discoverer of gravity and a pioneering voice in the study of optics (light), calculus, and physics.

More than any other scientist, Newton argued for (and proved) the idea of a mechanistic view of the world: You can see how the world works and prove how the world works through observation; if you can see these things with your own eyes, they must be so. Up to this time, people believed what other people told them; this is how the Church was able to keep control of people's lives for so long. Newton, following in the footsteps of Copernicus and Galileo, changed all that.

This naturally led to the **Enlightenment**, a period of intense self-study that focused on ethics and logic. More so than at any time before, scientists and philosophers questioned cherished truths, widely held beliefs, and their own sanity in an attempt to discover why the world worked—from within. "I think, therefore I am" was one of the famous sayings from the Enlightenment.

It was uttered by Rene Descartes, a French scientist-philosopher whose dedication to logic and the rigid rules of observation were a blueprint for the thinkers who came after him.

One of the giants of the era was England's **David Hume**. He was a pioneer in the doctrine of empiricism (believing things only when you've seen the proof for yourself). Hume was also a prime believer in the value of skepticism, in other words, he was naturally suspicious of things that other people told him to be true and constantly set out to discover the truth for himself. These two related ideas influenced many thinkers after Hume, and his writings (of which there are many) continue to inspire philosophers to this day.

Perhaps the most famous Enlightenment thinker is **Immanuel Kant** of Germany. He was both a philosopher and a scientist, and he took a definite scientific view of the world. He wrote the movement's most famous essay, "Answering the Question: What Is Enlightenment?" and he answered his famous question with the motto "Dare to Know." For Kant, the human being was a rational being capable of hugely creative thought and intense self-evaluation. He encouraged all to examine themselves and the world around them. He believed that the source of morality lay not in nature of in the grace of God but in the human soul itself. He believed that man believed in God for practical, not religious or mystical, reasons.

Also prevalent during the Enlightenment was the idea of the "**social contract,**" the belief that government existed because people wanted it to, that the people had an agreement with the government that they would submit to it as long as it protected them and didn't encroach on their basic human rights. This idea was first made famous by the Frenchman **Jean-Jacques Rousseau** but was also adopted by England's John Locke and America's Thomas Jefferson. **John Locke** was one of the most influential political writers of the seventeenth century who put great emphasis on human rights and put forth the belief that when governments violate those rights people should rebel. He wrote the book *Two Treatises of Government* in 1690. This book had tremendous influence on political thought in the American colonies and helped shaped the U.S. Constitution and Declaration of Independence

The **Age of Exploration** actually had its beginnings centuries before exploration actually took place. The rise and spread of Islam in the seventh century and its subsequent control over the holy city of Jerusalem led to the Christian European so-called holy wars, **the Crusades**, to free Jerusalem and the Holy Land from Muslim control. Even though the Crusades were not a success, those who survived and returned to their homes and countries in Western Europe brought back with them new products such as silks, spices, perfumes, new and different foods. Luxuries that were unheard of that gave new meaning to colorless, drab, dull lives.

New ideas, new inventions, better maps and charts, newer, more accurate navigational instruments, increased knowledge, great wealth and new methods also went to Western Europe with the returning Crusaders and from these new influences were the intellectual stimuli that led to the Renaissance. The revival of interest in classical Greek art, architecture, literature, science, astronomy, medicine and increased trade between Europe and Asia and the invention of the printing press helped to push the spread of knowledge and start exploring.

For many centuries, various cartographers made many maps and charts, which in turn stimulated curiosity and the seeking of more knowledge. At the same time, the Chinese were using the magnetic compass in their ships. Pacific islanders were going from island to island, covering thousands of miles in open canoes navigating by sun and stars. Arab traders were sailing all over the Indian Ocean in their **dhows**. The trade routes between Europe and Asia were slow, difficult, dangerous, and very expensive. Between sea voyages on the Indian Ocean and Mediterranean Sea and the camel caravans in central Asia and the Arabian Desert, the trade was still controlled by the Italian merchants in Genoa and Venice. It would take months and even years for the exotic luxuries of Asia to reach the markets of Western Europe. A faster, cheaper way had to be found. A way had to be found that would bypass traditional routes and end the control of the Italian merchants.

Prince Henry of Portugal (also called the Navigator) encouraged, supported, and financed the Portuguese seamen who led in the search for an all-water route to Asia. A shipyard was built along with a school teaching navigation. New types of sailing ships were built that would carry the seamen safely through the ocean waters. Experiments were conducted in newer maps, newer navigational methods, and newer instruments. These included the astrolabe and the compass enabling sailors to determine direction as well as latitude and longitude for exact location. Although Prince Henry died in 1460, the Portuguese kept on sailing along and exploring Africa's west coastline. In 1488, Bartholomew Diaz and his men sailed around Africa's southern tip and headed toward Asia. Diaz wanted to push on but turned back because his men were discouraged and weary from the long months at sea, extremely fearful of the unknown, and just refusing to travel any further.

However, the Portuguese were finally successful ten years later in 1498 when **Vasco da Gama** and his men, continuing the route of Diaz, rounded Africa's Cape of Good Hope, sailing across the Indian Ocean, reaching India's port of Calicut (Calcutta). Although, six years earlier, Columbus had reached the New World and an entire hemisphere, da Gama had proved Asia could be reached from Europe by sea.

Columbus' first transatlantic voyage was to try to prove his theory or idea that Asia could be reached by sailing west.

To a certain extent, his idea was true. It could be done but only after figuring how to go around or across or through the landmass in between. Long after Spain dispatched explorers and her famed conquistadors to gather the wealth for the Spanish monarchs and their coffers, the British were searching valiantly for the "Northwest Passage," a land-sea route across North America and open sea to the wealth of Asia. It wasn't until after the Lewis and Clark Expedition when Captains Meriwether Lewis and William Clark proved conclusively that the Northwest Passage did not exist.

However, this did not deter exploration and settlement. Spain, France, and England along with some participation by the Dutch led the way with expanding Western European civilization in the New World. These three nations had strong monarchical governments and were struggling for dominance and power in Europe. With the defeat of the Spanish Armada in 1588, England became undisputed master of the seas. Spain lost its power and influence in Europe and it was left to France and England to carry on the rivalry, leading to eventual British control in Asia as well.

With the increase in trade and travel, cities sprang up and began to grow. Craft workers in the cities developed their skills to a high degree, eventually organizing guilds to protect the quality of the work and to regulate the buying and selling of their products. City government developed and flourished centered on strong town councils. Active in city government and the town councils were the wealthy businessmen who made up the growing middle class.

In addition, there were a number of individuals and events during the time of exploration and discoveries. The **Vivaldo Brothers** and **Marco Polo** wrote of their travels and experiences, which signaled the early beginnings. From the Crusades, the survivors made their way home to different places in Europe bringing with them fascinating, new information about exotic lands, people, customs, and desired foods and goods such as spices and silks.

For France, claims to various parts of North America were the result of the efforts of such men as Verrazano, Champlain, Cartier, LaSalle, Father Marquette and Joliet. Dutch claims were based on the work of one Henry Hudson. John Cabot gave England its stake in North America along with John Hawkins, Sir Francis Drake, and the half-brothers Sir Walter Raleigh and Sir Humphrey Gilbert.

Actually, the first Europeans in the New World were Norsemen led by Eric the Red and later, his son Leif the Lucky. However, before any of these, the ancestors of today's Native Americans and Latin American Indians crossed the Bering Strait from Asia to Alaska, eventually settling in all parts of the Americas.

The **Native North and South American** could not have been more different, yet in some ways they were the same as well.

Differences in geography, economic focus, and the preponderance of visitors from overseas produced differing patterns of occupation, survival, and success.

In North America, the landscape was much more hospitable to settlement and exploration. The North American continent, especially in what is now the United States had a few mountain ranges and a handful of wide rivers but nothing near the dense jungles and staggeringly high mountains that South America did. The area that is now Canada was cold but otherwise conducive to settlement. As a result, the Native Americans in the northern areas of the Americas were more spread out and their cultures more diverse than their South American counterparts.

One of the best known of the North American tribes was the Pueblo, who lived in what is now the American Southwest. They are perhaps best known for the challenging vista-based villages that they constructed from the sheer faces of cliffs and rocks and for their *adobes*, mud-brick buildings that housed their living and meeting quarters. The Pueblos chose their own chiefs. This was perhaps one of the oldest representative governments in the world.

Known also for their organized government were the Iroquoi, who lived in the American Northeast. The famous Five Nations of the Iroquois made treaties among themselves and shared leadership of their peoples.

For the North Americans, life was all about finding and growing food. The people were great farmers and hunters. They grew such famous crops as *maize*, or corn, and potatoes and squash and pumpkins and beans; and they hunted all manner of animals for food, including deer, bears, and buffalo. Despite the preponderance of crop-growing areas, many Native Americans, however, did not domesticate animals except for dogs. They might have killed pigs and chickens for food, but they certainly made it easy on themselves by growing them in pens right outside their houses.

The Native Americans who lived in the wilds of Canada and in the Pacific Northwest lived off the land as well and, in this case, the nearby water. Fishing was a big business in these places. The people used fish to eat and for trade, exchanging the much-needed food for beads and other trinkets from neighboring tribes.

Religion was a personal affair for nearly all of these tribes, with beliefs in higher powers extending to Spirits in the sky and elsewhere in Nature. Native Americans had none of the one-god-only mentality that developed in Europe and the Middle East, nor did they have the wars associated with the conflict that those monotheistic religions had with one another.

Those people who lived in North America had large concentrations of people and houses, but they didn't have the kind of large civilization centers like the cities of elsewhere in the world. These people didn't have an exact system of writing, either. These were two technological advances that were found in many other places in the world, including, to varying degrees, South America.

We know the most about the empires of South America, the **Aztec**, **Inca**, and **Maya**. People lived in South America before the advent of these empires, of course. One of the earliest people of record was the Olmecs, who left behind little to prove their existence except a series of huge carved figures.

The Aztecs dominated Mexico and Central America. They weren't the only people living in these areas, just the most powerful ones. The Aztecs had many enemies, some of who were only too happy to help Hernan Cortes precipitate the downfall of the Aztec society. The Aztecs had access to large numbers of metals and jewels, and they used these metals to make weapons and these jewels to trade for items they didn't already possess. Actually, the Aztecs didn't do a whole lot of trading; rather, they conquered neighboring tribes and demanded tribute from them; this is the source of so much of the Aztec riches. They also believed in a handful of gods and believed that these gods demanded human sacrifice in order to continue to smile on the Aztecs. The center of Aztec society was the great city of Tenochtitlan, which was built on an island so as to be easier to defend and boasted a population of 300,000 at the time of the arrival of the conquistadors. Tenochtitlan was known for its canals and its pyramids, none of which survive today.

The Inca Empire stretched across a vast period of territory down the western coast of South America and was connected by a series of roads. A series of messengers ran along these roads, carrying news and instructions from the capital, Cuzco, another large city along the lines of but not as spectacular as Tenochtitlan. The Incas are known for inventing the *quipu*, a string-based device that provided them with a method of keeping records. The Inca Empire, like the Aztec Empire, was very much a centralized state, with all income going to the state coffers and all trade going through the emperor as well. The Incas worshiped the dead, their ancestors, and nature and often took part in what we could consider strange rituals.

The most advanced Native American civilization was the Maya, who lived primarily in Central America. They were the only Native American civilization to develop writing, which consisted of a series of symbols that has still not been deciphered. The Mayas also built huge pyramids and other stone figures and sculptures, mostly of the gods they worshiped. The Mayas are most famous, however, for their calendars and for their mathematics. The Mayan calendars were the most accurate on the planet until the sixteenth century. The Mayas also invented the idea of zero, which might sound like a small thing except that no other culture had thought of such a thing.

Maya worship resembled the practices of the Aztec and Inca, although human sacrifices were rare. The Mayas also traded heavily with their neighbors.

All of these civilizations were destroyed by the invading foreigners. The wealth of resources in these countries was desirable to the Europeans. Slaves were imported from the African countries to work in the Americas. It is estimated that in four centuries of the slave trade, more than 9.5 million slaves were sent to the Americas. The African sellers and leaders used slaves as a form of barter. They traded them for what the Europeans and others offered.

Skill 2.2b   Demonstrate knowledge of political and industrial revolutions 1750–1914

The overriding theme of the life in the eighteenth, nineteenth, and twentieth centuries was progress. Technological advancements brought great and terrible things in all aspects of life. New theories in economics brought great changes in the way the world does business. New theories in government brought about new nations, uprisings, and wars galore. New theories in art changed the landscape of painting forever.

During the eighteenth and especially the nineteenth Centuries, nationalism emerged as a powerful force in Europe and elsewhere in the world. Strictly speaking, nationalism is the belief in one's own nation, country, or people. More so than in previous centuries, the people of the European nations began to think in terms of a nation of people who had similar beliefs, concerns, and needs. This was partly a reaction to a growing discontent with the autocratic governments of the day and also just a general realization that there was more to life than the individual. People could feel a part of something like their nation, making themselves more than just an insignificant soul struggling to survive.

Nationalism precipitated several changes in government, most notably in France; it also brought large groups of people together, as with the unification of Germany and Italy. What it did not do, however, is provide sufficient outlets for this sudden rise in national fervor. Especially in the 1700s and 1800s, European powers and peoples began looking to Africa and Asia in order to find colonies: rich sources of goods, trade, and cheap labor. Africa, especially, suffered at the hands of European imperialists, bent on expanding their reach outside the borders of Europe. Asia also suffered from colonial expansion, most notably in India and Southeast Asia.

This colonial expansion would haunt the European imperialists in a very big way, as colonial skirmishes spilled over into alliance that dragged the European powers into World War I. Some of these colonial battles were still being fought as late as the start of World War II as well.

The **Industrial Revolution**, which began in Great Britain, was the development of power-driven machinery (fueled by coal and steam) leading to the accelerated growth of industry with large factories replacing homes and small workshops as work centers. The lives of people changed drastically and a largely agricultural society changed to an industrial one.

In Western Europe, the period of empire and colonialism began. The industrialized nations seized and claimed parts of Africa and Asia in an effort to control and provide the raw materials needed to feed the industries and machines in the "mother country". Later developments included power based on electricity and internal combustion, replacing coal and steam.

The use of machines in industry enabled workers to produce a large quantity of goods much faster than by hand. With the increase in business, hundreds of workers were hired, assigned to perform a certain job in the production process. This method of organization is called "**division of labor**." By increasing the rate of production, businesses lowered prices for their products making the products affordable for more people. As a result, sales and businesses were increasingly successful and profitable. A great variety of new products or inventions became available such as: the typewriter, the telephone, barbed wire, the electric light, the phonograph, and the gasoline automobile. From this list, the one that had the greatest effect on America's economy was the automobile.

The increase in business and industry was greatly affected by the many rich natural resources that were found throughout the nation. The industrial machines were powered by the abundant water supply. The construction industry as well as products made from wood depended heavily on lumber from the forests. An abundance of coal iron ore was needed for the steel industry, which profited and increased from the use of steel in such things as skyscrapers, automobiles, bridges, railroad tracks, and machines. Other minerals such as silver, copper, and petroleum played a large role in industrial growth, especially petroleum, from which gasoline was refined as fuel for the increasingly popular automobile.

The late 1800s and early 1900s were a period of the efforts of many to make significant reforms and changes in the areas of politics, society, and the economy. There was a need to reduce the levels of poverty and to improve the living conditions of those affected by it. Regulations of big business, ridding governmental corruption and making it more responsive to the needs of the people were also on the list of reforms to be accomplished. Until 1890, there was very little success, but from 1890 on, the reformers gained increased public support and were able to achieve some influence in government. Since some of these individuals referred to themselves as "**progressives**" the period of 1890 to 1917 is referred to by historians as the Progressive Era.

The **American Revolution** resulted in the successful efforts of the English colonists in America to win their freedom from Great Britain. After more than one hundred years of mostly self-government, the colonists resented the increased British meddling and control, they declared their freedom, won the Revolutionary War with aid from France, and formed a new independent nation.

The **French Revolution** was the revolt of the middle and lower classes against the gross political and economic excesses of the rulers and the supporting nobility. It ended with the establishment of the First in a series of French Republics. Conditions leading to revolt included extreme taxation, inflation, lack of food, and the total disregard for the impossible, degrading, and unacceptable condition of the people on the part of the rulers, nobility, and the Church.

Emboldened by the success of the American and French Revolutions, the Spanish and Portuguese colonies in Central and South America grew dissatisfied with their economic and political dependence on Europe, and in the early decades of the nineteenth century, several revolutionary movements gained momentum.

In Europe, France had moved into Spain and captured the Spanish King Ferdinand VII during the Napoleonic Wars, effectively weakening Spain's hold over its colonies in the Americas. The royal family of Portugal fled to Brazil, its South American colony, before Napoleon's armies reached them. Efforts by the mother countries to suppress the independence movements were thwarted by junta forces led by such figures as Miguel Hidalgo and Simon Bolivar. They were further discouraged by other countries such as the United States and Great Britain that were eager to gain access to South America's natural resources and lucrative markets.

By 1822, Argentina, Chile, Colombia, Mexico, Paraguay, Venezuela, Peru, Ecuador and Brazil had all succeeded in their battles for independence, and looked to the rest of the world for recognition and assistance. In the United States, President James Monroe announced the Monroe Doctrine, which stated that any designs by European countries to take control of the former colonies in the Western Hemisphere would be interpreted as attacks on the United States.

Socialism is a fairly recent political phenomenon though its roots can be traced pretty far back in time in many respects. At its core, both socialism and communism are fundamentally economic philosophies that advocate public rather than private ownership, especially over means of production, yet even here, there are many distinctions. Karl Marx basically concentrated his attention on the industrial worker and on state domination over the means of production.

In practice, this Marxian dogma has largely been followed the most in those countries that profess to be communist. The emphasis in communism is the massive programs for the development of heavy industry regardless of the wants or comforts of the individual in the given society. Socialism by contrast, usually occurring where industry has already been developed has concerned itself more with the welfare of the individual and the fair distribution of whatever wealth is available.

Communism has a rigid theology, and a bible (*Das Capital*) that sees communism emerging as a result of almost cosmic laws. Modern socialism is much closer to the ground. It too sees change in human society and hopes for improvement, but there is no unchanging millennium at the end of the road. Communism aims to achieve the perfect state and in this certainty it is willing to use any and all means, however ruthless, to bring it about.

Socialism on the other hand, confident only that the human condition is always changing, makes no easy approximation between ends and means and so cannot justify brutalities. This distinction in philosophy, of course, makes for an immense conflict in methods. Communism believes that revolution is inevitable, works toward it by emphasizing class antagonisms. Socialism, meanwhile, insists on the use of democratic procedures within the existing social order of a given society while seeking change. In it, the upper classes and capitalists are not to be violently overthrown but instead won over by logical persuasion.

It is interesting to note that in every perfect, idealized community or society that people have dreamed about throughout history, human beings are pictured living in a special harmony that transcends their natural instincts, have been elements of socialism. This tendency was especially found in the **Utopian-Socialists** of the early nineteenth century, whose basic aim was the repudiation of the private property system with its economic inefficiency and social injustice. Their criticisms rather than any actual achievements would linger after them.

Like Marx, they envisioned industrial capitalism as becoming more and more inhumane and oppressive. They could not imagine the mass of workers prospering in such a system. Yet the workers soon developed their own powerful organizations and institutions. They began to bend the economic system to their own benefit, creating factions. The first was between those who after the growing success of the labor movement rejected the earlier utopian ideas as being impractical. Second were those who saw in this newfound political awareness of the working class the key to organizing a realistic ability of revolution, who saw this as inevitable based on their previous observations and study of history. Having reached a point where it has managed to jeopardize its very own survival, the inevitable revolution of those opposed to the present capitalist system had to occur, history has proven this so, and history is always right and irrefutable.

These believers in the absolute correctness of this doctrine gathered around Marx in what he called **Scientific Socialism**. He had contempt for all other kinds of socialism, which he considered to be unscientific and, therefore, useless as a realistic political philosophy.

The next split would occur between those who believed in the absolute inevitability of the coming revolution (the **Revolutionary Socialists** or as they came to be known, the **communists**), and those who accepted the basic idea that the current capitalist system could not last. They saw the growing political awareness of the working class and the beginnings of an ability to effect peaceful and gradual change in the social order. They believed this is better in the long run for everyone concerned as opposed to a cataclysmic, apocalyptic uprising (the **Democratic-Socialists**).

Major strides for the **democratic-socialists** were made before the First World War—a war that the Socialists, as philosophical pacifists, initially resisted, giving only reluctant support only once the struggle had begun. During the conflict, public sentiment against pacifism tended generally to weaken the movement, but with peace, reaction set in. The cause of world socialism leaped forward, often overcompensating by adhering to revolutionary communism, which in the Revolution of 1917 had taken hold of in Russia.

The between wars period saw the sudden spurt of socialism, whether their leanings were democratic or not, all socialists were bound together for a time in their resistance to fascism.

In London in 1864, Karl Marx organized the first Socialist International. This radical leftist organization died off after limping along for twelve years, by which time its headquarters had moved to New York. The **Second Socialist International** met twelve years later in Paris to celebrate the anniversary of the fall of the Bastille in the French Revolution. By this time, serious factions were developing. There were the **anarchists**, who wanted to tear down everything, **communists** who wanted to tear down the established order and build another in its place, and the **democratic-socialist** majority who favored peaceful political action.

Struggling for internal peace and cohesion right up to the First World War, socialism would remain largely ineffectual at this critical international time. Peace brought them all together again in Bern, Switzerland, but by this time the Soviet Union had been created, and the Russian communists refused to attend the meeting on the ground that the Second Socialist International opposed the type of dictatorship it saw as necessary in order to achieve revolutions. Thus the **Communist International** was created in direct opposition to the Socialist International. While the socialists went on to advocate the "triumph of democracy, firmly rooted in the principles of liberty." The main objective of this new Socialist International was to maintain the peace, an ironic and very elusive goal in the period between the two world wars.

At the international level, socialism seeks a world of free peoples living together in peace and harmony for the mutual benefit of all. That freedom, at least from colonial rule, has largely been won. Peace throughout the world, however, is still as far off in most respects as it has ever been. According to the socialist doctrine, putting an end to capitalism will reduce the likelihood of war. Armies and businesses are seen to need each other in a marriage of the weapons-mentality and devotion to private profit through the economic exploitation of weaker countries.

All socialism denies certain freedoms. This denial is sometimes hidden in what it considers favorable terms. It deprives the minority of special economic privileges for the benefit of majority. The more left wing, communistic socialism may deny the democratic process entirely. Traditionally defined, democracy holds to the idea that the people, exercising their majority opinion at the polls, will arrive at the common good by electing representative individuals to govern them. Communists would interpret this to mean the tyranny of an uneducated majority is obliged to decide between a politically selected group of would-be leaders.

The last important historical economic system to arise was fascism. It has been called a reaction against communism and socialism. It can, at times, cooperate with a monarchy if it has to.

Fascist movements often had socialist origins. For example, in Italy, where fascism first arose in place of socialism, **Benito Mussolini**, sought to impose what he called "*corporativism*". A fascist "*corporate*" state would theoretically run the economy for the benefit of the whole country like a corporation. It would be centrally controlled and managed by an elite who would see that its benefits would go to everyone.

In general, Fascism is the effort to create, by dictatorial means, a viable national society in which competing interests were to be adjusted to each other by being entirely subordinated to the service of the state. The following features have been characteristic of Fascism in its various manifestations:

(1) An origin during a time of serious economic disruption and of rapid and bewildering social change.

(2) A philosophy that rejects democratic and humanitarian ideals and glorifies the absolute sovereignty of the state, the unity and destiny of the people, and their unquestioning loyalty and obedience to the dictator.

(3) Aggressive nationalism calls for the mobilization and regimentation of every aspect of national life and makes open use of violence and intimidation.

(4) The simulation of mass popular support, accomplished by outlawing all but a single political party and by using suppression, censorship, and propaganda.

(5) A program of vigorous action including economic reconstruction, industrialization, pursuit of economic self-sufficiency, territorial expansion and war which is dramatized as bold, adventurous, and promising a glorious future.

Fascism has always declared itself the uncompromising enemy of communism. However, fascist actions have much in common with communism. (In fact, many of the methods of organization and propaganda used by fascists were taken from the experience of the early Russian communists, along with the belief in a single strong political party, secret police, etc.) The propertied interests and the upper classes, fearful of revolution, often gave their support to fascism on the basis of promises by the fascist leaders to maintain the status quo and safeguard property. (In effect, accomplishing a revolution from above with their help as opposed from below against them. However, fascism did consider itself a revolutionary movement of a different type).

Once established, a fascist regime ruthlessly crushes communist and socialist parties as well as all democratic opposition. It regiments the propertied interests to its national goals and wins the potentially revolutionary masses to fascist programs by substituting a rabid nationalism for class conflict. Thus fascism may be regarded as an extreme defensive expedient adopted by a nation faced with the sometimes-illusionary threat of communist subversion or revolution. Under fascism, capital is regulated as much as labor and fascist contempt for legal or constitutional guarantees effectively destroyed whatever security the capitalistic system had enjoyed under pre-fascist governments.

In theory, the chief distinction between fascism and communism is that fascism is *nationalist*, exalting the interests of the state and glorifying war between nations, whereas communism is *internationalist,* exalting the interests of a specific economic class (the proletariat) and glorifying worldwide class warfare. In practice, however, this fundamental distinction loses some of its validity. In its heyday, fascism was also an internationalist movement dedicated to world conquest (like communism), as evidenced by the events prior to and during World War II. At the same time, many elements in communism as it evolved came to be very nationalistic as well.

The time from 1830 to 1914 is characterized by the extraordinary growth and spread of patriotic pride in a nation along with intense, widespread imperialism. Loyalty to one's nation included national pride, extending and maintaining sovereign political boundaries, and unification of smaller states with common language, history, and culture into a more powerful nation. As part of a larger multicultural empire, there were smaller groups who wished to separate into smaller, political, cultural nations. Examples of major events of this time resulting from the insurgence of nationalism include:

In the United States, territorial expansion occurred in the expansion westward under the banner of "Manifest Destiny." In addition, the U.S. was involved in the War with Mexico, the Spanish-American War, and support of the Latin American colonies of Spain in their revolt for independence. In Latin America, the Spanish colonies were successful in their fight for independence and self-government.

Prior to the Industrial Revolution, most urban centers were either ports or centers of government. With the sudden and rapid growth of industry, which started in England, urban centers began growing based on industrial production and proximity to power resources, such as coal and water power. During the 1700s, the population of England went from a majority living in rural areas to a majority living in cities. As industrialization spread to other countries, a similar pattern of urbanization followed. With the advent of the railroad, moving raw materials over land became easier and less expensive, further fueling urban growth.

In Europe, Italy and Germany were each totally united into one nation from many smaller states. There were revolutions in Austria and Hungary, the Franco-Prussian War, the division of Africa among the strong European nations, interference and intervention of Western nations in Asia, and the breakup of Turkish dominance in the Balkans.

In Africa; France, Great Britain, Italy, Portugal, Spain, Germany, and Belgium controlled the entire continent except Liberia and Ethiopia. In Asia and the Pacific Islands, only China, Japan, and Siam (present-day Thailand) kept their independence. The others were controlled by the strong European nations. An additional reason for European imperialism was the harsh, urgent demand for the raw materials needed to fuel and feed the great Industrial Revolution. These resources were not available in the huge quantity so desperately needed, which necessitated (and rationalized) the partitioning of the continent of Africa and parts of Asia. In turn, these colonial areas would purchase the finished manufactured goods.

Things changed in the worlds of literature and art as well. The main development in the nineteenth century was **Romanticism**, an emphasis on emotion and the imagination that was a direct reaction to the logic and reason so stressed in the preceding Enlightenment. Famous Romantic authors included John Keats, William Wordsworth, Victor Hugo, and Johann Wolfgang von Goethe. The horrors of the Industrial Revolution gave rise to the very famous realists Charles Dickens, Fyodor Dostoevsky, Leo Tolstoy, and Mark Twain, who described life as they saw it, for better or for worse (and it was usually worse).

The most famous movement of the 1800s, however, was **Impressionism**. The idea was to present an interpretation of a specific moment in time; one of life's fleeting moments memorialized on canvas. A list of famous impressionists is a who's who of the most famous painters in the world: Monet, Degas, van Gogh, Manet, Cezanne, and Renoir. More than any other time in the history of the arts, Impressionism produced famous faces and famous canvases.

Echoing Dickens's dislike of an industrialized world, twentieth century authors stressed individual action and responsibility. The giants of the 1900s include James Joyce, T.S. Eliot, John Steinbeck, Ernest Hemingway, William Faulkner, and George Orwell, all of whom to varying degrees expressed distrust at the power of machines and weapons and most of modern society.

One of the main places for European imperialist expansion was Africa. Britain, France, Germany, and Belgium took over countries in Africa and claimed them as their own. The resources (including people) were then shipped back to the mainland and claimed as colonial gains. The Europeans made a big deal about "civilizing the savages," reasoning that their technological superiority gave them the right to rule and "educate" the peoples of Africa.

Southeast Asia was another area of European expansion at this time, mainly by France. So, too, was India, colonized by Great Britain. These two nations combined with Spain to occupy countries in Latin America. Spain also seized the rich lands of the Philippines.

Competency 2.3   1914 to the Present

Skill 2.3a   Evaluate conflicts, ideologies, and changes in the twentieth century

The **Russian Revolution** began in March (or February on the old calendar) 1917 with the abdication of Tsar Nicholas II and the establishment of a democratic government. Those who were the extreme Marxists and had a majority in Russia's Socialist Party, the Bolsheviks, overcame opposition, and in November (October on the old calendar), did away with the provisional democratic government and set up the world's first Marxist state.

The conditions in Russia in previous centuries led up to this. Russia's harsh climate, tremendous size, and physical isolation from the rest of Europe, along with the brutal despotic rule and control of the Tsars over enslaved peasants, contributed to the final conditions leading to revolution. Despite the tremendous efforts of Peter the Great during the late seventeenth and early eighteenth centuries to bring his country up to the social, cultural, and economic standards of the rest of Europe, Russia always remained a hundred years or more behind. Autocratic rule, the existence of the system of serfdom or slavery of the peasants, lack of money, defeats in wars, lack of enough food and food production, little if any industrialization--all of these contributed to conditions ripe for revolt.

By 1914, Russia's industrial growth was even faster than Germany's and agricultural production was improving, along with better transportation. However, poverty was rampant. The Orthodox Church was steeped in political activities, and the Tsars had absolute rule. By the time the nation entered World War I, conditions were just right for revolution. Marxist socialism seemed to be the solution or answer to all the problems. Russia had to stop participation in the war, although winning a big battle. Industry could not meet the military's needs.

Transportation by rail was severely disrupted, and it was most difficult to procure supplies from the Allies. The people had had enough of war, injustice, starvation, poverty, slavery, and cruelty. The support for and strength of the Bolsheviks were mainly in the cities. After two to three years of civil war, fighting foreign invasions, and opposing other revolutionary groups, the Bolsheviks were finally successful in making possible a type of "pre-Utopia" for the workers and the people.

As succeeding Marxist or communist leaders came to power, the effects of this violent revolution were felt all around the earth. From 1989 until 1991, communism eventually gave way to various forms of democracies and free enterprise societies in Eastern Europe and the former Soviet Union. The foreign policies of all free Western nations were directly and immensely affected by the Marxist-communist ideology. Its effect on Eastern Europe and the former Soviet Union was felt politically, economically, socially, culturally, and geographically. The people of ancient Russia simply exchanged one autocratic dictatorial system for another, and its impact on all of the people on the earth is still being felt to this day.

World War I 1914 to 1918
The causes of World War I include the surge of nationalism, the increasing strength of military capabilities, massive colonization for raw materials needed for industrialization and manufacturing, and military and diplomatic alliances.
The initial spark that started the war was the assassination of Austrian Archduke Franz Ferdinand and his wife in Sarajevo.

There were 28 nations involved in the war, not including colonies and territories. It began July 28, 1914 and ended November 11, 1918 with the signing of the Treaty of Versailles. Economically speaking, the war cost a total of $337 billion, increased inflation and created huge war debts, and caused a loss of markets, goods, jobs, and factories. Politically, old empires collapsed. Many monarchies disappeared and smaller countries gained temporary independence. Communists seized power in Russia and, in some cases, nationalism increased. Socially, total populations decreased because of war casualties and low birth rates. There were millions of displaced persons and villages and farms were destroyed. Cities grew while women made significant gains in the work force and the ballot box. There was less social distinction and classes. Attitudes completely changed, and old beliefs and values were questioned. The peace settlement established the League of Nations to ensure peace, but it failed to do so.

Fascism arose following WWI. In general, Fascism is the effort to create, by dictatorial means, a viable national society in which competing interests were to be adjusted to each other by being entirely subordinated to the service of the state. The following features have been characteristic of Fascism in its various manifestations: **(1)** An origin at a time of serious economic disruption and of rapid and bewildering social change. **(2)** A philosophy that rejects democratic and humanitarian ideals and glorifies the absolute sovereignty of the state, the unity and destiny of the people, and their unquestioning loyalty and obedience to the dictator. **(3)** Aggressive nationalism calls for the mobilization and regimentation of every aspect of national life and makes open use of violence and intimidation. **(4)** The simulation of mass popular support, accomplished by outlawing all but a single political party and by using suppression, censorship, and propaganda. **(5)** A program of vigorous action including economic reconstruction, industrialization, pursuit of economic self-sufficiency, territorial expansion and war that is dramatized as bold, adventurous, and promising a glorious future.

Fascist movements often had socialist origins. For example, in Italy, where fascism first arose in place of socialism, **Benito Mussolini**, sought to impose what he called "*corporativism.*" A fascist "*corporate*" state would, in theory, run the economy for the benefit of the whole country like a corporation. It would be centrally controlled and managed by an elite who would see that its benefits would go to everyone.

Fascism has always declared itself the uncompromising enemy of communism, with which, however, fascist actions have much in common. (In fact, many of the methods of organization and propaganda used by fascists were taken from the experience of the early Russian communists, along with the belief in a single strong political party, secret police, etc.) The propertied interests and the upper classes, fearful of revolution, often gave their support to fascism on the basis of promises by the fascist leaders to maintain the status quo and safeguard property. (In effect, this accomplished a revolution from above with their help as opposed from below against them. However, fascism did consider itself a revolutionary movement of a different type).

In addition, fascist or similar regimes are at times anti-communist, as evidenced by the Soviet-German Treaty of 1939. During the period of alliance created by the treaty, Italy, Germany, and their satellite countries ceased their anti-communist propaganda. They emphasized their own revolutionary and proletarian origins and attacked the so-called plutocratic western democracies.

In theory at least, the chief distinction between fascism and communism is that fascism is *nationalist*, exalting the interests of the state and glorifying war between nations, whereas communism is *internationalist,* exalting the interests of a specific economic class (the proletariat) and glorifying worldwide class warfare. In practice, however, this fundamental distinction loses some of its validity. For in its heyday, fascism was also an internationalist movement, a movement dedicated to world conquest, (like communism), as evidenced by the events prior to and during the Second World War. At the same time, many elements in communism as it evolved came to be very nationalistic as well.

World War II 1939 to 1945

Ironically, the Treaty of Versailles, which ended World War I, ultimately led to the World War II. Countries that fought in the first war were either dissatisfied over the "spoils" of war, or were punished so harshly that resentment continued building to an eruption twenty years later.

The economic problems of both winners and losers of the first war were never resolved, and the worldwide Great Depression of the 1930s dealt the final blow to any immediate rapid recovery. Democratic governments in Europe were severely strained and weakened, which in turn gave strength and encouragement to those political movements that were extreme and made promises to end the economic chaos in their countries.

Nationalism, which was a major cause of World War I, grew even stronger and seemed to feed the feelings of discontent, which became increasingly rampant.

Because of unstable economic conditions and political unrest, harsh dictatorships arose in several of the countries, especially where there was no history of experience in democratic government.

Countries such as Germany, Japan, and Italy began to aggressively expand their borders and acquire additional territory.

In all, 59 nations became embroiled in World War II, which began September 1, 1939 and ended September 2, 1945. These dates include both the European and Pacific front of the war. The horrible tragic results of this second global conflagration were more deaths and more destruction than in any other armed conflict. It completely uprooted and displaced millions of people. The end of the war brought renewed power struggles, especially in Europe and China, with many Eastern European nations as well as China coming under complete control and domination of the Communists, supported and backed by the Soviet Union. With the development of and two-time deployment of an atomic bomb against two Japanese cities, the world found itself in the nuclear age. The peace settlement established the United Nations Organization, still existing and operating today.

The post WWII years have seen many changes in society. Nations have been involved in a global community since then, partly due to the existence of the United Nations. Since then, governments have been more concerned with the rights of various groups, such as women and minorities. The role of women has changed throughout the world, taking on a more important role in economies. For the most part, they no longer leave the workforce when they have children so they now have a more important role as leaders, consumers and workers. They are also better educated than in the past and have assumed their roles in industry and commerce, as well as politics and government.

Gains have been made in the treatment of minorities and human rights. Much of this is due to the United Nations, which provides a forum for discussion and enforcement by its member nations. International treaties have also come into being to protect the rights of people. The Cold War, came out of tensions between the United States and the Soviet Union after WWII.

The Cold War was, more than anything else, an ideological struggle between proponents of democracy and those of communism. The two major players were the United States and the Soviet Union, but other countries were involved as well. It was a "cold" war because no direct large-scale fighting took place between the US and USSR.

It was not just forms of government that was driving this war, either. Economics were a main concern as well. Both countries had access to precious resources (such as oil and food) from other like-minded countries. They would not allow the resources to flow to "the other side."

The Soviet Union kept much more of a tight leash on its supporting countries, including all of Eastern Europe, which made up a military organization called the Warsaw Pact. The Western nations responded with a military organization of their own, the North Atlantic Treaty Organization (NATO). The prime battleground was Asia, where the Soviet Union had allies in China, North Korea, and North Vietnam. The United States had allies in Japan, South Korea, Taiwan, and South Vietnam. The Korean War and Vietnam War were major conflicts in which both big protagonists played big roles but didn't directly fight each other. The main symbol of the Cold War was the arms race, a continual buildup of missiles, tanks, and other weapons that became ever more technologically advanced and increasingly more deadly. The ultimate weapon, which both sides had in abundance, was the nuclear bomb. Spending on weapons and defensive systems eventually occupied great percentages of the budgets of the U.S. and the U.S.S.R., and some historians argue that this high level of spending played a large part in the end of the latter.

The war was a cultural struggle as well. Adults brought up their children to hate "the Americans" or "the Communists." Cold War tensions spilled over into many parts of life in countries around the world. The ways of life in countries on either side of the divide were so different that they seemed entirely foreign to outside observers.

The Cold War continued in varying degrees from 1947 to 1991, when the Soviet Union collapsed. Other Eastern European countries had seen their communist governments overthrown by this time as well, marking the shredding of the "Iron Curtain" (a term coined by Winston Churchill).

The major thrust of U.S. foreign policy from the end of World War II to 1991 was the post-war struggle between non-Communist nations, led by the United States, and the Soviet Union and the Communist nations who were its allies. It was referred to as a "Cold War" because its conflicts did not lead to a major war of fighting, or a "hot war." Both the Soviet Union and the United States embarked on an arsenal buildup of atomic and hydrogen bombs as well as other nuclear weapons. Both nations had the capability of destroying each other but because of the continuous threat of nuclear war and accidents, extreme caution was practiced on both sides. The efforts of both sides to serve and protect their political philosophies and to support and assist their allies resulted in a number of events during this 46-year period.

The problem the world has been dealing with since WWII is population growth, especially in the less developed countries. Economies and the food supply have to expand to accommodate a growing population. This has not been the case in many of the less developed countries and as a result they suffer extreme poverty and have a poor quality of life.

Skill 2.3b   Understand contemporary trends—1991 to the present

The struggle between the communist world under Soviet Union leadership and the non-communist world under Anglo-American leadership resulted in what became known as the Cold War. Communism crept into the Western Hemisphere with Cuban leader Fidel Castro and his regime. Most colonies in Africa, Asia, and the Middle East gained independence from European and Western influence and control. In South Africa in the early 1990s, the system of racial segregation, called "apartheid," was abolished.

The Soviet Union was the first industrialized nation to successfully begin a program of space flight and exploration, launching Sputnik and putting the first man in space. The United States also experienced success in its space program successfully landing space crews on the moon. In 1989, the Berlin Wall was torn down. From 1989 until 1991, communism dissolved in the Soviet Union and Eastern Europe. The 15 republics of the former U.S.S.R. became independent nations with varying degrees of freedom and democracy in government and together formed the Commonwealth of Independent States (CIS). The former communist nations of Eastern Europe also emphasized their independence with democratic forms of government.

Tremendous progress in communication and transportation has tied all parts of the earth and drawn them closer. There are still vast areas of the former Soviet Union that have unproductive land, extreme poverty, food shortages, rampant diseases, violent friction between cultures, the ever-present nuclear threat, environmental pollution, rapid reduction of natural resources, urban over-crowding, acceleration in global terrorism and violent crimes, and a diminishing middle class.

New technologies have changed the way of life for many. This is the computer age and in many places, computers are even in the grade schools. Technology makes the world seem a much smaller place. Even children have cell phones today. The existence of television and modern technology has us watching a war while it is in progress. Outsourcing is now popular because of technological advances. Call centers for European, American and other large countries are now located in India, Pakistan, etc. Multinational corporations located plants in foreign countries to lower costs.

In many places technology has resulted in a mobile population. Popular culture has been shaped by mass production and the mass media. Mass production and technology has made electronic goods affordable to most. This is the day of the cell phone and the Personal Digital Assistant, or PDA. The **Internet** and email allow people anywhere in the world to be in touch and allows people to learn about world events. In the industrial countries and in many others, the popular culture is oriented towards the electronic era.

COMPETENCY 3.0   BASIC POLITICAL CONCEPTS

Skill 3.0a   Demonstrate understanding of why government is needed

Historically the functions of government, or people's concepts of government and its purpose and function, have varied considerably. In the theory of political science, the function of government is to secure the common welfare of the members of the given society over which it exercises control. In different historical eras, governments have attempted to achieve the common welfare by various means in accordance with the traditions and ideology of the given society. Among *primitive peoples*, systems of control were rudimentary at best. They arose directly from the ideas of right and wrong that was established in the group and was common in that particular society. Control was exercised most often by means of group pressure, most often in the forms of taboos and superstitions and in many cases by ostracism or banishment from the group. Thus, because of the extreme tribal nature of society in those early times, this led to very unpleasant circumstances for the individual so treated. Without the protection of the group, a lone individual was most often in for a sad and very short fate. (No other group would accept such an individual into their midst, and survival alone was extremely difficult if not impossible).

Among more *civilized peoples*, governments began to assume more institutional forms. They rested on a well-defined legal basis. They imposed penalties on violators of the social order. They used force, which was supported and sanctioned by their people. The government was charged to establish the social order and was supposed to do so in order to be able to discharge its functions.

Eventually the ideas of government, who should govern and how, came to be considered by various thinkers and philosophers. The most influential of these and those who had the most influence on our present society were the ancient Greek philosophers such as Aristotle and Plato.

Aristotle's conception of government was based on a simple idea. The function of government was to provide for the general welfare of its people. A good government, and one that should be supported, was one that did so in the best way possible, with the least pressure on the people.   Bad governments were those that subordinated the general welfare to that of the individuals who ruled. At no time should any function of any government be that of personal interest of any one individual, no matter who that individual was. This does not mean that Aristotle had no sympathy for the individual or individual happiness (as at times Plato has been accused by those who read his **Republic,** which was the first important philosophical text to explore these issues). Rather, Aristotle believed that a society is greater than the sum of its parts, or that "the good of the many outweighs the good of the few and also of the one."

Yet, a good government and one that functions well will always weigh the relative merits of what is good for a given individual in society and what is good for the society as a whole.

This basic concept has continued to our own time and has found its fullest expression in the idea of representative democracy and political and personal freedom. In addition, it is a government that maintains good social order, while allowing the greatest possible exercise of autonomy for individuals to achieve.

Skill 3.0b   Demonstrate knowledge of political theory

POLITICAL SCIENCE is the study of political life, different forms of government including elections, political parties, and public administration. In addition, political science studies the values of justice, freedom, power, and equality. There are six main fields of political-study in the United States:

1. Political theory and philosophy,
2. Comparative governments,
3. International relations,
4. Political behavior,
5. Public administration, and
6. American government and politics.

Some contributors to political theory include:

Aristotle and Plato were Greek philosophers who believed that political order was to be the result of political science and that this political order would ensure maximum justice while at the same time remaining totally stable.

Saint Thomas Aquinas elaborated further on Aristotle's theories and adapted them to Christianity, emphasizing certain duties and rights of individuals in the governmental processes. He also laid emphasis on government rule according to those rights and duties. Aquinas helped lay the foundation of the idea of modern constitutionalism by stating that government was limited by law.

Niccolo Machiavelli was the famous politician from Florence who disregarded the ideals of Christianity in favor of realistic power politics, and author of *The Prince.*

Thomas Hobbes who's most famous work was *Leviathan,* believed that a person's life was a constant unceasing search for power and believed in the state's supremacy to combat this.

John Locke was one of the most influential political writers of the seventeenth century who put great emphasis on human rights and put forth the belief that when governments violate those rights, people should rebel. He wrote the *Two Treatises of Government* in 1690. This had tremendous influence on political thought in the American colonies and helped shaped the U.S. Constitution and Declaration of Independence.

Montesquieu and Rousseau were proponents of "liberalism," the willingness to change ideas, policies, and proposals to solve current problems. They also believed that individual freedom was just as important as any community's welfare. In his 1762 work, *The Social Contract,* Rousseau also described the "general will" leading to socialism.

David Hume and Jeremy Bentham believed that "the greatest happiness of the greatest number was the goal of politics."

John Stuart Mill wrote extensively of the liberal ideas of his time.

Johann Gottlieb Fichte and Friedrich Hegel were well-known German philosophers who contributed significantly in the eighteenth century. Johann Gottlieb Fichte and Friedrich Hegel supported a liberalism, which included ideas about nationalism and socialism. Immanuel Kant's liberalism included the idea of universal peace through world organization.

Law is the set of established rules or accepted norms of human conduct in their relationship with other individuals, organizations and institutions. The rule of law recognizes that the authority of the government is to be exercised only within the context and boundaries established by laws that are enacted according to established procedure and publicly disclosed. As a Constitutional government and political system, the basis of all laws and all decisions and enforcement of laws is the U.S. Constitution. The Constitution establishes the process by which law can be written and enacted, the basis by which their legitimacy within the context of the principles documented in the Constitution, and the means of interpretation and enforcement of those laws by the police and the courts.

All federal law begins in the Constitution, which grants the Congress of the U.S. the power to enact laws for certain purposes. These statutes are gathered and published in the United States Code. Since ratification of the Constitution, laws have been enacted that give agencies of the executive branch of government the power to create regulations that carry the force of law. The meaning of these laws and regulations when challenged or questioned is determined by the courts, those decisions then assuming the force of law.

The Constitution defines the process by which laws and regulations can be enacted within the protection of the balance of powers of the branches of government. Laws are introduced, debated, and passed by the United States Congress, with both houses of Congress passing the same version of the law.

The President of the United States then must sign the law. Once signed, the law is considered enacted and is enforced. Challenges to the constitutionality of the law and questions of interpretation of the law are handled by the federal court system. Each state has the authority to make laws covering anything not reserved to the federal government. These laws cannot negate federal laws.

In order to structure and maintain the functionality of a society and the various safeties of the people, the rule of adherence to the law is considered universal for all who live within the jurisdiction to which laws apply. Failure to adhere to the laws of the state or the nation is punishable under the legal code. Civil disobedience, however, is the refusal to obey certain laws, regulations, or requirements of a government because those laws are believed to be detrimental to the freedom or right of the people to exercise government-guaranteed personal and civil liberties. Civil disobedience, in principle, can be nonviolent in the steps taken to resist or refuse to obey these laws. Notable examples of the exercise of civil disobedience have included Henry David Thoreau's refusal to pay taxes in protest against slavery and against the Mexican-American War. Dr Martin Luther King, Jr. led the Civil Rights Movement of the 1960s on the principle and within the established techniques of non-violent civil disobedience.

Skill 3.0c Demonstrate understanding of political concepts such as legitimacy, power, authority, and responsibility

The American nation was founded with the idea that the people would have a large degree of autonomy and liberty. The famous maxim "no taxation without representation" was a rallying cry for the Revolution, not only because the people did not want to suffer the increasingly oppressive series of taxes imposed on them by the British Parliament, but also because the people could not in any way influence the lawmakers in Parliament in regard to those taxes. No American colonist had a seat in Parliament, and no American colonist could vote for members of Parliament.

One of the most famous words in the Declaration of Independence is **liberty**, the pursuit of which all people should be free to attempt. That idea, that a people should be free to pursue their own course, even to the extent of making their own mistakes, has dominated political thought in the 200-plus years of the American republic.

Another key concept in the American ideal is **equality**, the idea that every person has the same rights and responsibilities under the law. The Great Britain that the American colonists knew was one of a stratified society, with social classes firmly in place. Not everyone was equal under the law or in the coffers. It was clear for all to see that the more money and power a person had, the easier it was for that person to avoid such things as serving in the army and being charged with a crime. The goal of the Declaration of Independence and the Constitution was to provide equality for all who read those documents. The reality, though, was vastly different for large sectors of society, including women and non-white Americans.

This feeds into the idea of basic opportunity. The so-called "American Dream" is that every individual has an equal chance to make his or her fortune in a new land and that the country that is the United States will welcome and even encourage that opportunity. The history of the U.S. is filled with stories of people who ventured to America and made their fortunes in the Land of Opportunity. Unfortunately for anyone who was not a white male, that basic opportunity was sometimes a difficult thing to achieve.

The political concepts of legitimacy, **power, authority and responsibility** are all inter-related. Legitimacy refers to the moral correctness of political system. If the political system is deemed to be morally correct then it will be accepted by its' citizens. The citizen will agree to obey the laws and rules of that system because he/she accepts its legitimacy. When the citizens no longer accept the legitimacy of a regime, then the political system is overthrown—which is different than an election. An election is a part of the political system. A political system's legitimacy is enhanced when it is recognized or acknowledged by another government. Capitalism is a political system with legitimacy. Democracy is a political system with legitimacy.

Political authority refers to the people in the various offices within the political system. Their political authority lies in their ability to coerce people to comply with the wishes of the political system. Their political authority stems from the acceptance of the legitimacy of the political system or the citizens would not accept their ability to coerce.

Political power refers to the ability of those with political authority to do or to influence. If a legitimate representative of the political system doesn't have his orders obeyed, there is always the military to enforce those orders.

Political responsibility is the moral obligation of citizens and government to do the morally correct thing. For example in the case of genocide and other atrocities, the political responsibility is to speak out and fight the atrocities.

There is no such thing as political authority and political power with legitimacy.

Skill 3.0d   Demonstrate understanding of various political orientations

In regards to the American political system, it is important to realize that political parties are never mentioned in the United States Constitution. In fact, George Washington himself warned against the creation of "factions" in American politics that cause "jealousies and false alarms" and the damage they could cause to the body politic. Thomas Jefferson echoed this warning, yet he would come to lead a party himself.

Americans had good reason to fear the emergence of political parties. They had witnessed how parties worked in Great Britain. Parties are called "factions" in Britain, thus Washington's warning, were made up of a few people who schemed to win favors from the government. They were more interested in their own personal profit and advantage than in the public good. Thus, the new American leaders were very interested in keeping factions from forming. Ironically, it was disagreements between two of Washington's chief advisors, Thomas Jefferson and Alexander Hamilton that spurred the formation of the first political parties in the newly formed United States of America.

The two parties that developed through the early 1790s were led by Jefferson as the Secretary of State and Alexander Hamilton as the Secretary of the Treasury. Jefferson and Hamilton were different in many ways. Not the least was their views on what should be the proper form of government of the United States. This difference helped to shape the parties that formed around them.

Hamilton wanted the federal government to be stronger than the state governments. Jefferson believed that the state governments should be stronger. Hamilton supported the creation of the first Bank of the United States, while Jefferson opposed it because he felt that it gave too much power to wealthy investors who would help run it. Jefferson interpreted the Constitution strictly and argued that the Constitution does not grant the federal government the power to create a national bank. Hamilton interpreted the Constitution much more loosely. He pointed out that the Constitution gave Congress the power to make all laws "necessary and proper" to carry out its duties. He reasoned that since Congress had the right to collect taxes, then Congress had the right to create the bank. Hamilton wanted the government to encourage economic growth. He favored the growth of trade, manufacturing, and the rise of cities as the necessary parts of economic growth. He favored the business leaders and mistrusted the common people.

Jefferson believed that the common people, especially the farmers, were the backbone of the nation. He thought that the rise of big cities and manufacturing would corrupt American life.

Finally, Hamilton and Jefferson had their disagreements only in private. But when Congress began to pass many of Hamilton's ideas and programs, Jefferson and his friend James Madison decided to organize support for their own views. They moved quietly and very cautiously in the beginning. In 1791, they went to New York telling people that they were going to just study its wildlife. Actually, Jefferson was more interested in meeting with several important New York politicians such as its governor, George Clinton, and Aaron Burr, a strong critic of Hamilton. Jefferson asked Clinton and Burr to help defeat Hamilton's program by getting New Yorkers to vote for Jefferson's supporters in the next election. Before long, leaders in other states began to organize support for either Jefferson or Hamilton. Jefferson's supporters called themselves Democratic-Republicans (often this was shortened just to Republicans, though in actuality it was the forerunner of today's Democratic Party). Meanwhile, Hamilton and his supporters were known as Federalists, because they favored a strong federal government. The Federalists had the support of the merchants and ship owners in the Northeast and some planters in the South. Small farmers, craft workers, and some of the wealthier landowners supported Jefferson and the Democratic-Republicans.

By the time Washington retired from office in 1796, the new political parties would come to play an important role in choosing his successor. Each party would put up its own candidates for office. The election of 1796 was the first one in which political parties played a role. This role would continue to be played in various forms for all of American history. By the beginning of the 1800s, the Federalist Party, torn by internal divisions, began suffering a decline. The election in 1800 saw Thomas Jefferson as President, Hamilton's bitter rival, and after its leader Alexander Hamilton was killed in 1804 in a duel with Aaron Burr, the Federalist Party began to collapse. By 1816, after losing a string of important elections, (Jefferson was reelected in 1804, and James Madison, a Democratic-Republican was elected in 1808), the Federalist Party ceased to be an effective political force and soon passed off the national stage.

By the late 1820s, new political parties had grown up. The **Democratic-Republican** Party, or simply the **Republican Party**, had been the major party for many years, but differences within it about the direction the country was headed in caused a split after 1824. Those who favored strong national growth took the name **Whigs** after a similar party in Great Britain and united around then President John Quincy Adams. Many business people in the Northeast as well as some wealthy planters in the South supported it.

Those who favored slower growth and were more worker and small farmer oriented went on to form the new Democratic Party, with Andrew Jackson being its first leader as well as becoming the first President from it. It is the forerunner of today's present party of the same name.

In the mid-1850s, slavery was beginning to heat up as a political issue. In 1854, the Whigs, and some Northern Democrats opposed to slavery, united to form the Republican Party. Before the Civil War, the Democratic Party was more heavily represented in the South and was thus pro-slavery for the most part.

By the time of the Civil War, the present form of the major political parties had been formed. Though there would sometimes be drastic changes in ideology and platforms over the years, no other political parties would manage to gain enough strength to seriously challenge the "Big Two" parties.

In fact, they have shown themselves adaptable to changing times. In many instances, they have managed to shut out other parties by simply adapting their platforms. For example, in 1930s during the Great Depression, the Democratic Party adapted much of the Socialist Party platform and, under Franklin Roosevelt, put much of it into effect, thus managing to eliminate it as any serious threat. Since the Civil War, no other political party has managed to gain enough support to either elect substantial members to Congress or elect a President. Some have come closer than others, but barring any unforeseen circumstances, the absolute monopoly on national political debate seems very secure in the hands of the Republican and Democratic parties.

Other political parties existed during this period. The Anti-Masonic Party came into being to oppose the Freemasons who they accused of being a secret society trying to take over the country. The Free Soil Party existed for the 1848 and 1852 elections only. They opposed slavery in the lands acquired from Mexico. The Liberty Party of this period was also abolitionist.

In the mid-1850s, the slavery issue was beginning to heat up and in 1854, those opposed to slavery, the Whigs, and some Northern Democrats opposed to slavery, united to form the Republican Party. Before the Civil War, the Democratic Party was more heavily represented in the South and was thus pro-slavery for the most part. The American Party was called the Know Nothings, and they lasted from 1854 to 1858 and were opposed to Irish-Catholic immigration. The Constitution Union Party was formed in 1860, and was made up of entities from other extinguished political powers. They claim to support the Constitution above all and thought this would do away with the slavery issue. The National Union Party of 1864 was formed only for the purpose of the Lincoln election. That was the only reason for its existence.

Other political parties came and went in the post-Civil War era. The Liberal Republican Party formed in 1872 to oppose Ulysses S. Grant. They thought that Grant and his administration were corrupt and sought to displace them. The Anti-Monopoly Party of 1789 was more short-lived than the previous one. It billed itself as progressive and supported such ideas as a graduated income tax system and the direct election of senators. The Greenback Party was formed in 1878 and advocated the use of paper money. The Populist Party was a party consisting mostly of farmers who opposed the gold-standard.

The process of political parties with short life spans continued in the twentieth century. Most of this is due to the fact that these parties come into existence in opposition to some policy or politician. Once the "problem" is gone, so is the party that opposed it. For example, the **Farmer-Labor Party** was a Minnesota based political party. It supported farmers and labor and social security. It had moderate success in electing officials in Minnesota and merged with the Democratic Party in 1944. The **Progressive Party** was formed under the name the Bull-Moose Party, in 1912 due to a rift in the Republican Party that occurred when Theodore Roosevelt lost the nomination. This is not the same as the Progressive Party formed in 1924 to back LaFollette of Wisconsin. The **Social Democratic Party** was an outgrowth of a social movement and didn't have much political success.

There have also been other parties that have had a short life in the years following the Great Depression. The **American Labor Party** was a socialist party that existed in New York for a while. The **American Workers Party** was another socialist party based on Marxism. They also were short-lived. A third **Progressive Party** came into being in 1948 to run candidates for President and Vice-President. The **Dixiecrats** or States Rights Democratic Party also formed in 1948. They were a splinter group from the Democrats who supported Strom Thurmond. They also supported George Wallace in 1968. There have been various Workers' Parties that have come and gone. Most of these have had left-wing tendencies.

There are other political parties but they are not as strong as the Republicans and the Democrats. The **Libertarian Party** represents belief in the free rights of individuals to do as they wish without the interference of government. They favor a small government and propose a much lower level of government spending and services. The Libertarians are the third largest political party in America. The **Socialist Party** is also a political party. They run candidates in the elections. They favor the establishment of a radical democracy in which people control production and communities for all, not for the benefit of a few. The **Communist Party** is also a political party advocating very radical changes in American society. They are concerned with the revolutionary struggle and moving through Marx's stages of history. The American First Party is conservative as is the American Party. The American Nazi Party is also active in politics. Preaching fascism, they run candidates for elections and occasionally win. The Constitution Party is also representative of conservative views. The **Reform Party** was founded by Ross Perot, after his bid for President as an Independent. The list goes on and on. Many of these parties are regional and small and not on the national scene. Many of them form for a purpose, such as an election, and then dwindle.

Time will tell if the Republicans and Democrats remain the "Big Two" parties. History and political science both teach us that the American people are quite willing to change their support from one area or group to another, especially if it means a better way of doing things or will give them more opportunity and freedoms. As conservative as some might think Americans have become, there has always been and always will be, something of the revolutionary spirit about them.

COMPETENCY 3.1   UNITED STATES POLITICAL SYSTEM

Skill 3.1a   Demonstrate understanding of the constitutional foundation of the United States government, including knowledge of the basic content and structure of the United States Constitution, and of the processes of constitutional interpretation and amendment

The Magna Carta—This charter has been considered the basis of English constitutional liberties. It was granted to a representative group of English barons and nobles on **June 15, 1215** by the British King John, after they had forced it on him. The English barons and nobles sought to limit what they had come to perceive as the overwhelming power of the Monarchy in public affairs. The Magna Carta is considered to be the first modern document that sought to try to limit the powers of the given state authority. It guaranteed feudal rights, regulated the justice system, and abolished many abuses of the King's power to tax and regulate trade. It said that the king could not raise new taxes without first consulting a Great Council, made up of nobles, barons, and Church people. Significantly, the Magna Carta dealt only with the rights of the upper classes of the nobility, and all of its provisions excluded the rights of the common people. However, gradually the rights won by the nobles were given to other English people.

The Great Council grew into a representative assembly called the Parliament. By the 1600s, Parliament was divided into the House of Lords, made up of nobles and the House of Commons. Members of the House of Commons were elected to office. In the beginning, only a few wealthy men could vote. Still English people firmly believed that the ruler must consult Parliament on money matters and obey the law. Thus, it did set a precedent that there was a limit to the allowed power of the state. A precedent, which would have no small effect on the history of political revolution, is notably the American Revolution.

The Petition of Right—In English history, it was the title of a petition that was addressed to the King of England **Charles I,** by the British parliament in **1628.** The Parliament demanded that the king stop proclaiming new taxes without its consent. Parliament demanded that he cease housing soldiers and sailors in the homes of private citizens, proclaiming martial law in times of peace, and that no subject should be imprisoned without a good cause being shown. After some attempts to circumvent these demands, Charles finally agreed to them. They later had an important effect on the demands of the revolutionary colonists, as these were some of the rights that as Englishmen, were being denied to them. The Petition of Right was also the basis of specific protections that the designers of the Constitution made a point of inserting in the document.

British Bill of Rights—Also known as the **Declaration of Rights**, it spelled out the rights that were considered to belong to Englishmen. It was granted by **King William III** in 1869. It had previously been passed by a convention of the Parliament and it came out of the struggle for power that took place in Great Britain and at that time was known as **The Glorious Revolution**. It was known as a revolution that was accomplished with virtually no bloodshed and led to King William III and Queen Mary II becoming joint sovereigns.

The Declaration itself was very similar in style to the later American Bill of Rights. It protected the rights of individuals and gave anyone accused of a crime the right to trial by jury. It outlawed cruel punishments and stated that a ruler could not raise taxes or an army without the consent of Parliament. The colonists as Englishmen were protected by these provisions. The colonists considered abridgments of these rights that helped to contribute to the revolutionary spirit of the times.

All of these events and the principles that arose from them are of the utmost importance in understanding the process that eventually led to the ideals that are inherent in the Constitution of the United States. In addition, the fact is that all of these ideals are universal in nature and have become the basis for the idea of human freedoms throughout the world.

Eleven states finally ratified the U.S. Consitution. The new national government went into effect. It was no small feat that the delegates were able to produce a workable document that satisfied all opinions, feelings, and viewpoints. The separation of powers of the three branches of government and the built-in system of checks and balances to keep power balanced were a stroke of genius.

In the United States, checks and balances refers to the ability of each branch of government (Executive, Legislative, and Judicial) to "check" or limit the actions of the others. Examples of checks and balances would be the Executive branch limiting the Legislature by power of veto over bills and appointments in the court system. The Judicial branch limits the power of the Legislature by judicial review and the ability to rule laws unconstitutional and may also determine executive orders unconstitutional. The Legislature checks the Executive by power of impeachment.

It provided for the individuals and the states as well as an organized central authority to keep a new inexperienced young nation on track. They created a system of government so flexible that it has continued in its basic form to this day. In 1789, the Electoral College unanimously elected George Washington as the first President, and the new nation was on its way.

The Declaration of Independence is an outgrowth of both ancient Greek ideas of democracy and individual rights and the ideas of the European Enlightenment and the Renaissance, especially the ideology of the political thinker **John Locke**.

Thomas Jefferson (1743-1826), the principal author of the Declaration, borrowed much from Locke's theories and writings.

Essentially, Jefferson applied Locke's principles to the contemporary American situation. Jefferson argued that the currently reigning King George III had repeatedly violated the rights of the colonists as subjects of the British Crown. Disdaining the colonial petition for redress of grievances (a right guaranteed by the Declaration of Rights of 1689), the King seemed bent on establishing an "absolute tyranny" over the colonies. Such disgraceful behavior itself violated the reasons for which government had been instituted. The American colonists were left with no choice. As Thomas Jefferson wrote, *"it is their right, it is their duty, to throw off such a government, and to provide new guards for their future security."*

Yet, though his fundamental principles were derived from Locke's, Jefferson was bolder than his intellectual mentor was. Jefferson's view of natural rights was much broader than Locke's and less tied to the idea of property rights and more on personal rights.

For instance, though both Jefferson and Locke believed very strongly in property rights, especially as a guard for individual liberty, the famous line in the Declaration about people being endowed with the inalienable right to "life, liberty and the pursuit of happiness", was originally Locke's idea. It was "life, liberty, and *private property"*. Jefferson did not want to tie the idea of rights to any one particular circumstance however. Thus, he changed Locke's original specific reliance on property and substituted the more general idea of human happiness as being a fundamental right that is the duty of a government to protect.

Locke and Jefferson both stressed that the individual citizen's rights are prior to and more important than any obligation to the state. Government is the servant of the people. The officials of government hold their positions at the sufferance of the people. Their job is to ensure that the rights of the people are preserved and protected by that government. The citizens come first, the government comes second. The Declaration thus produced turned out to be one of the most important and historic documents that expounded the inherent rights of all peoples; it is a document still looked up to as an ideal and an example.

An amendment is a change or addition to the United States Constitution. Two-thirds of both houses of Congress must propose and then pass one. Or two-thirds of the state legislatures must call a convention to propose one and then it must be ratified by three-fourths of the state legislatures.

To date there are only 27 amendments to the Constitution that have passed. An amendment may be used to cancel out a previous one, such as the 18th Amendment (1919) known as Prohibition, nullified by the 21st Amendment (1933). Amending the United States Constitution is an extremely difficult thing to do.

An **amendment** must start in Congress. One or more lawmakers propose it, and then each house votes on it in turn. The Amendment must have the support of two-thirds of each house separately in order to progress on its path into law. (It should be noted here that this two-thirds need be only two-thirds of a quorum, which is just a simple majority.

Thus, it is theoretically possible for an Amendment to be passed and be legal even though it has been approved by less than half of one or both houses.)

The final and most difficult step for an Amendment is the ratification of state legislatures. A total of three-fourths of those must approve the Amendment. Approvals there need be only a simple majority, but the number of states that must approve the Amendment is 38. Hundreds of Amendments have been proposed through the years, but only 27 have become part of the Constitution.

A key element in some of those failures has been the time limit that Congress has the option to put on Amendment proposals. A famous example of an Amendment that got close but did not reach the threshold before the deadline expired was the Equal Rights Amendment. This Amendment was proposed in 1972 but could not muster enough support for passage, even though its deadline was extended from seven to ten years.

The first ten Amendments are called the Bill of Rights and were approved at the same time, shortly after the Constitution was ratified. The 11th and 12th Amendments were ratified around the turn of the nineteenth century and, respectively, voided foreign suits against states and revised the method of presidential election. The 13th, 14th, and 15th Amendments were passed in succession after the end of the Civil War. Slavery was outlawed by the 13th Amendment, and the 14th and 15th Amendments provided for equal protection and for voting rights, respectively, without consideration of skin color.

The first twentieth century Amendment was the 16th. This provided for a federal income tax. Direct election to the Senate was the 17th Amendment. (Before this, Senators were appointed by state leaders, not elected by the public at large.)

The 18th Amendment prohibited the use or sale of alcohol across the country. The long battle for voting rights for women ended in success with the passage of the 19th Amendment. The date for the beginning of terms for the President and the Congress was changed from March to January by the 20th Amendment.

With the 21st Amendment came the only instance in which an Amendment was repealed. In this case, it was the 18th Amendment and its prohibition of alcohol consumption or sale.

The 22nd Amendment limited the number of terms that a President could serve to two. Presidents since George Washington had followed the practice of not running for a third term; this changed when Franklin D. Roosevelt ran for a third term, in 1940. He was re-elected that time, and again for a fourth term. He did not live out his fourth term, but he did convince Congress and most of the state legislature that some sort of term limit should be in place.

The 23rd Amendment provided for representation of Washington, D.C., in the Electoral College. The 24th Amendment prohibited poll taxes, which people had had to pay in order to vote.

Presidential succession is the focus of the 25th Amendment, which provides a blueprint of what to do if the president is incapacitated or killed. The 26th Amendment lowered the legal voting age for Americans from 21 to 18. The final Amendment, the 27th, prohibits members of Congress from substantially raising their own salaries. This Amendment was one of 12 originally proposed in the late 18th Century. Ten of those 12 became the Bill of Rights, and one has yet to become law.

A host of potential Amendments have made news headlines in recent years. A total of six Amendments have been proposed by Congress and passed muster in both houses but have not been ratified by enough state legislatures. The aforementioned Equal Rights Amendment is one. Another one, which would grant the District of Columbia full voting rights equivalent to states, has not passed; like the Equal Rights Amendment, its deadline has expired. A handful of others remain on the books without expiration dates, including an amendment to regulate child labor.

The Bill of Rights consists of the first ten Amendments to the U.S. Constitution. These amendments were passed almost immediately upon ratification of the Constitution by the states. They reflect the concerns that were raised throughout the country and by the Founding Fathers during the ratification process. These Amendments reflect the fears and concerns of the people that the power and authority of the government be restricted from denying or limiting the rights of the people of the nation. The experiences of the founders of the nation as colonists formed the foundation of the concern to limit the power of government.

The Bill of Rights has been interpreted in different ways at different times by different interpreters. These, and other Constitutional Amendments may be interpreted very strictly or very loosely. The terms of the amendments may be defined in different ways to enfranchise or to disenfranchise individuals or groups of persons.

The Bill of Rights are:

1. Freedom of Speech, Religion, Press, and Assembly.
2. Right To Bear Arms.
3. Security from the quartering of troops in homes.
4. Right against unreasonable search and seizures.
5. Right against self-incrimination.
6. Right to trial by jury and the right to legal council.
7. Right to jury trial for civil actions.
8. No cruel or unusual punishment allowed.
9. These rights shall not deny other rights the people enjoy.
10. Powers not mentioned in the Constitution shall be retained by the states or the people.

Skill 3.1b   Demonstrate knowledge of the functions and powers of the legislative, executive, and judicial branches of government, and of the relationships among them

In the United States, the three branches of the federal government mentioned earlier, the **Executive**, the **Legislative**, and the **Judicial**, divide up their powers thus:

Legislative – Article I of the Constitution established the legislative or law-making branch of the government called the Congress. It is made up of two houses, the House of Representatives and the Senate. Voters in all states elect the members who serve in each respective House of Congress. The legislative branch is responsible for making laws, raising and printing money, regulating trade, establishing the postal service and federal courts, approving the President's appointments, declaring war and supporting the armed forces. The Congress also has the power to change the Constitution itself, and to *impeach* (bring charges against) the President. Charges for impeachment are brought by the House of Representatives and are then tried in the Senate.

Executive – Article II of the Constitution created the Executive branch of the government, headed by the President, who leads the country, recommends new laws, and can veto bills passed by the legislative branch. As the chief of state, the President is responsible for carrying out the laws of the country and the treaties and declarations of war passed by the legislative branch. The President also appoints federal judges and is commander-in-chief of the military when it is called into service. Other members of the Executive branch include the Vice-President (also elected) and various appointed cabinet members (such as ambassadors, presidential advisors, members of the armed forces, and other appointed and civil servants of government agencies, departments and bureaus). Though the President appoints them, they must be approved by the legislative branch.

Judicial – Article III of the Constitution established the judicial branch of government headed by the Supreme Court. The Supreme Court has the power to rule that a law passed by the legislature or an act of the Executive branch is illegal and unconstitutional. Citizens, businesses, and government officials can, in an appeal capacity, ask the Supreme Court to review a decision made in a lower court if someone believes that the ruling by a judge is unconstitutional. The Judicial branch also includes lower federal courts known as federal district courts that have been established by the Congress. These courts try lawbreakers and review cases referred from other courts. Supreme Court justices must also be approved by the Senate.

Skill 3.1c   Demonstrate knowledge of the formation and operation of political institutions not established by the Constitution, such as political parties and interest groups, and of the role of the media and public opinion in American political life

From the earliest days of political expression in America, efforts were a collaborative affair. One of the first of the democratic movements was the **Sons of Liberty**, an organization that made its actions known but kept the identity of its members a secret. Famous members of this group included John and Samuel Adams. Other patriotic movements sprang up after the success of the Sons of Liberty was assured, and the overall struggle against British oppression was a collaborative effort involving thousands of people throughout the American colonies.

American political discussion built on the example of the British Parliament, which had two houses of its legislative branch of government containing representatives who had great debates on public policy before making laws. Although this process isn't anywhere near as wide open and public and spirited as it is today, the lawmakers nonetheless had their chance to make their views known on the issues of the day. Some laws, such as those implementing the infamous taxes following the British and American victory in the French and Indian War, required relatively little debate, since they were so popular and were obviously wanted by the Prime Minister and other heads of the government. Other laws enjoyed spirited debate and took months to pass.

The Assemblies of the American colonies inherited this tradition and enjoyed spirited debate as well, even though they met just one or a few times a year. One of the most famous examples of both collaboration and deliberation was the Stamp Act Congress, a gathering of fed-up Americans who drafted resolutions demanding that Great Britain repeal the unpopular tax on paper and documents. The Americans who met at both of the Continental Congresses and the Constitutional Convention built on this tradition as well.

Thanks to the voluminous notes taken diligently by James Madison, we have a clear record of just how contentious at times the debate over the shape and scope of the American federal government was. Still, every interest was advanced, every argument put forward, and every chance given to repeal the main points of the government document. The result was a blueprint for government approved by the vast majority of the delegates and eventually approved by people in all of the American colonies.

This ratification process has continued throughout the history of the country, through passage by both houses of Congress to ratification by state legislatures and finally to approval by a majority of the people of a majority of states.

With this sometimes spirited and sometimes virulent debate have come countless opportunities to influence that debate. Even in the earliest times, people having special interests were trying to influence political debates in their favor. Plenty of people who were not delegates to the Constitutional Convention favored a strong central government or its opposite, a weak central government. No doubt these people were in communication with the delegates.

Also developing at this time were the nation's first political parties, the Federalists and the Democratic-Republicans. It wasn't elected officials who were members of these political parties, although those elected officials were the most famous members. The people who joined these political parties wanted to see their political interests protected and were sometimes very effective in making sure that the people that they voted for did the things that they were elected to do. As the nation grew, so did the number of political parties and so did the number of people who were pursuing the so-called "special interests." Actually, a special interest is nothing more than a subject that a person or people who pursue one issue above all others. As more and more people gained more and more money, they began to pressure their lawmakers more and more to pass laws that favored their interests. Exporters of goods from ports to destinations overseas would not want to see heavy taxes on such exports. People who owned large amounts of land wouldn't want to see a sharp increase in property taxes. The list goes on and on. These special interests can be found today. These days, it's just more money and more ways to influence lawmakers that distinguish special interest pursuits from those made in years past. So, too, can we draw a straight line from the deliberative-collaborative traditions of today to the secret meetings and political conventions of colonial days.

Americans are free and encouraged to join non-business organizations both public and private. America is a land full of groups—religious, political, social, and economic groups. All these groups meet in public and in private, and the people who belong to these groups are free to associate with any groups that they choose, again as long as the practices of those groups are not illegal or harmful to other people.

Social groups are encouraged as well. The First Amendment gives the American people the right to peaceable assemble. This certainly describes the meetings of most social organizations in America, from clubs to interest groups to veterans organizations. Groups, made up of people with similar interests or experiences, may come together on a regular basis to discuss those interests and experiences and to pursue a joint appreciation. So long as those people in those groups assemble peacefully and don't become violent or speak out in the name of fomenting rebellion, they can go on meeting as often as they like.

One very public interest that many people pursue is politics. Theoretically, anyone who is a U.S. citizen can get on a ballot *somewhere* running for *something*. Participation in politics is encouraged in America and more and more people are getting involved—at the local, state, and federal levels—all the time. The federal and state governments, in particular, will provide money and opportunities for candidates who reach certain thresholds of monetary support of their own

If there's one thing that drives American politics more than any other, it's money. More often than not, the candidate who has the most money at his or her disposal has the best chance of getting or keeping political office. Money can buy so many things that are necessary to a successful campaign that is entirely indispensable. Money drives the utilization of every other factor in the running of a campaign. First and foremost, money is needed to pay the people who will run a candidate's campaign. A candidate cannot expect people to give up, in some cases, years of their lives without monetary compensation. Volunteers on a political campaign are plentiful, but they are not at the top levels. The faithful lieutenants of a campaign are paid performers. Money is also needed to buy or rent all of the tangible and intangible *things* that are needed to power a political campaign: office supplies, meeting places, transportation vehicles, and many more. The inventory of these items can add up frighteningly quickly, and money can appear to disappear like water down a drain.

Of course, the expense that gets the most exposure in modern times is **media advertising**, specifically television advertising. This is the most expensive kind of advertising, but it also has the potential to reach the widest audience. TV ad prices can run into the hundreds of thousands of dollars, depending on when they run; but they have the potential to reach perhaps millions of viewers. Here, too, money can disappear quickly. A political campaign is also a fashion show and candidates cannot afford to go without showing their friendly faces to as wide an audience as possible on a regular basis. Other forms of advertising include radio and Web ads, signs and billboards, and good old-fashioned flyers.

The sources of all this money that is needed to run a successful political campaign are varied. A candidate might have a significant amount of money in his or her own personal coffers. In rare cases, the candidate finances the entire campaign. However, the most prevalent source of money is outside donations. A candidate's friends and family might donate funds to the campaign, as well as the campaign workers themselves. State and federal governments will also contribute to most regional or national campaigns, provided that the candidate can prove that he or she can raise a certain amount of money first. The largest source of campaign finance money, however, comes from "special interest." A large company such as an oil company or a manufacturer of electronic goods will want to keep prices or tariffs down and so will want to make sure that laws lifting those prices or tariffs are not passed.

To this end, the company will contribute money to the campaigns of candidates who are likely to vote to keep those prices or tariffs down. Of course, a candidate is not obligated to accept such a donation, and further, is not obligated to vote in favor of the interests of the special interest; however, doing the former might create a shortage of money and doing the latter might ensure that no further donations come from that or any other special interest. An oil company wants to protect its interests, and its leaders don't very much care which political candidate is doing that for them as long as it is being done.

Another powerful source of support for a political campaign is **special interest groups** of a political nature. These are not necessarily economic powers but rather groups whose people want to effect political change (or make sure that such change doesn't take place, depending on the status of the laws at the time). A good example of a special interest group is an anti-abortion group or a pro-choice group. The abortion issue is still a divisive one in American politics, and many groups will want to protect or defend or ban—depending on which side they're on—certain rights and practices. An anti-abortion group, for example, might pay big money to candidates who pledge to work against laws that protect the right for women to have abortions. As long as these candidates continue to assure their supporters that they will keep on fighting the fight, the money will continue to flow. This kind of social group usually has a large number of dedicated individuals who do much more than vote: They organize themselves into political action committees, attend meetings and rallies, and work to make sure that their message gets out to a wide audience. Methods of spreading the word often include media advertising on behalf of their chosen candidates. This kind of expenditure is no doubt welcomed by the candidates, who will get the benefit of the exposure but won't have to spend that money because someone else is signing the checks.

A free press is essential to maintaining responsibility and civic-mindedness in government and in the rest of society. The broadcast, print, and electronic media in America serve as societal and governmental watchdogs, showcasing for the rest of America and for the world what kinds of brilliant and terrible things the rich, powerful, and elected are doing.

First and foremost, the media report on the actions taken and encouraged by leaders of the government. In many cases, these actions are common knowledge. Policy debates, discussions on controversial issues, struggles against foreign powers in economic and wartime endeavors—all are fodder for media reports. The First Amendment guarantees press in America the right to report on these things, and the media reporters take full advantage of that right and privilege in striving not only to inform the American public but also to keep the governmental leaders in check.

The most extreme kind of action that needs reporting on is an illegal one. Officials who perform illegal actions will, in most cases, find those actions part of the public record. These officials are expected to be models of society or, at the very least, following the very laws that they were elected to pass or erase. This is largely a trust issue as well: If you can't trust your elected leaders, who can you trust? Many people would answer that question with the skeptical, "No one can be trusted, especially those in government." Others would say, more simply, that greater scrutiny is needed for those in legislative power, since they are more easily able to hide questionable actions. No one is above the law, especially those charged with making those laws. If a lawmaker thinks that he or she is above the law, then in most cases he or she will be sadly mistaken to discover that that assumption is incorrect. In the vast majority of cases, lawmakers who break the law in a big way are caught and informed on, especially because of reporting done by newspapers, radio stations, magazines, and websites.

The flip side of this is that lawmakers often do positive, noteworthy, and newsworthy things that should be reported on as well. The official who spearheads a campaign to get a certain wide-ranging bill passed will want to take the appropriate credit for those efforts, making his actions known to the media so those actions can be reported to his or her constituents. The scandals and jail terms that get most of the screaming headlines in mass media today, but praise-worthy actions are no less important in a national understanding of who the lawmakers are and why they take the actions that they do.

Owners of large companies and charities and especially recognizable figures in popular entertainment are continually under scrutiny for signs of questionable actions or behavior. In the same way that lawmakers are responsible for public legislative policy, many company owners are responsible for public economic policy. If a corporation is stealing money from its employees or shareholders, then those employees and shareholders and the American public at large need to know about it. Such reporting is not only informative but also usually leads to indictments, prosecutions, and jail terms for the perpetrators of such economic crimes.

One time when a free press is not exactly a good idea, however, is when a country is at war. Troop movements and battle plans aren't the sort of thing that needs to be broadcast. Such broadcasts have a way of making their way into the hands of the very people that the country's armed forces are attempting to defeat on the battlefield. (An excellent example of this was seen by all in the lead up and prosecution of the Gulf War, when Iraqi leader Saddam Hussein and his allies and followers kept up with Allied actions by watching CNN.) The government, and especially its armed forces, has the right to refuse to provide information that is vital to national security. This right has been validated time and again by the U.S. Supreme Court and is the law of the land.

Of course, the key word in all of this is *free*. American media reporters are *free* to report on such things as lawmakers' actions (good or bad), company owners' practices (good or bad), and goings-on at the local country club or American Legion house because the Constitution—specifically, the First Amendment—guarantees them the right to do so. This freedom of reporting is a right that is enjoyed by reporters in other countries, to varying degrees. In other countries, most notably modern day China, reporters are *not* free to report on everything they see, especially things that the government does not want its people to know. If such reporting is banned, then the government can conceivably conduct all sorts of illegal transactions or escapades without fear of those actions being exposed by the mainstream media. If a country's citizens do not have a handle on how badly their government is behaving on the world stage, then they have no basis for demanding that things change.

It was this idea, after all, which was at the heart of the American Revolution — the idea that a people could stand up and say that they had had enough of their government and its leaders and their actions.

Public officials have an overwhelming need to communicate. They want other people to know what they're doing and why. They want to make sure that the voters who elected know what great jobs they're doing pursuing the agendas that are closest to their hearts. Ultimately, they want to do as much as they can to get themselves re-elected or, if terms limit won't allow such re-election, to leave a memorable public legacy.

This is the key thing to remember if you are reading things on Web pages: They might not have undergone the same sort of scrutiny as comparable efforts released by major media outlets to newspapers, radio, and television. Those media processes have built-in safety measures called editors who will verify information before it is released to the wide world; to be a blogger, all you need is access to a Web-enabled computer and time to write a column. Bloggers routinely do not use editors or run their copy by anyone else before publishing it; as such, they have lower standards of professionalism overall and need to be regarded as such. What they write might be totally true; the blog, however, is known as a *log*, a chronicle of thoughts and opinions about the affairs of the day, not so much a blow-by-blow of facts and figures.

Public officials will hire one or more people or perhaps a whole department or an entire business to conduct **public relations**, which are efforts intended to make the lawmakers look good in the eyes of their constituents. A public relations person or firm will have as its overreaching goal the happiness of the lawmaker who hired her or them and will gladly write press releases, arrange media events (such as tours of schools or soup kitchens), and basically do everything else to keep their employer's name in the public eye in a good way. This includes making the lawmaker's position on important issues known to the public.

Especially controversial issues will be embraced on the other side by lawmakers, and those lawmakers will want their constituents to know how they intend to vote those issues. It's also a good idea to find out what your constituents think about these issues of the day, since the fastest way to get yourself bad publicity or thrown out at re-election time is to ignore the weight of public opinion.

Another inherent part of the public official-media relationship is the need to appear to be open and above-board. Even if a politician isn't forthcoming with all the details of what he is doing, he or she needs to look like that is what is happening. A lawmaker who communicates with the public is one who appears to be on the level, since an absence of information seems to imply guilt or complicity in the minds of many people. To this end, lawmakers will go out of their way to make their actions, intentions, and political views known to the people who will vote for them and support them by sending them money.

All of these things are true as well for potential lawmakers who are running for office against those already in office. Since incumbents can often call on the "weight of the office" to give them free publicity just for participating in such activities as voting on bills or attending local ribbon-cutting or other public functions, challengers routinely face an uphill battle to get their names, views, and deeds into the public debate and will work extra hard to do so.

On the other side of the coin, members of the media will want the public to know what their lawmakers are saying and doing. Many reporters and editors consider it in the best interest of the country to report on the dealings and actions of those in government, especially if those dealings or actions are of a questionable legal or moral nature. It works both ways, and the smart politicians understand the nature of that dichotomy and use it to their advantage.

Skill 3.1d   Demonstrate understanding of the relationship among federal, state, and local governments

Powers delegated to the federal government	Powers reserved to the states:
1. To tax.	1. To regulate intrastate trade.
2. To borrow and coin money	2. To establish local governments.
3. To establish postal service.	3. To protect general welfare.
4. To grant patents and copyrights.	4. To protect life and property.
5. To regulate interstate & foreign commerce.	5. To ratify amendments.
6. To establish courts.	6. To conduct elections.
7. To declare war.	7. To make state and local laws.
8. To raise and support the armed forces.	
9. To govern territories.	
10. To define and punish felonies and piracy on the high seas.	
11. To fix standards of weights and measures.	
12. To conduct foreign affairs.	

Concurrent powers of the federal government and states.

1. Both Congress and the states may tax.
2. Both may borrow money.
3. Both may charter banks and corporations.
4. Both may establish courts.
5. Both may make and enforce laws.
6. Both may take property for public purposes.
7. Both may spend money to provide for the public welfare.

Implied powers of the federal government.

1. To establish banks or other corporations, implied from delegated powers to tax, borrow, and to regulate commerce.
2. To spend money for roads, schools, health, insurance, etc. implied from powers to establish post roads, to tax to provide for general welfare and defense, and to regulate commerce.
3. To create military academies, implied from powers to raise and support an armed force.
4. To locate and generate sources of power and sell surplus, implied from powers to dispose of government property, commerce, and war powers.
5. To assist and regulate agriculture, implied from power to tax and spend for general welfare and regulate commerce.

Skill 3.1e **Demonstrate understanding of political behavior at both the individual and group levels, including elections and other forms of political participation**

The most basic way for citizens to participate in the political process is to vote. Since the passing of the 23rd Amendment in 1965, US citizens who are at least 18 years old are eligible to vote. Elections are held at regular intervals at all levels of government, allowing citizens to weigh in on local matters as well as those of national scope.

The sad reality for most Americans is that they do not play a large role in governmental decision-making, except perhaps at the local level. Only there, in the towns and cities in which they live, can they afford the time and money to personally lobby their lawmakers in the name of passage or defeat of laws. At the state and the national level, the country is just too big for one poor person to have much of a difference individually. Where people make a difference at the higher levels is in joining political parties and, more importantly, citizen action groups or political action committees. Only in the larger numbers that make up these groups can individual people make a difference in government. In such cases, however, people tend to lose their individual voices and are more easily swayed by the will of their peers.

Citizens wishing to engage in the political process to a greater degree have several paths open, such as participating in local government. Counties, states, and sometimes neighborhoods are governed by locally elected boards or councils that meet publicly. Citizens can usually address these boards, bringing their concerns and expressing their opinions on matters being considered. Citizens may even wish to stand for local election and join a governing board or seek support for higher office.

This is not to say that the avenues of lobbying lawmakers are closed to the average American. Letters are still read, phone calls are still taken, and donations are still appreciated. More cutting-edge methods of communication include e-mail, fax, and SMS. Personal office visits are definitely appreciated as well. If enough people write or call or visit their lawmakers and say the same thing, those lawmakers will listen. That's why it's still important for people to speak out, not only to their neighbors but also their elected officials. And of course, the ultimate way of expressing one's political views is to elect or oust a lawmaker through the power of the ballot.

This kind of open access and potentially direct role in the political decision-making of the country has not always been with us, though. In the early days of the American colonies, the British settlers could disagree all they wanted with the kind of policies, laws, and taxes that were being impressed on them by the Parliament across the Atlantic. The settlers also couldn't very well decide who their colonial governors were. The British Government appointed those officials.

Supporting a political party is another means by which citizens can participate in the political process. Political parties endorse certain platforms that express general social and political goals, and support member candidates in election campaigns. Political parties make use of much volunteer labor, with supporters making telephone calls, distributing printed material and campaigning for the party's causes and candidates. Political parties solicit donations to support their efforts as well. Contributing money to a political party is another form of participation citizens can undertake.

Another form of political activity is to support an issue-related political group. Several political groups work actively to sway public opinion on various issues or on behalf of a segment of American society. These groups may have representatives who meet with state and federal legislators to "lobby" them—to provide them with information on an issue and persuade them to take favorable action.

The colonies were not totally void of representative government, though. Beginning in 1619, the Virginia colony had such an entity, the House of Burgesses. This was one of the most famous governing bodies in colonial American history. Among its members over time were some of the shining lights of the American Revolution, including George Washington, Thomas Jefferson, James Madison, and Patrick Henry. It was Henry who introduced the resolutions that ultimately resulted in the repeal of the dreaded Stamp Act, the devastating tax on paper goods.

The people of Virginia elected a total of 15 of the 22 members of the House of Burgesses. (The governor, of course, was appointed.) The Burgesses could make laws, and the governor could veto them. The Burgesses also met just once a year. But the elements of representative government were there.

Other lawmaking bodies followed. Generally, each colony had one. They had various names; most were called the Assembly. As with the Virginia House of Burgesses, these Assemblies met just once a year and dealt with financial matters, such as taxes and budgets. The governor, however, had the power to dissolve the Assembly, keeping it from meeting even once, which was done relatively frequently during the months leading up to the Revolutionary War.

Representative is a relative term, however. Although it is true that the Assembly had members who were voted in by their peers, those peers were *true* peers in the sense that they all looked exactly alike. Serving in government and voting for those who did was limited to white, property-owning males. Women could neither vote nor own property. African-American men and women certainly could not do either of those things, even if they were not enslaved. It is one thing to say that the members of the Burgesses or Assembly were elected by *the people*; it is another thing entirely to say that *the people* included *everyone in the colonies*.

Still, the cry for representation was a key rallying point of the Revolution and the War to preserve it, and eventually the Colonial Army had its day in the sun. The Constitution was a blueprint of a representative government such that the world had never seen. The reality, though, was still that white, property-owning males were the ones doing the voting and the legislating.

One holdover from the colonial appointing days was that Senators, who made up the upper house of Government, were appointed by the Legislature of each state. This practice lasted until the passage of the 12th Amendment, in the early nineteenth century. African-American men, however, had to wait to vote and run for office until the 14th Amendment, ratified in 1868, and women of any color had to wait until the twentieth century to vote for nationwide office.

A person who lives in a democratic society theoretically has an entire laundry list guaranteed to him or her by the government. In the United States, this is the Constitution and its Amendments. Among these very important rights are:

- the right to speak out in public;
- the right to pursue any religion;
- the right for a group of people to gather in public for *any* reason that doesn't fall under a national security cloud;
- the right *not* to have soldiers stationed in your home;
- the right *not* to be forced to testify against yourself in a court of law;
- the right to a speedy and public trial by a jury of your peers;
- the right *not* to the victim of cruel and unusual punishment; and
- the right to avoid unreasonable search and seizure of your person, your house, and your vehicle.

The average citizen of an authoritarian country has little if any of these rights and must watch his or her words, actions, and even magazine subscriptions and Internet visits in order to avoid *the appearance* of disobeying one of the many oppressive laws that help the government govern its people.

Both the democratic-society and the authoritarian-society citizens can serve in government. They can even run for election and can be voted in by their peers. One large difference exists, however: In an authoritarian society, the members of government will most likely be of the same political party. A country with this setup, such as China, will have a government that includes representatives elected by the Chinese people, but all of those elected representatives will belong to the Communist Party, which runs the government and the country. When the voters vote, they see only Communist Party members on the ballot. In fact, in many cases, only one candidate is on the ballot for each office. China, in fact, chooses its head of government through a meeting of the Party leaders. In effect, the Party is higher in the governmental hierarchy than the leader of the country. Efforts to change this governmental structure and practice are clamped down and discouraged.

On the other side of this spectrum is the citizen of the democratic society, who can vote for whomever he or she wants to and can run for any office he or she wants to. On those ballots will appear names and political parties that run the spectrum, including the Communist Party. Theoretically, *any* political party can get its candidates on ballots locally, statewide, or nationwide; varying degrees of effort have to be put in to do this, of course. Building on the First Amendment freedom to peacefully assembly, American citizens can have political party meetings, fund-raisers, and even conventions without fearing reprisals from the Government.

COMPETENCY 3.2   OTHER FORMS OF GOVERNMENT

Skill 3.2a   Demonstrate understanding of the structures of various forms of government

Parliamentary System is a system of government with a legislature, usually involving a multiplicity of political parties and often coalition politics. There is division between the head of state and head of government. Head of government is usually known as a Prime Minister who is also usually the head of the largest party. The head of government and cabinet usually both sit and vote in the parliament. Another head of state is most often an elected president (though in the case of a constitutional monarchy such as Great Britain, the sovereign may take the place of a president as head of state). A government may fall when a majority in parliament votes "no confidence" in the government.

Anarchism—Political movement believing in the elimination of all government and its replacement by a cooperative community of individuals. Sometimes it has involved political violence such as assassinations of important political or governmental figures. The historical banner of the movement is a black flag.

Communism—A belief as well as a political system, characterized by the ideology of class conflict and revolution, one party state and dictatorship, repressive police apparatus, and government ownership of the means of production and distribution of goods and services. Communism is a revolutionary ideology preaching the eventual overthrow of all other political orders and the establishment of one world communist government.   Marxism is very similar. The historical banner of the movement is a red flag and variation of stars, hammer and sickles, representing the various types of workers.

Dictatorship—The rule by an individual or small group of individuals (Oligarchy) that centralizes all political control in itself and enforces its will with a terrorist police force.

Fascism—A belief as well as a political system, opposed ideologically to Communism, though similar in basic structure, with a one party state, centralized political control and a repressive police system. It however tolerates private ownership of the means of production, though it maintains tight overall control. Central to its belief is the idolization of the Leader, a "Cult of the Personality," and most often an expansionist ideology. Examples have been German Nazism and Italian Fascism. (See: Fascism, Section 5.4)

Monarchy—The rule of a nation by a Monarch, (a non-elected usually hereditary leader), most often a king, or queen. It may or may not be accompanied by some measure of democracy open institutions and elections at various levels. A modern example is Great Britain, where it is called a Constitutional Monarchy.

Socialism—Political belief and system in which the state takes a guiding role in the national economy and provides extensive social services to its population. It may or may not own outright means of production, but even where it does not, it exercises tight control. It usually promotes democracy, (Democratic Socialism), though the heavy state involvement produces excessive bureaucracy and usually inefficiency. Taken to an extreme, it may lead to communism as government control increases and democratic practices decrease. Ideologically, the two movements are very similar in both belief and practice, as socialists also preach the superiority of their system to all others and that it will become the eventual natural order. It is also considered for that reason a variant of Marxism. It also has used a red flag as a symbol.

COMPETENCY 3.3   INTERNATIONAL RELATIONS

Skill 3.3a   Demonstrate knowledge of the functions and powers of international organizations, such as the United Nations

Individuals and societies have divided the earth's surface through conflict for a number of reasons:

- The domination of peoples or societies, e.g., colonialism
- The control of valuable resources, e.g., oil
- The control of strategic routes, e.g., the Panama Canal

Religion, political ideology, national origin, language, and race can spur conflicts. Conflicts can result from disagreement over how land, ocean or natural resources will be developed, shared, and used. Conflicts have resulted from trade, migration, and settlement rights. Conflicts can occur between small groups of people, between cities, between nations, between religious groups, and between multi-national alliances.

Today, the world is primarily divided by political/administrative interests into state sovereignties. A particular region is recognized to be controlled by a particular government, including its territory, population and natural resources. The only area of the earth's surface that today is not defined by state or national sovereignty is Antarctica.

Alliances are developed among nations on the basis of political philosophy, economic concerns, cultural similarities, religious interests, or for military defense. Some of the most notable alliances today are:

- The United Nations
- The North Atlantic Treaty Organization
- The Caribbean Community
- The Common Market
- The Council of Arab Economic Unity
- The European Union

Large companies and multi-national corporations also compete for control of natural resources for manufacturing, development, and distribution.

Throughout human history there have been conflicts on virtually every scale over the right to divide the Earth according to differing perceptions, needs and values. These conflicts have ranged from tribal conflicts to urban riots, to civil wars, to regional wars, to world wars. While these conflicts have traditionally centered on control of land surfaces, new disputes are beginning to arise over the resources of the oceans and space.

On smaller scales, conflicts have created divisions between rival gangs; use zones in cities, water supply, school districts; economic divisions include franchise areas and trade zones.

DOMAIN IV.   **GEOGRAPHY**

COMPETENCY 4.0   THEMES

Skill 4.0a   Identify relative and absolute location and the physical and human characteristics of "place"

Human communities subsisted initially as gatherers – gathering berries, leaves, etc. With the invention of tools it became possible to dig for roots, hunt small animals, and catch fish from rivers and oceans. Humans observed their environments and soon learned to plant seeds and harvest crops. As people migrated to areas with abundant game and fertile soil, communities began to develop. When people had the knowledge to grow crops and the skills to hunt game, they began to understand division of labor. Some of the people in the community tended to agricultural needs while others hunted game.

As habitats attracted larger numbers of people, environments became crowded and there was competition. The concept of division of labor and sharing of food soon came, in more heavily populated areas, to be managed. Groups of people focused on growing crops while others concentrated on hunting. Experience led to the development of skills and of knowledge that make the work easier. Farmers began to develop new plant species and hunters began to protect animal species from other predators for their own use. This ability to manage the environment led people to settle down, to guard their resources, and to manage them.

Camps soon became villages. Villages became year-round settlements. Animals were domesticated and gathered into herds that met the needs of the village. With the settled life it was no longer necessary to "travel light." Pottery was developed for storing and cooking food.

By 8000 BCE, culture was beginning to evolve in these villages. Agriculture was developed for the production of grain crops, which led to a decreased reliance on wild plants. Domesticating animals for various purposes decreased the need to hunt wild game. Life became more settled. It was then possible to turn attention to such matters as managing water supplies, producing tools, making cloth, etc. There was both the social interaction and the opportunity to reflect upon existence. Mythologies arose and various kinds of belief systems. Rituals arose that re-enacted the mythologies that gave meaning to life.

As farming and animal husbandry skills increased, the dependence on wild game and food gathering declined. With this change came the realization that a larger number of people could be supported on the produce of farming and animal husbandry.

Two things seem to have come together to produce cultures and civilizations: a society and culture based on agriculture and the development of centers of the community with literate social and religious structures. The members of these hierarchies then managed water supply and irrigation, ritual and religious life, and exerted their own right to use a portion of the goods produced by the community for their own subsistence in return for their management.

Sharpened skills, development of more sophisticated tools, commerce with other communities, and increasing knowledge of their environment, the resources available to them, and responses to the needs to share good, order community life, and protect their possessions from outsiders led to further division of labor and community development.

As trade routes developed and travel between cities became easier, trade led to specialization. Trade enables a people to obtain the goods they desire in exchange for the goods they are able to produce. This, in turn, leads to increased attention to refinements of technique and the sharing of ideas. The knowledge of a new discovery or invention provides knowledge and technology that increases the ability to produce goods for trade.

As each community learns the value of the goods it produces and improves its ability to produce the goods in greater quantity, industry is born.

Skill 4.0b   Demonstrate understanding of human-environment interactions

Ecology is the study of how living organisms interact with the physical aspects of their surroundings (their environment), including soil, water, air, and other living things. **Biogeography** is the study of how the surface features of the earth – form, movement, and climate – affect living things.

Three levels of environmental understanding are critical:

1. An **ecosystem** is a community (of any size) consisting of a physical environment and the organisms that live within it.

2. A **biome** is a large area of land with characteristic climate, soil, and mixture of plants and animals. Biomes are made up of groups of ecosystems. Major biomes are: desert, chaparral, savanna, tropical rain forest, temperate grassland, temperate deciduous forest, taiga, and tundra.

3. A **habitat** is the set of surroundings within which members of a species normally live. Elements of the habitat include soil, water, predators, and competitors.

Within habitats interactions between members of the species occur. These interactions occur between members of the same species and between members of different species. Interaction tends to be of three types:

1. **Competition**. Competition occurs between members of the same species or between members of different species for resources required to continue life, to grow, or to reproduce. For example, competition for acorns can occur between squirrels or it can occur between squirrels and woodpeckers. One species can either push out or cause the demise of another species if it is better adapted to obtain the resource. When a new species is introduced into a habitat, the result can be a loss of the native species and/or significant change to the habitat. For example, the introduction of the Asian plant Kudzu into the American South has resulted in the destruction of several species because Kudzu grows and spreads very quickly and smothers everything in its path.

2. **Predation**. Predators are organisms that live by hunting and eating other organisms. The species best suited for hunting other species in the habitat will be the species that survives. Larger species that have better hunting skills reduce the amount of prey available for smaller and/or weaker species. This affects both the amount of available prey and the diversity of species that are able to survive in the habitat.

3. **Symbiosis** is a condition in which two organisms of different species are able to live in the same environment over an extended period of time without harming each other. In some cases, one species may benefit without harming the other. In other cases, both species benefit.

Different organisms are by nature best suited for existence in particular environments. When an organism is displaced to a different environment or when the environment changes for some reason, its ability to survive is determined by its ability to *adapt* to the new environment. Adaptation can take the form of structural change, physiological change, or behavioral modification.

Biodiversity refers to the variety of species and organisms, as well as the variety of habitats available on the earth. Biodiversity provides the life-support system for the various habitats and species. The greater the degree of biodiversity, the more species and habitats will continue to survive.

When human and other population and migration changes, climate changes, or natural disasters disrupt the delicate balance of a habitat or an ecosystem, species either adapt or become extinct.

Natural changes can occur that alter habitats – floods, volcanoes, storms, earthquakes. These changes can affect the species that exist within the habitat, either by causing extinction or by changing the environment in a way that will no longer support the life systems. Climate changes can have similar effects.

Inhabiting species, however, can also alter habitats, particularly through migration. Human civilization, population growth, and efforts to control the environment can have many negative effects on various habitats. Humans change their environments to suit their particular needs and interests. This can result in changes that result in the extinction of species or changes to the habitat itself. For example, deforestation damages the stability of mountain surfaces. One particularly devastating example is in the removal of the grasses of the Great Plains for agriculture. Tilling the ground and planting crops left the soil unprotected. Sustained drought dried out the soil into dust. When windstorms occurred, the topsoil was stripped away and blown all the way to the Atlantic Ocean.

Skill 4.0c   Identify significant types of movement such as migration, trade, and the spread of ideas

The Agricultural Revolution, initiated by the invention of the plow, led to a transformation of human society by making large-scale agricultural production possible and facilitating the development of agrarian societies. During the period during which the plow was invented, the wheel, numbers, and writing were also invented. Coinciding with the shift from hunting wild game to the domestication of animals, this period was one of dramatic social and economic change.

Numerous changes in lifestyle and thinking accompanied the development of stable agricultural communities. Rather than gathering a wide variety of plants as hunter-gatherers, agricultural communities became dependent on a limited number of plants or crops that are harvested. Subsistence becomes vulnerable to the weather and dependent upon planting and harvesting times. Agriculture also required a great deal of physical labor and the development of a sense of discipline. Agricultural communities become sedentary or stable in terms of location. This makes the construction of dwellings appropriate. These tend to be built relatively close together, creating villages or towns. Stable communities also free people from the need to carry everything with them and the move from hunting ground to hunting ground. This facilitates the invention of larger, more complex tools. As new tools are envisioned and developed, it begins to make sense to have some specialization within the society. Skills begin to have greater value, and people begin to do work on behalf of the community that utilizes their particular skills and abilities. Settled community life also gives rise to the notion of wealth. It is now possible to keep possessions.

In the beginning of the transition to agriculture, the tools that were used for hunting and gathering were adequate for the tasks of agriculture. The initial challenge was in adapting to a new way of life. Once that challenge was met, attention turned to the development of more advanced tools and sources of energy. Six thousand years ago, the first plow was invented in Mesopotamia, and it was pulled by animals. Agriculture was now possible on a much larger scale.

Soon tools were developed that make such basic tasks as gathering seeds, planting, and cutting grain faster and easier.

It also becomes necessary to maintain social and political stability to ensure that planting and harvesting times are not interrupted by internal discord or a war with a neighboring community. It also becomes necessary to develop ways to store the crop and prevent its destruction by the elements and animals. And then it must be protected from thieves.

Settled communities that produce the necessities of life are self-supporting. Advances in agricultural technology and the ability to produce a surplus of produce create two opportunities: first, the opportunity to trade the surplus goods for other desired goods, and second, the vulnerability to others who steal to take those goods. Protecting domesticated livestock and surplus, as well as stored, crops become an issue for the community. This, in turn, leads to the construction of walls and other fortifications around the community.

The ability to produce surplus crops creates the opportunity to trade or barter with other communities in exchange for desired goods. Traders and trade routes begin to develop between villages and cities. The domestication of animals expands the range of trade and facilitates an exchange of ideas and knowledge.

Competition for control of areas of the earth's surface is a common trait of human interaction throughout history. This competition has resulted in both destructive conflict and peaceful and productive cooperation. Societies and groups have sought control of regions of the earth's surface for a wide variety of reasons including religion, economics, politics and administration. Numerous wars have been fought through the centuries for the control of territory for each of these reasons.

Individuals and societies have divided the earth's surface through conflict for a number of reasons:

- The domination of peoples or societies, e.g., colonialism
- The control of valuable resources, e.g., oil
- The control of strategic routes, e.g., the Panama Canal

Religion, political ideology, national origin, language, and race can spur conflicts. Conflicts can result from disagreement over how land, ocean or natural resources will be developed, shared, and used. Conflicts have resulted from trade, migration, and settlement rights. Conflicts can occur between small groups of people, between cities, between nations, between religious groups, and between multi-national alliances.

Large companies and multi-national corporations also compete for control of natural resources for manufacturing, development, and distribution.

Throughout human history there have been conflicts on virtually every scale over the right to divide the Earth according to differing perceptions, needs and values. These conflicts have ranged from tribal conflicts to urban riots, to civil wars, to regional wars, to world wars. While these conflicts have traditionally centered on control of land surfaces, new disputes are beginning to arise over the resources of the oceans and space.

On smaller scales, conflicts have created divisions between rival gangs, use zones in cities, water supply, school districts; economic divisions include franchise areas and trade zones.

COMPETENCY 4.1   MAP SKILLS

Skill 4.1a   Read and interpret various types of maps

We use **illustrations** of various sorts because it is often easier to demonstrate a given idea visually instead of orally. Sometimes it is even easier to do so with an illustration than a description. This is especially true in the areas of education and research because humans are visually stimulated. It is a fact that any idea presented visually in some manner is always easier to understand and to comprehend than simply getting an idea across verbally, by hearing it or reading it. Among the more common illustrations used in political and social sciences are various types of **maps, graphs and charts**.

Photographs and **globes** are useful as well; but because they are limited in what kind of information that they can show, they are rarely used—unless, as in the case of a photograph, it is of a particular political figure or a time that one wishes to visualize.

Although maps have advantages over globes and photographs, they do have a major disadvantage. This problem must be considered as well. The major problem of all maps comes about because most maps are flat and the Earth is a sphere. It is impossible to reproduce exactly on a flat surface an object shaped like a sphere. In order to put the earth's features onto a map they must be stretched in some way. This stretching is called **distortion.**

Distortion does not mean that maps are wrong it simply means that they are not perfect representations of the Earth or its parts. **Cartographers,** or mapmakers, understand the problems of distortion. They try to design their maps so that there is as little distortion as possible.

The process of putting the features of the Earth onto a flat surface is called **projection**. All maps are really map projections. There are many different types. Each one deals in a different way with the problem of distortion. Map projections are made in a number of ways. Some are done using complicated mathematics. However, the basic ideas behind map projections can be understood by looking at the three most common types:

> (1) <u>**Cylindrical Projections**</u>—These are done by taking a cylinder of paper and wrapping it around a globe. A light is used to project the globe's features onto the paper. Distortion is least where the paper touches the globe. For example, suppose that the paper was wrapped so that it touched the globe at the equator; the map from this projection would have just a little distortion near the equator.
> However, in moving north or south of the equator, the distortion would increase as you moved further away from the equator.

The best known and most widely used cylindrical projection is the **Mercator Projection.** Gerardus Mercator, a Flemish cartographer, first developed it in 1569.

(2). <u>**Conical Projections**</u>—The name for these maps come from the fact that the projection is made onto a cone of paper. The cone is made so that it touches a globe at the base of the cone only. It can also be made so that it cuts through part of the globe in two different places. Again, there is the least distortion where the paper touches the globe. If the cone touches at two different points, there is some distortion at both of them. Conical projections are most often used to map areas in the **middle latitudes**. Maps of the United States are most often conical projections. This is because most of the country lies within these latitudes.

(3). <u>**Flat-Plane Projections**</u> —These are made with a flat piece of paper. It touches the globe at one point only. Areas near this point show little distortion. Flat-plane projections are often used to show the areas of the north and south poles. One such flat projection is called a **Gnomonic Projection**. On this kind of map all meridians appear as straight lines, Gnomonic projections are useful because any straight line drawn between points on it forms a Great-Circle Route.

Great-Circle Routes can best be described by thinking of a globe and when using the globe the shortest route between two points on it can be found by simply stretching a string from one point to the other. However, if the string was extended in reality, so that it took into effect the globe's curvature, it would then make a great-circle. A great-circle is any circle that cuts a sphere, such as the globe, into two equal parts. Because of distortion, most maps do not show great-circle routes as straight lines. Gnomonic projections, however, do show the shortest distance between the two places as a straight line; because of this they are valuable for navigation. They are called Great-Circle Sailing Maps.

Maps have four main properties. They are (1) the size of the areas shown on the map, (2) the shapes of the areas, (3) consistent scales, and (4) straight line directions. A map can be drawn so that it is correct in one or more of these properties. No map can be correct in all of them.

Equal areas—One property that maps can have is the property of equal areas. In an equal area map, the meridians and parallels are drawn so that the areas shown have the same proportions as they do on the Earth. For example, Greenland is about 118th the size of South America, thus it will be show as 118th the size on an equal area map. The **Mercator projection** is an example of a map that does not have equal areas. In it, Greenland appears to be about the same size of South America. This is because the distortion is very bad at the poles and Greenland lies near the North Pole.

Conformal Map—A second map property is conformal, or correct shapes. There are no maps that can show very large areas of the earth in their exact shapes. Only globes can really do that. However, Conformal Maps are as close as possible to true shapes. The United States is often shown by a Lambert Conformal Conic Projection Map.

Consistent Scales—Many maps attempt to use the same scale on all parts of the map. Generally, this is easier when maps show a relatively small part of the earth's surface. For example, a map of Florida might be a Consistent Scale Map. Generally, maps showing large areas are not consistent-scale maps. This is because of distortion. Often, such maps will have two scales noted in the key. One scale, for example, might be accurate to measure distances between points along the Equator. Another might be then used to measure distances between the North Pole and the South Pole.

Maps showing physical features often try to show information about the elevation or **relief** of the land. **Elevation** is the distance above or below the sea level. The elevation is usually shown with colors, for instance, all areas on a map that are at a certain level will be shown in the same color.

Relief Maps—Show the shape of the land surface: flat, rugged, or steep. Relief maps usually give more detail than simply showing the overall elevation of the land's surface. Relief is also sometimes shown with colors, but another way to show relief is by using **contour lines**. These lines connect all points of a land surface that are the same height surrounding the particular area of land.

Thematic Maps—These are used to show more specific information, often on a single **theme**, or topic. Thematic maps show the distribution or amount of something over a certain given area for example, things such as population density, climate, economic information, cultural, political information, etc.

Skill 4.1b   Determine distance, direction, latitude, longitude, and the location of physical features

Distance is the measurement between two points of location on a map. Measurement can be in terms of a number of units such as feet, yards, miles, meters, or kilometers. Distance is often correct on equidistant maps only in the direction of latitude.

On a map that has a large scale, 1:125,000 or larger, distance distortion is usually insignificant. An example of a large-scale map is a standard topographic map. On these maps measuring straight line distance is simple. Distance is first measured on the map using a ruler. This measurement is then converted into a real world distance using the map's scale. For example, if we measured a distance of 10 centimeters on a map that had a scale of 1:10,000, we would multiply 10 (distance) by 10,000 (scale). Thus, the actual distance in the real world would be 100,000 centimeters.

Measuring distance along map features that are not straight is a little more difficult. One technique that can be employed for this task is to use a number of straight-line segments. The accuracy of this method is dependent on the number of straight-line segments used. Another method for measuring curvilinear map distances is to use a mechanical device called an **opisometer**. This device uses a small rotating wheel that records the distance traveled. The recorded distance is measured by this device either in centimeters or inches.

Direction is usually measured relative to the location of North or South Pole. Directions determined from these locations are said to be relative to True North or True South. The magnetic poles can also be used to measure direction. However, these points on the Earth are located in spatially different spots from the geographic North and South Pole. The North Magnetic Pole is located at 78.3° North, 104.0° West. In the Southern Hemisphere, the South Magnetic Pole is located in Commonwealth Day, Antarctica, and has a geographical location of 65° South, 139° East. The magnetic poles are also not fixed overtime but shift their spatial position overtime.

There are many different climates throughout the earth. It is most unusual if a country contains just one kind of climate. Regions of climates are divided according to **latitudes**:

0 – 23½° are the "low latitudes"
23½° - 66½° are the "middle latitudes"
66½ ° to the Poles are the "high latitudes"

The **low latitudes** are composed of the rainforest, savanna, and desert climates. The tropical rainforest climate is found in equatorial lowlands and is hot and wet. There is sun, extreme heat and rain every day. Although daily temperatures rarely rise above 90° F, the daily humidity is always high, leaving everything sticky and damp. North and south of the tropical rainforests are the tropical grasslands called "savannas," the "lands of two seasons" – a winter dry season and a summer wet season. Further north and south of the tropical grasslands or savannas are the deserts. These areas are the hottest and driest parts of the earth, receiving less than 10 inches of annual rainfall. These areas have extreme temperatures between night and day. After the sun sets, the land cools quickly dropping the temperature as much as 50° F.

The **middle latitudes** contain the Mediterranean, humid-subtropical, humid-continental, marine, steppe, and desert climates. Lands containing the Mediterranean climate are considered "sunny" lands found in six areas of the world: lands bordering the Mediterranean Sea, a small portion of southwestern Africa, areas in southern and southwestern Australia, a small part of the Ukraine near the Black Sea, central Chile, and Southern California. Summers are hot and dry with mild winters. The growing season usually lasts all year and what little rain falls are during the winter months. What is rather unusual is that the Mediterranean climate is located between 30 and 40 degrees north and south latitude on the western coasts of countries.

Longitude measures the north-south position of locations on the Earth's surface relative to a point found at the center of the Earth. This central point is also located on the Earth's rotational or **polar axis**. The equator is the starting point for the measurement of latitude. The equator has a value of zero degrees. A line of latitude or **parallel** of 30° North has an angle that is 30° north of the plane represented by the equator. The maximum value that latitude can attain is either 90° North or South. These lines of latitude run parallel to the rotational axis of the Earth. There are 180° of longitude on either side of a starting meridian, which is known as the **Prime Meridian**. The Prime Meridian has a designated value of 0°. Measurements of longitude are also defined as being either west or east of the Prime Meridian.

Skill 4.1c Recognize and describe spatial patterns

Maps come in a variety of formats. A thematic map, also known as a statistical or special purpose map, displays the spatial pattern of a theme or series of attributes, for example, population, age and income levels. In contrast to reference maps, which show many geographic features (forests, roads, and political boundaries), thematic maps emphasize spatial variation of one or a small number of geographic distributions. These distributions may be physical phenomena such as climate or human characteristics such as population density and health issues. These types of maps are sometimes referred to as graphic essays that portray spatial variations and interrelationships of geographical distributions. Location is important to provide a reference base of where selected phenomena are occurring. While general reference maps show where something is in relation to other points, thematic maps describe attribute(s) about that place.

Skill 4.1d Using a legend or key

To properly analyze a given map, one must be familiar with the various parts and symbols that most modern maps use. For the most part, these parts and symbols are standardized, with different maps using similar parts and symbols, which can include the following:

The Title—All maps should have a title, just like all books should. The title tells you what information is to be found on the map.

The Legend—Most maps have a legend. A legend tells the reader about the various symbols that are used on that particular map and what the symbols represent (also called a **map key**).

The Grid—A grid is a series of lines that are used to find exact places and locations on the map. Several different kinds of grid systems are in use; however, most maps do use the longitude and latitude system, known as the **Geographic Grid System**.

Directions—Most maps have some directional system to show which way the map is being presented. Often on a map, a small compass will be present, with arrows showing the four basic directions: north, south, east, and west.

The Scale—The scale is used to show the relationship between a unit of measurement on the map and the real world measure on the Earth. Maps are drawn to many different scales. Some maps show a lot of detail for a small area. Others show a greater span of distance. In any event, one should always be aware of just what scale is being used. For instance, for a small area, the scale might be 1 inch = 10 miles. For a map showing the whole world, the scale might be 1 inch = 1,000 miles. One must look at the map key in order to see what units of measurements the map is using.

COMPETENCY 4.2   PHYSICAL GEOGRAPHY

Skill 4.2a   **Demonstrate knowledge of landforms and water, climate, and vegetation and natural resources**

A landform comprises a geomorphologic unit. Landforms are categorized by characteristics such as elevation, slope, orientation, stratification, rock exposure, and soil type. Landforms by name include berms, mounds, hills, cliffs, valleys, and others. Oceans and continents exemplify highest-order landforms. Landform elements are parts of a landform that can be further identified. The generic landform elements are: pits, peaks, channels, ridges, passes, pools, planes, etc., and can be often extracted from a digital elevation model using some automated or semi-automated techniques.

Elementary landforms (segments, facets, relief units) are the smallest homogeneous divisions of the land surface, at the given scale/resolution. A plateau or a hill can be observed at various scales ranging from a few hundred meters to hundreds of kilometers. Hence, the spatial distribution of landforms is often fuzzy and scale-dependent, as is the case for soils and geological strata.

A number of factors, ranging from plate tectonics to erosion and deposition, can generate and affect landforms. Biological factors can also influence landforms, for example, the role of plants in the development of dune systems and salt marshes, and the work of corals and algae in the formation of coral reefs.

Weather is the condition of the air, which surrounds the day-to-day atmospheric conditions including temperature, air pressure, wind and moisture or precipitation which includes rain, snow, hail, or sleet.

Climate is average weather or daily weather conditions for a specific region or location over a long or extended period of time. Studying the climate of an area includes information gathered on the area's monthly and yearly temperatures and its monthly and yearly amounts of precipitation. In addition, a characteristic of an area's climate is the length of its growing season.

In northern and central United States, northern China, south central and southeastern Canada, and the western and southeastern parts of the former Soviet Union is found the "climate of four seasons," the humid continental climate – spring, summer, fall, and winter. Cold winters, hot summers, and enough rainfall to grow a variety of crops are the major characteristics of this climate. In areas where the humid continental climate is found are some of the world's best farmlands as well as important activities such as trading and mining. Differences in temperatures throughout the year are determined by the distance a place is inland, away from the coasts.

The steppe or prairie climate is located in the interiors of the large continents such as Asia and North America. These dry flatlands are far from ocean breezes and are called prairies or the Great Plains in Canada and the United States and steppes in Asia. Although the summers are similar to the humid continental climate, with hot and the winters, the big difference is with annual rainfall. In the steppe climate, rainfall is light and uncertain, 10 to 20 inches a year mainly in spring and summer and is considered normal. Where rain is more plentiful, grass grows; in areas of less, the steppes or prairies gradually become deserts. These are found in the Gobi Desert of Asia, central and western Australia, southwestern United States, and in the smaller deserts found in Pakistan, Argentina, and Africa south of the Equator.

The two major climates found in the high latitudes are **tundra** and **taiga**. The word tundra meaning marshy plain is a Russian word and aptly describes the climatic conditions in the northern areas of Russia, Europe, and Canada. Winters are extremely cold and very long. For most of the year, the ground is frozen but becomes rather mushy during the very short summer months. Surprisingly less snow falls in the area of the tundra than in the eastern part of the United States. However, due to the harshness of the extreme cold, very few people live there and no crops can be raised. Despite having a small human population, many plants and animals are found there.

The taiga is the northern forest region and is located south of the tundra. The world's largest forestlands are found here along with vast mineral wealth and fur bearing animals. The climate is extreme that very few people live here, not being able to grow crops due to the extremely short growing season. The winter temperatures are colder and the summer temperatures are hotter than those in the tundra are because the taiga climate region is farther from the waters of the Arctic Ocean. The taiga is found in the northern parts of Russia, Sweden, Norway, Finland, Canada, and Alaska with most of their lands covered with marshes and swamps.

The humid subtropical climate is found north and south of the tropics and is moist indeed. The areas having this type of climate are found on the eastern side of their continents and include Japan, mainland China, Australia, Africa, South America, and the United States – the southeastern coasts of these areas. An interesting feature of their locations is that warm ocean currents are found there. The winds that blow across these currents bring in warm moist air all year round. Long, warm summers; short, mild winters; a long growing season allows for different crops to be grown several times a year.   All contribute to the productivity of this climate type that supports more people than any of the other climates.

The marine climate is found in Western Europe, the British Isles, the U.S. Pacific Northwest, the western coast of Canada, southern Chile, southern New Zealand and southeastern Australia. A common characteristic of these lands is their proximity to water. The ocean winds are wet and warm bringing a mild, rainy climate to these areas. In the summer, the daily temperatures average at or below 70 degrees Fahrenheit. The temperatures rarely fall below freezing during the winter because of the warming effect of the ocean waters.

In northern and central United States, northern China, south central and southeastern Canada, and the western and southeastern parts of the former Soviet Union the "climate of four seasons" is found. This is the humid continental climate with spring, summer, fall, and winter. Cold winters, hot summers, and enough rainfall to grow a variety of crops are the major characteristics of this climate. In areas where the humid continental climate is found are some of the world's best farmlands as well as important activities such as trading and mining. Differences in temperatures throughout the year are determined by the distance a place is inland,

In certain areas of the earth there exists a type of climate unique to areas with high mountains, usually different from their surroundings. This type of climate is called a "vertical climate" because the temperatures, crops, vegetation, and human activities change and become different as one ascends the different levels of elevation. At the foot of the mountain, a hot and rainy climate is found with the cultivation of many lowland crops. As one climbs higher, the air becomes cooler, the climate changes sharply and different economic activities change, such as grazing sheep and growing corn. At the top of many mountains, snow is found year-round.

Natural resources are naturally occurring substances that are considered valuable in their natural form. A commodity is generally considered a natural resource when the primary activities associated with it are extraction and purification, as opposed to creation. Thus, mining, petroleum extraction, fishing, and forestry are generally considered natural-resource industries, while agriculture is not.

Natural resources are often classified into renewable and non-renewable resources. Renewable resources are generally living resources (fish, coffee, and forests, for example) that can restock (renew) themselves if they are sustained and not over-harvested. Once renewable resources are consumed at a rate that exceeds their natural rate of replacement, the standing stock will diminish and eventually run out. The rate of sustainable use of a renewable resource is determined by the replacement rate and amount of standing stock of that particular resource. Non-living renewable natural resources include soil, as well as water, wind, tides and solar radiation. Natural resources include soil, timber, oil, minerals, and other goods taken more or less as they are from the Earth.

In recent years, the depletion of natural capital and attempts to move to sustainable development has been a major focus of development agencies. This is of particular concern in rainforest regions, which hold most of the Earth's natural biodiversity—irreplaceable genetic natural capital. Conservation of natural resources is the major focus of Natural Capitalism, environmentalism, the ecology movement, and Green Parties. Some view this depletion as a major source of social unrest and conflicts in developing nations.

Skill 4.2b   Demonstrate understanding of human impact on the environment

By nature, people are essentially social creatures. They generally live in communities or settlements of some kind and of some size. Settlements are the cradles of culture, political structure, education, and the management of resources. The relative placement of these settlements or communities are shaped by the proximity to natural resources, the movement of raw materials, the production of finished products, the availability of a work force, and the delivery of finished products. Shared values, language, culture, religion, and subsistence will at least to some extent, determine the composition of communities.

Settlements begin in areas that offer the natural resources to support life – food and water. With the ability to manage the environment one finds a concentration of populations. With the ability to transport raw materials and finished products, comes mobility. With increasing technology and the rise of industrial centers comes a migration of the workforce.

Cities are the major hubs of human settlement. Almost half of the population of the world now lives in cities. These percentages are much higher in developed regions. Established cities continue to grow. The fastest growth, however, is occurring in developing areas. In some regions there are "metropolitan areas" made up of urban and sub-urban areas. In some places cities and urban areas have become interconnected into "megalopoli" (e.g., Tokyo-Kawasaki-Yokohama).

The concentrations of populations and the divisions of these areas among various groups that constitute the cities can differ significantly. North American cities are different from European cities in terms of shape, size, population density, and modes of transportation. While in North America, the wealthiest economic groups tend to live outside the cities, whereas the opposite is true in Latin American cities.

There are significant differences among the cities of the world in terms of connectedness to other cities. While European and North American cities tend to be well linked both by transportation and communication connections, there are other places in the world in which communication between the cities of the country may be inferior to communication with the rest of the world.

Rural areas tend to be less densely populated because of the needs of agriculture. More land is needed to produce crops or for animal husbandry than for manufacturing, especially in a city in which the buildings tend to be taller. Rural areas, however, must be connected via communication and transportation in order to provide food and raw materials to urban areas.

Social policy aims to improve human welfare and to meet basic human needs within the society and addresses basic human needs for the sustainability of the individual and the society. The concerns of social policy, then, include food, clean water, shelter, clothing, education, health, and social security. Social policy is part of public policy, determined by the city, the state, the nation, or the multi-national organization responsible for human welfare in a particular region.

Environmental policy is concerned with the sustainability of the earth, the region under the administration of the governing group or individual or a local habitat. The concern of environmental policy is the preservation of the region, habitat or ecosystem.

Because humans, both individually and communally, rely upon the environment to sustain human life, social and environmental policy must be mutually supported. Especially since humans rely on the environment to draw upon the natural resources of the earth, affect the environment in many ways, and live upon the earth.

If modern societies have no understanding of the limitations on natural resources or how their actions affect the environment, and they act without regard for the sustainability of the earth, it will become impossible for the earth to sustain human existence. At the same time, the resources of the earth are necessary to support the human welfare. Environmental policies must recognize that the planet is the home of humans and other species.

For centuries, social, economic, and political policies have ignored the impact of human existence and human civilization on the environment. Human civilization has disrupted the ecological balance, contributed to the extinction of animal and plant species, and destroyed ecosystems through uncontrolled harvesting.

In an age of global warming, unprecedented demand on natural resources, and a shrinking planet, social and environmental policies must become increasingly interdependent if the planet is to continue to support life and human civilization.

COMPETENCY 4.3   HUMAN GEOGRAPHY

Skill 4.3a   Demonstrate knowledge of human geography, including cultural geography; economic geography; political geography; and population geography

The **Industrial Revolution** of the eighteenth and nineteenth centuries resulted in even greater changes in human civilization and even greater opportunities for trade, increased production, and the exchange of ideas and knowledge.

The first phase of the Industrial Revolution (1750-1830) saw the mechanization of the textile industry, vast improvements in mining, with the invention of the steam engine, and numerous improvements in transportation, with the development and improvement of turnpikes, canals, and the invention of the railroad.

The second phase (1830-1910) resulted in vast improvements in a number of industries that had already been mechanized through such inventions as the Bessemer steel process and the invention of steam ships. New industries arose as a result of the new technological advances, such as photography, electricity, and chemical processes. New sources of power were harnessed and applied, including petroleum and hydroelectric power. Precision instruments were developed, and engineering was launched. It was during this second phase that the Industrial Revolution spread to other European countries, to Japan, and to the United States.

The direct results of the Industrial Revolution, particularly as they affected industry, commerce, and agriculture, included:

- Enormous increase in productivity,
- Huge increase in world trade,
- Specialization and division of labor,
- Standardization of parts and mass production,
- Growth of giant business conglomerates and monopolies, and
- A new revolution in agriculture facilitated by the steam engine, machinery, chemical fertilizers, processing, canning, and refrigeration.

The political results included:

- Growth of complex government by technical experts,
- Centralization of government, including regulatory administrative agencies, and

- Advantages to democratic development, including extension of franchise to the middle class, and later to all elements of the population, mass education to meet the needs of an industrial society, the development of media of public communication, including radio, television, and cheap newspapers.
- Dangers to democracy included the risk of manipulation of the media of mass communication, facilitation of dictatorial centralization and totalitarian control, subordination of the legislative function to administrative directives, efforts to achieve uniformity and angles, and social impersonalization.

The economic results were numerous:

- The conflict between free trade and low tariffs and protectionism,
- The issue of free enterprise against government regulation,
- Struggles between labor and capital, including the trade-union movement,
- The rise of socialism, utopian socialists, and Marxian or scientific socialism.

The social results of the Industrial Revolution include:

- Increase of population, especially in industrial centers,
- Advances in science applied to agriculture, sanitation and medicine,
- Growth of cities,
- Disappearance of the difference between city dwellers and farmers,
- Faster tempo of life and increased stress from the monotony of the work routine,
- The emancipation of women,
- The decline of religion,
- Rise of scientific materialism, and
- Darwin's theory of evolution.

Increased mobility produced a rapid diffusion of knowledge and ideas. Increased mobility also resulted in wide-scale immigration to industrialized countries, while cultures clashed and cultures melded.

COMPETENCY 4.4   REGIONAL GEOGRAPHY

Skill 4.4a   Demonstrate knowledge of the geography of the major regions of the world

The earth's surface is 70 percent water and 30 percent land. Physical features of the land surface include mountains, hills, plateaus, valleys, and plains. Other minor landforms include deserts, deltas, canyons, mesas, basins, foothills, marshes and swamps. Earth's water features include oceans, seas, lakes, rivers, and canals.

Mountains are landforms with rather steep slopes at least 2,000 feet or more above sea level. Mountains are found in groups called mountain chains or mountain ranges. At least one range can be found on six of the earth's seven continents. North America has the Appalachian and Rocky Mountains; South America the Andes; Asia the Himalayas; Australia the Great Dividing Range; Europe the Alps; and Africa the Atlas, Ahaggar, and Drakensburg Mountains.

Hills are elevated landforms rising to an elevation of about 500 to 2000 feet. They are found everywhere on earth including Antarctica, where they are covered by ice.

Plateaus are elevated landforms and usually level on top. Depending on location, they range from being an area that is very cold to one that is cool and healthful. Some plateaus are dry because mountains that keep out any moisture surround them. Some examples include the Kenya Plateau in East Africa, which is very cool. The plateau extending north from the Himalayas is extremely dry while those in Antarctica and Greenland are covered with ice and snow.

Plains are described as areas of flat or slightly rolling land, usually lower than the landforms next to them. Sometimes called lowlands (and sometimes located along **seacoasts**), they support the majority of the world's people. Some are found inland, and many have been formed by large rivers. This resulted in extremely fertile soil for successful cultivation of crops and numerous large settlements of people. In North America, the vast plains areas extend from the Gulf of Mexico north to the Arctic Ocean and between the Appalachian and Rocky Mountains. In Europe, rich plains extend east from Great Britain into central Europe on into the Siberian region of Russia. Plains in river valleys are found in China (the Yangtze River valley), India (the Ganges River valley), and Southeast Asia (the Mekong River valley).

Valleys are land areas found between hills and mountains. Some have gentle slopes containing trees and plants; others have steep walls and are referred to as canyons. One example is Arizona's Grand Canyon of the Colorado River.

Deserts are large dry areas of land receiving ten inches or less of rainfall each year.

Among the better known deserts are Africa's large Sahara Desert, the Arabian Desert on the Arabian Peninsula, and the desert Outback covering roughly one third of Australia.

Deltas are areas of lowlands formed by soil and sediment deposited at the mouths of rivers. The soil is generally very fertile and most fertile river deltas are important crop-growing areas. One well-known example is the delta of Egypt's Nile River, known for its production of cotton.

Mesas are the flat tops of hills or mountains usually with steep sides. Sometimes plateaus are also called mesas. Basins are considered to be low areas drained by rivers or low spots in mountains. Foothills are generally considered a low series of hills found between a plain and a mountain range. Marshes and swamps are wet lowlands providing growth of such plants as rushes and reeds.

Oceans are the largest bodies of water on the planet. The four oceans of the earth are the **Atlantic Ocean**, one-half the size of the Pacific and separating North and South America from Africa and Europe; the **Pacific Ocean**, covering almost one-third of the entire surface of the earth and separating North and South America from Asia and Australia; the **Indian Ocean**, touching Africa, Asia, and Australia; and the ice-filled **Arctic Ocean,** extending from North America and Europe to the North Pole. The waters of the Atlantic, Pacific, and Indian Oceans also touch the shores of Antarctica.

Seas are smaller than oceans and are surrounded by land. Some examples include the Mediterranean Sea found between Europe, Asia, and Africa; and the Caribbean Sea, touching the West Indies, South and Central America. A lake is a body of water surrounded by land. The Great Lakes in North America are a good example.

Rivers, considered a nation's lifeblood, usually begin as very small streams, formed by melting snow and rainfall, flowing from higher to lower land, emptying into a larger body of water, usually a sea or an ocean. Examples of important rivers for the people and countries affected by and/or dependent on them include the Nile, Niger, and Zaire Rivers of Africa; the Rhine, Danube, and Thames Rivers of Europe; the Yangtze, Ganges, Mekong, Hwang He, and Irrawaddy Rivers of Asia; the Murray-Darling in Australia; and the Orinoco in South America. River systems are made up of large rivers and numerous smaller rivers or tributaries flowing into them. Examples include the vast Amazon Rivers system in South America and the Mississippi River system in the United States.

Canals are man-made water passages constructed to connect two larger bodies of water. Famous examples include the **Panama Canal** across Panama's isthmus, connecting the Atlantic and Pacific Oceans and the **Suez Canal** in the Middle East between Africa and the Arabian Peninsula, connecting the Red and Mediterranean Seas.

DOMAIN V.   **ECONOMICS**

COMPETENCY 5.0   MICROECONOMICS I

Skill 5.0a   Understand the definition of economics and identify the factors of production and explain how they are used

Economics is a study of how a society allocates its scarce **resources** to satisfy what are basically unlimited and competing **wants**. Economics can also be defined as the study of the production, distribution and consumption of goods and resources subject to the constraint of scarce resources. Each of these definitions may look as if they are defining different things, but both of them are the same. A resource is an input into the production process. Resources are limited in supply; they are scarce. There are not enough of them to produce all of the goods and services that society wants. Resources are called factors of production, and there are four factors of production: **labor, capital, land, and entrepreneurs**.

Labor refers to all kinds of labor used in the production process. It doesn't matter if the labor is skilled or unskilled, part-time or full-time. All laborers are selling their ability to produce goods and services. Capital refers to anything that is made or manufactured to be used in the production process. Included in this definition are plant, equipment, machines, tools, etc. Land is not only land itself, but also all natural resources such as lumber, minerals, and oil. The entrepreneur is the individual that has the ability to combine the land, labor, and capital to produce a good or service. They bear the risks of failure and loss, and he is the one who will gain from the profits if the product is successful. Each of these four resources is combined in the production of every good and service.

Every good and service that is produced uses some combination of each of the four inputs. The combination used is called the production process. The production process refers to the way the four factors are combined to produce the output. If the production technique uses a lot of machinery with very few laborers, then the production process is called capital-intensive. If the production process requires many workers with very little machinery, then it is said to be a labor-intensive production process.

Whatever the production technique is, there are not enough resources to produce all of the goods and services that a society wants. The scarcity of resources functions as a constraint on the amounts and kinds of goods and services that the economy can produce and consume. The scarcity of resources then affects the production, distribution and consumption decisions of the society. The available resource supply, both quantity and quality, determines production.

For example, if there are not enough workers for a particular productive technique, then the smart owner will find machinery that requires fewer workers if he is going to stay in business in that area. Since the scarcity of resources determines what can be produced, distributed and consumed, than defining economics as a study of how a society allocates its scarce resources to satisfy unlimited and competing desires is saying the same thing. Consumers want more consumer goods, businesses want more investments, and government wants more public goods.

More capital goods mean fewer consumer goods because there are not enough resources to produce more of both.

Skill 5.0b   Demonstrate understanding of scarcity, choice and opportunity cost

The scarcity of resources is the basis for the existence of economics. Economics is defined as a study of how scarce resources are allocated to satisfy unlimited wants. Resources refer to the four factors of production: labor, capital, land and entrepreneurs. Labor refers to anyone who sells his ability to produce goods and services. Capital is anything that is manufactured to be used in the production process. Land refers to the land itself and everything occurring naturally on it, such as soil, minerals, and lumber. Entrepreneurship is the ability of an individual to combine the three inputs with his or her own talents to produce a viable good or service. The entrepreneur takes the risk and experiences the losses or profits.

The fact that the supply of these resources is finite means that society cannot have as much of everything that it wants. There is a constraint on production and consumption and on the kinds of goods and services that can be produced and consumed. **Scarcity** means that choices have to be made. If society decides to produce more of one good, this means that there are fewer resources available for the production of other goods. Assume a society can produce two goods, good X and good Y. The society uses resources in the production of each good. For example, producing one unit of good X results in using three units of resources needed to make good Y, then producing one more unit of good X results in a decrease of three units of good Y. In effect, one unit of good X "costs" three units of good Y. This cost is referred to as opportunity cost. **Opportunity cost** is the value of the sacrificed alternative, the value of what had to be given up in order to have the output of good X. Opportunity cost does not refer just to production. Your opportunity cost of studying with this guide is the value of what you are not doing because you are studying, whether it is watching TV, spending time with family, working, or whatever. Every **choice** has an opportunity cost.

If wants were limited and/or if resources were unlimited, then the concepts of choice and opportunity cost would not exist, and neither would the field of economics. There would be enough resources to satisfy the wants of consumers, businesses, and governments. The allocation of resources wouldn't be a problem. Society could have more of both good X and good Y without having to give up anything. There would be no opportunity cost. But this is not the situation that societies are faced with.

Because resources are scarce, society doesn't want to waste them. Society wants to obtain the most satisfaction it can from the consumption of the goods and services produced with its scarce resources. The members of the society don't want their scarce resources wasted through inefficiency.

Producers must, therefore, choose an efficient production process, which is the lowest cost means of production. High costs mean wasted resources, and we then have the situation given above with good X and good Y. Consumers also don't want society's resources wasted by producing goods that they don't want. How do producers know what goods consumers want? Consumers buy the goods they want and vote with their dollar spending. A desirable good, one that consumers want, earns profits. A good that incurs losses is a good that society doesn't want its resources wasted on. This loss signals the producer that society wants their resources used in another way.

Skill 5.0c   Demonstrate knowledge and application of the production possibilities curve to illustrate efficiency, unemployment, and tradeoffs

The scarcity of resources places a constraint on the kinds and amounts of goods and services that a society can produce, distribute, and consume. Because resources are limited in supply, society wants to use them efficiently. They do not want to waste them. They want to obtain the greatest amount of output possible for their available supply of resources. In order to achieve efficiency, two conditions must be fulfilled: full-employment and full-production. **Full-employment** refers to having all resources employed. Idle resources result in lower levels of output. **Full-production** means that resources should be employed in their most productive capacity. A resource should be doing what it does best in order to make the greatest contribution to output. Full-production cannot be achieved without allocative and productive efficiency. A society has achieved allocative efficiency when its resources are being used to produce the goods wanted by that society. Productive efficiency means those goods are being produced without waste, that the lowest cost method of production is being used.

All of these concepts come together in the Production Possibilities Curve (PPC). If we assume a two-good economy, capital goods and consumer goods, with fixed resources and fixed technology, the PCC then represents the maximum amounts of output that the society can achieve given efficient production. For example, if the economy uses all of its resources to produce capital goods, it can have 500 units of capital goods and no consumer goods. Its choices are as follows: If it produces 100 consumer goods, then it can have only 450 capital goods; 200 consumer goods and 375 capital goods, 300 consumer goods and 275 capital goods, 400 consumer goods and 150 capital goods, and 500 consumer goods and no capital goods. The opportunity cost is the amount of capital goods given up to produce consumer goods.

The first 100 consumer goods have an opportunity cost of 50 capital goods, the second 100 have an opportunity cost of 75 capital goods, and so on. Plotting the above capital-good/consumer-good combinations results in a downward sloping curve that is bowed outward. This is the PPC.

Every point on it represents efficient production. Every point on the curve represents a trade-off between capital goods and consumer goods. If society wants more consumer goods, it must give up some capital goods.

Points to the left of the curve represent inefficient production. If society is at a point inside the curve, then there is underemployment or unemployment. If society has unemployed resources, it is producing a lower level of output. Employing those unemployed resources means a higher quantity of output, and society will move from the point inside the curve to the curve itself. Society may have full employment of its resources, but not all the resources are employed in their most productive capacity. If this is the case, society is not obtaining the most output it can with its available supply of resources and is still at a point to the left of the PPC. Employing these resources in the most productive capacity will move them to a point on the curve where they are efficient. Points to the right of or outside the PPC are unattainable. The society must experience economic growth by an increase in the supply of factors and/or technological progress.

Skill 5.0d   Demonstrate knowledge of economic systems

Economic systems refer to the arrangements a society has devised to answer what are known as the Three Questions: What goods to produce, How to produce the goods, and For Whom are the goods being produced, or how the allocation of the output is determined. Different economic systems answer these questions in different ways. These are the different "isms" that define the method of resource and output allocation.

A market economy answers these questions in terms of demand and supply and the use of markets. Consumers vote for the products they want with their dollar spending. Goods acquiring enough dollar votes are profitable, signaling to the producers that society wants their scarce resources used in this way. This is how the "What" question is answered. The producer then hires inputs in accordance with the goods consumers want, looking for the most efficient or lowest cost method of production. The lower the firm's costs for any given level of revenue, the higher the firm's profits. This is the way in which the "How" question is answered in a market economy. The "For Whom" question is answered in the marketplace by the determination of the equilibrium price. Price serves to ration the good to those that can and will transact at the market price of better. Those who can't or won't are excluded from the market. The United States has a **market economy**.

The opposite of the market economy is the **centrally planned economy**. This used to be called communism, even though the term is not correct in a strict Marxian sense. In a planned economy, the means of production are publicly owned with little, if any public ownership. Instead of the Three Questions being solved by markets, they have a planning authority that makes the decisions in place of markets.

The planning authority decides what will be produced and how. Since most planned economies directed resources into the production of capital and military goods, there was little remaining for consumer goods and the result was chronic shortages. Price functioned as an accounting measure and did not reflect scarcity. The former Soviet Union and most of the Eastern Bloc countries were planned economies of this sort.

In between the two extremes is **market socialism**. This is a mixed economic system that uses both markets and planning. Planning is usually used to direct resources at the upper levels of the economy, with markets being used to determine prices of consumer goods and wages. This kind of economic system answers the three questions with planning and markets. The former Yugoslavia was a market socialist economy.

You can put each nation of the world on a continuum in terms of these characteristics and rank them from most capitalistic to the most planned. The United States would probably rank as the most capitalistic, and North Korea would probably rank as the most planned, but this doesn't mean that the United States does not engage in planning or that economies such as mainland China do not use markets.

Skill 5.0e   Demonstrate understanding of the concepts of absolute and comparative advantage, free trade, and the impacts of trade barriers such as tariffs and quotas

Trade theory is based on prices and costs. A nation has an absolute advantage in the production of a good when it can produce that good more efficiently than the other nations can. It is comparative advantage that is the basis for international trade. Trade that takes place on the basis of comparative advantage results in lower output prices and higher resource prices. According to trade theory, nations or regions should specialize in the production of the good that they can produce at a relatively lower cost than the other country can. In other words, if in country A one unit of X costs one unit of Y and in country B one unit of X costs three units of Y, good X is cheaper in country A and good Y is cheaper in country B. It takes only one third of a unit of X to produce one unit of Y in country B, whereas it takes one unit of Y in country A. Therefore, country B has the comparative advantage in the production of Y and country A has the comparative advantage in the production of good X. Economic theory states that each country should specialize in the production of the good in which it has the comparative advantage and trade for the other good. This means country B should use all of its resources to produce good Y and trade for good X. Country A should do the opposite and specialize in the production of good X and trade for good Y. Specialization and trade on this basis result in lower prices in both countries/regions and greater efficiency in the use of resources.

Each country will also experience increased consumption, since it is getting the maximum amount of output from its given inputs by specializing according to comparative advantage. Each country or region can consume its own goods and the goods it has traded for.

The introduction of national or international competition into a market can result in greater efficiency if the trade is without restrictions, such as tariffs or quotas. Trade barriers cause inefficiencies by resulting in higher prices and lower quantities. A **tariff** is a tax that is added to the price of the import or export. The purpose is to raise the price of the import so people will buy the domestic good. This leads to higher employment levels in the domestic industry and unemployment in the foreign industry. Resources have shifted in the wrong direction because of the tariff. Tariffs are a way of exporting unemployment to the foreign country.

Quotas are limits set on the physical number of units on imports or exports. An import quota limits the number of units entering a country; an export quota limits the number of units leaving the country. The result of limiting the quantity is to cause a higher price. Whether the trade barrier is a tariff or a quote, the result is to lower the volume of international trade. All of the benefits that were achieved with free trade are being lost. The results of trade barriers are lower levels of production, consumption, employment, and income.

Trade theory says that free trade is best. It results in the highest level of efficiency for the world. It results in the greatest levels of output, production, consumption, income, and employment. Any form of interference with free trade, such as tariffs and quotas, deters from the highest level of efficiency. The world has less output from its available inputs. There are lower levels of income and employment. This is why there is a movement on for trade liberalization.

Skill 5.0f   Demonstrate understanding of property rights, incentives, and the role of markets

Property rights perform an important function in our economy. The assignment of property rights entitles the owner to a payment for the use of his property. It is when the assignment of property rights is lacking that problems result. Pollution is an example of this situation. Assume a factory is dumping its wastes in a river. If the factory had to dispose of the wastes in another manner, it would have to pay a price for the disposal. It does not have to pay to dump its wastes in the river; the river is treated as a **free input**. The pollution is affecting other people in the area. They have dirty water, they can't swim or fish in it, vegetation is dying, there are odors, etc. If property rights for the river were assigned, the owner would charge for its use and the factory would have higher production costs. The pollution results from the river being a free input and the result is overproduction of the factory's product.

Incentives are part of a market economy that are absent in planned economies. All market participants are willing to take a risk for the opportunity of being a financial success. Entrepreneurs are willing to undertake the risk of new business ventures for the purpose of monetary gain. Resources move into higher than normal rate of return industries because they are attracted by the profit potential. Inventors are willing to take the risk of spending time and money trying to come up with new products in the hope of monetary gain. All of these represent the ways financial incentives operate in a market economy. Without a profit incentive, there would be no reason for firms to spend millions and billions on research and development and technological progress would be almost nonexistent. This was a problem in the planned economies in the Soviet era. Since the means of production were owned by the state, there was no incentive to improve technology or to develop new production processes. The individual had no reason to take the risks involved in entrepreneurial activities because there was nothing in it for him but a letter of commendation. The results were slow, inefficient production processes. In a market economy, the entrepreneur is willing to take the risks and knows there is a good probability that his business will fail but there is also a chance that it will succeed.

The existence of economic profits in an industry functions as a market signal to firms to enter the industry. Economic profits means there is an above normal rate of return in this industry. As the number of firms increases, the market supply curve shifts to the right. Assuming that cost curves stay the same, the expansion continues until the economic profits are eliminated and the industry is earning a normal rate of return. Depending on the level of capital intensity, this process might take a few or many years. The easier it is to shift resources from one industry to another, the faster the process will be. Resources will go where they earn the highest rate of return, especially if they are in a situation earning a lower than normal rate of return.

Profits are the market signal that indicates the proper allocation of resources in accordance with consumer preferences.

Skill 5.0g Demonstrate understanding of the supply and demand model and its application in the determination of equilibrium price in competitive markets

In a market economy, the markets function on the basis of supply and demand and, if markets are free, the result is an efficient allocation of resources. The seller's supply curve represents the different quantities of a good or service the seller is willing and able to bring to the market at different prices during a given period of time. The seller has to have the good and has to be willing to sell it. If either of these isn't true, then he isn't a part of the relevant market supply. The supply curve represents the selling and production decisions of the seller and is based on the costs of production. The costs of production of a product are based on the costs of the resources used in its production. The costs of resources are based on the scarcity of the resource. The scarcer a resource is, relatively speaking, the higher its price. A diamond costs more than paper because diamonds are scarcer than paper is. All of these concepts are embodied in the seller's supply curve.

The same thing is true on the buying side of the market. The buyer's preferences, tastes, income, etc. – all of the buying decisions – are embodied in the demand curve. The demand curve represents the various quantities of a good or a service the buyer is willing and able to buy at different prices during a given period of time. The buyer has to want the good and be willing and able to purchase it. He may want a Ferrari but can't afford one; therefore, he is not a part of the relevant market demand.

The demand side of the market is showing us what buyers are willing and able to purchase, and the supply side of the market is showing us what sellers are willing and able to supply. But we don't know anything about what buyers and sellers actually do buy and sell without putting the two sides together. If we compare the buying decisions of buyers with the selling decisions of sellers, the place where they coincide represents the market equilibrium. This is where the demand and supply curves intersect. At this one point of intersection, the buying decisions of buyers are equal to the selling decisions of sellers. The quantity that buyers want to buy at that particular price is equal to the quantity that sellers want to sell at that particular price. This is the market equilibrium. At this one point, the quantity demanded is equal to the quantity supplied. This price–quantity combination represents an efficient allocation of resources.

Consumers are basically voting for the goods and services that they want with their dollar spending. When a good accumulates enough dollar votes, the producer earns a profit. The existence of profits is the way the market signals the seller that he is using society's resources in a way that society wants them used. Consumers are obtaining the most satisfaction that they can from the way their society's scarce resources are being used. When consumers do not want a good or service, they don't purchase it and the producers don't accumulate enough dollar votes to have profits. **Losses** are the markets' way of signaling that consumers don't want their scarce resources used in the production of that particular good or service and that they want their resources used in some other manner. Firms that incur losses eventually go out of business. They either have a product that consumers don't want or they have an inefficient production process that results in higher costs and, therefore, higher prices. Higher costs than the competitors' means that there is inefficiency in production. All of this occurs naturally in markets in a market economy.

Skill 5.0h   Demonstrate understanding of market surpluses and shortages

A market is in equilibrium when there is a price that equates quantity demanded and quantity supplied. The demand curve is based on consumer preferences and represents the different quantities of a good a consumer is willing and able to purchase at different prices during a given period of time. The supply curve is based on costs of production and represents the different quantities of a good that sellers are willing and able to sell at different prices during a given period of time. The point of intersection of demand and supply represents the price that equates quantity demanded and quantity supplied. It is the only price where quantity demanded is equal to quantity supplied. The market is in equilibrium. The equilibrium price is the price that is said to clear the market, and there is no tendency for this price-quantity combination to change. The price that clears the market results in no imbalances between quantities demanded and quantity supplied. The buying decisions of buyers coincide exactly with the selling decisions of sellers.

Market surpluses and shortages exist when the market in not in equilibrium. This occurs when there is an inequality between quantity supplied and quantity demanded. In other words, the market price does not equate quantity demanded with quantity supplied. Let's look at a situation with a price above the market equilibrium price. The higher price results in a larger quantity supplied, as sellers are willing to supply larger quantities at higher prices than they are at lower prices. The higher price also means that buyers don't want as many units of output. Buyers are willing and able to buy larger quantities at lower prices, not at higher prices. So the higher price results in a situation where quantity supplied is greater than quantity demanded, or there is a surplus of the good. The seller begins to offer the surplus goods at a lower price.

As price comes down, more buyers are willing to buy the good. A lower price results in a larger quantity demanded.

So price continues to fall until the surplus is eliminated and the market is back at equilibrium, where quantity demanded is equal to quantity supplied.

Let's consider the effects of a price below the market equilibrium. At the lower price, sellers do not want to sell as much. The lower price results in a smaller quantity supplied by sellers. The lower price means an increase in quantity demanded by buyers, who want to buy larger quantities at lower prices than at higher prices. The result is a situation where quantity demanded exceeds quantity supplied. There is a shortage in the market. Because of the shortage of the good, buyers who want the good begin to bid up the price.
The higher price results in more producers willing to sell the good. As the price rises, there is a decrease in the quantity demanded of consumers, who will buy fewer units of a good at higher prices than at lower prices. This process of bidding up prices continues until the shortage has been eliminated and that market is back in equilibrium, where quantity demanded equals quantity supplied.

Whenever there is a situation of disequilibrium in a market, the market will function to eliminate the inequality. A surplus of goods will cause the price to fall; a shortage of goods will cause the price to rise. A disequilibrium situation will never last for long in a market because the market functions in such a way that it will eliminate the disequilibrium. This is called the rationing function of prices.

Skill 5.0i **Demonstrate understanding of the role of government and the impact of price ceilings, price floors, and taxes on market outcomes**

Price controls interfere with the market's ability to arrive at an equilibrium price that equates supply and demand. Price controls rob the market of what is called the rationing function of prices—the ability to adjust to equate demand and supply because they are administratively imposed prices above or below the market equilibrium.

A price imposed above the market equilibrium price is called a **price floor**. It represents the highest price that can be charged for the good. The price of the good cannot rise above the price floor. At the imposed floor price, the market cannot equate supply and demand. The higher legally mandated price results in a larger quantity supplied, as sellers are willing to supply larger quantities at higher prices than they are at lower prices. The higher price also means that buyers don't want as many units of output. Buyers are willing and able to buy larger quantities at lower prices than at higher prices.

So the legally imposed floor price results in a situation where quantity supplied is greater than quantity demanded, or there is a surplus of the good and there is no way that the market can function to eliminate the surplus because it can't lower prices to attract more buyers. This has been the situation in agriculture for years.

A **price ceiling** is a legally imposed price below the market equilibrium. Its purpose is to keep prices from rising, as in periods of severe inflation. With a price ceiling, the lower price results in a smaller quantity supplied by sellers. The lower price means an increase in quantity demanded by buyers, who want to buy larger quantities at lower prices than at higher prices. The result is a situation where quantity demanded exceeds quantity supplied, or a shortage. There is no way for the market to eliminate the shortage with buyers bidding up the price for the available quantity. The legally imposed price means that the price can't rise to eliminate the shortage and the shortage will remain as long as the price controls are in effect. When the price ceilings are lifted, prices usually shoot upwards as buyers and sellers try to make up for lost time.

Price controls, whether they are ceilings or floors, are never a good way to deal with economic problems. The market cannot function to remove the distortion in it. They result in misallocations of resources. Price floors, as in agriculture, result in an overallocation of resources to that industry and an overproduction of output that the market cannot eliminate by lowering prices. The resources used in agriculture are not being used elsewhere where they might be more productive. The price ceiling causes the opposite – an underallocation of resources and underproduction of output. Society is not getting enough of the output that it wants and is not having its resources used in the manner it wants them used in. Any interference with the market results in a misallocation.

A tax imposed on goods results in an additional cost to the producer. The higher costs mean the firm produces less output at that level of costs. The result is a decrease, or leftward shift, in the supply curve, causing new market equilibrium with a higher price and smaller quantity. This also results in a misallocation of resources.

Skill 5.0j   Demonstrate understanding of the concept of market failure and public policy

Market failure is a situation where the price system doesn't function properly and results in a misallocation of resources. Even though the market is in equilibrium, the market isn't tabulating all of the costs of production and is causing the wrong quantity of a good to be produced. This is where a role for government is defined in the area of public policy.

Pollution is an example of market failure. Pollution is referred to as a negative externality, a situation where the effects of the market are affecting a non-involved third party. Assume a factory is dumping its wastes in a river. If the factory had to dispose of the wastes in another manner, it would have to pay a price for the disposal. It does not have to pay to dump its wastes in the river; the river is treated as a free input. The pollution is affecting other people in the area. They have dirty water they can't swim or fish in, vegetation is dying, there are odors, etc.

If property rights for the river were assigned, the owner would charge for its use and the factory would have higher production costs. The pollution results from the river being a free input, and the result is overproduction of the factory's product. Another role for government here is to shift the cost onto the producer with a tax or a fine. This raises the costs to the firm and results in a decrease in supply. This corrects somewhat for the overallocation of resources. The government can also outlaw the pollution.

Another form of market failure concerns public goods. These are goods that the market cannot produce or will not produce because it they are not profitable. The best example of a public good is national defense. A public good is indivisible or incapable of being consumed on an individual basis. There is no such thing as buying one unit of national defense. The public good is consumed on a collective basis. No one can be excluded from the public good. The role for government is to provide the public goods that the market can't provide.

Market economies result in some firms acquiring market power. In some cases, called natural monopoly, the cost structure is such that there can be only one firm in the industry, such as the electric company. Monopoly results in higher prices and lower levels of output, which is a misallocation of resources. The role for government here is to regulate the natural monopolist so there is more output at an equitable price. In situations where the firm isn't a natural monopolist but has too much market power, government uses anti-trust laws to protect and promote the competitiveness of the marketplace.

Public policy is also required in the areas of income inequality and macro instability. These are also forms of market failure. The market doesn't result in an equal or equitable distribution of income. Government tries to remedy this situation with income redistribution through programs such as welfare or food stamps and also through the progressive federal income tax system. Since the business cycle results in periods of inflation and unemployment, government uses monetary and/or fiscal policy to promote stability in the macroeconomy. Whenever the price system doesn't function properly and results in inefficiency, there is a role defined for government and public policy.

COMPETENCY 5.1 MICROECONOMICS II

Skill 5.1a **Demonstrate knowledge of types of market structure and the characteristics and behavior of firms in perfect competition, monopoly, oligopoly, and monopolistic competition**

Firms sell their outputs in different output market structures. There are four kinds of market structures in the output market: **perfect competition, monopoly, monopolistic competition, and oligopoly**. Each of these market structures differs in terms of competition. Perfect competition is the most competitive of all market structures. For the most part, perfect competition is a theoretical extreme, most closely approximated by agriculture. Products are homogenous in this market structure. The numerous firms sell a product identical to that sold by all other firms in the industry and have no control over the price. There are a large number of buyers and a large number of sellers, and no one buyer or seller is large enough to affect market price. The price is determined by supply and demand, and the price is a given to the firm. This means the individual firm faces a horizontal or perfectly elastic demand curve. Buyers and sellers have full market information, and there are no barriers to entry. A barrier to entry is anything that makes it difficult for firms to enter or leave the industry.

The opposite of perfect competition is a **monopoly**, a market structure in which only one seller sells a unique product for which there are no substitutes. The firm is the only supplier of the good. The firm can control the price because it is equal to the industry. High barriers to entry allow monopolies to exist and remain the only producer of a certain product. These barriers to entry, such as a very high fixed cost structure, function to keep new firms from entering the industry. Pure monopolies are rare and are illegal in the U.S. economy.

In between the two extremes are the two market structures that all U.S. firms fall into. An **Oligopoly** is a market structure in which there are a few sellers of products that may be either homogeneous, such as steel, or heterogeneous, such as automobiles. There are high barriers to entry, which is why there are only a few firms in each industry. Each firm has some degree of monopoly power but not as much as a monopolist.

The firms of an oligopoly are dependent on one another. Each firm must consider the actions of its rivals when making any decisions. This is referred to as a mutual interdependence in decision making. If Ford offers rebates, Chrysler will also offer rebates to keep its customers. Monopolistic competition is the market structure you see in shopping centers. There are numerous firms, each selling similar products, but not identical, such as brand name shoes or clothing. Products are close substitutes for one another. Each firm has a small market share, since no one firm is large enough to dominate the industry. Barriers to entry are not as high as in oligopoly, which is why there are more firms. It is relatively easy for most firms to enter or leave the industry.

When products are close substitutes for one another, firms engage in advertising, or non-price competition, to try to differentiate their product from their competitors. Advertising and non-price competition occur in monopolistic competition and homogeneous oligopoly.

Skill 5.1b   Demonstrate understanding of factor markets and the determination of income distributions and the returns to factors of production

There are input and output markets in the economy. **Output markets** refer to the market in which goods and services are sold. The **input market** is the market in which factors of production, or resources, are bought and sold. Inputs, or factors of production, fall into four broad categories: land, labor, capital, and entrepreneurs. Each of these four inputs is used in the production of every good and service. When the consumer goes to the local shoe store to buy a pair of shoes, the shoes are the output and the consumer is taking part in the output market. However, the shoe store is a participant in both the input and output market. The sales clerk and store's workers are hiring out their resource of labor in return for a wage rate. They are participating in the input market. In a market-oriented economy, all of these markets function on the basis of supply and demand, whether they are input or output markets. The equilibrium price is determined where the buying decisions of buyers coincide with the selling decision of sellers. This is true whether the market is an input market with a market rate of wage or an output market with a market price of the output. This results in the most efficient allocation of resources.

A firm's production decisions are based on its costs. Every product is produced using inputs or resources. As said above, these are called factors of production and there are four that are used in the production of every good and service. They are labor, land, capital, and entrepreneurs. The firm hires these factors in the input or resource market. The production process refers to the method in which resources are combined to produce a good or service. Each factor of production earns its factor income in the resource market.

Labor earns income, also called wages, capital earns interest, land earns rent, and the entrepreneur earns profit. The labor market illustrates the variation in market structure. There can be a competitive market structure, such as the market for unskilled labor. The laborer is the wage-taker with the wage rate more or less given. Labor markets can also be unionized. When there is a union, the wage rate and benefits are negotiated by the employer and the union representatives.

The factor income for capital is the interest rate, which is determined by the intersection of the demand for loanable funds curve and the supply of loanable funds curve. The supply of loanable funds comes from savings. When people save their money, they are delaying consumption. They must receive a payment to induce them to save. This payment is called the **interest rate**. Lenders pay a price for borrowed funds, which is also the interest rate. The interest rate equates the quantity demanded of loanable fund with the quantity supplied of loanable funds and represents the payment to owners of capital.

Land is a factor that is fixed in supply, so it has a perfectly inelastic supply curve. No matter what the price is, it can't result in an increased supply of land. Rent, then, the factor payment to land, is determined solely by demand.

Profit is the factor income for the entrepreneur. Profit is equal to total revenue minus total cost. It is the entrepreneur's reward for the risk he incurs.

COMPETENCY 5.2 MACROECONOMICS I

Skill 5.2a Demonstrate understanding of gross domestic product (GDP) and its components

Macroeconomics refers to the functioning of the economy on the national level and the functioning of the aggregate units that comprise the national economy. It is concerned with a study of the economy's overall economic performance, or what is called the **Gross Domestic Product,** or **GDP.** The GDP is a monetary measure of the economy's output during a specified time period. Tabulating the economy's output can be measured in two ways, both of which give the same result: the expenditures approach and the incomes approach. Basically, what is spent on the national output by each sector of the economy is equal to what is earned producing the national output by each of the factors of production. The two methods have to be equal.

The macro economy consists of four broad sectors: **consumers, businesses, government** and the **foreign sector**. In the expenditures approach, GDP is determined by the amount of spending in each sector. GDP is equal to the consumption expenditures of consumers plus the investment expenditures of businesses plus spending of all three levels of government plus the net export spending in the foreign sector.

$$GDP = C + I + G + (X-M)$$

The above formula is called the GDP identity. The computation of GDP includes only final goods and services, not the value of intermediate goods. An intermediate good is a good that is used in the production of other goods. It is an input, and its value is included in the price of the final good. If the value of intermediate goods is included, there would be double counting and GDP would be overstated.

What is spent buying the national output has to be equal to what is earned in producing the national output. This basically involves computing the incomes of the four factors with several adjustments being made. Labor earns wages, which is called Compensation of Employees. Land earns Rental Income, and capital earns Interest Income. The first three are pretty straightforward. Since entrepreneurial ability can be in the form of individual effort or corporations, there are two different categories here. The return to the individual entrepreneur is called Proprietor's Income. The return to the corporation is called **Corporate Profit**. Corporations do three things with their profits: they pay the corporate profits tax, they pay dividends and the rest is kept as retained earnings. So these are the three components of corporate profits.

To complete the tabulation of GDP from the incomes approach, we have to adjust for two non-income charges. First are Indirect Business Taxes, such as property taxes and sales taxes. Second is depreciation or the amount of capital that is worn out producing the current term's output. Both Indirect Businesses Taxes and depreciation are subtracted, and the figure remaining is GDP. This figure is identical to the figure computed in the expenditures approach.

Skill 5.2b Demonstrate understanding of how unemployment is measured and its causes and consequences

When the economy is functioning smoothly, the amount of national output produced, or the aggregate supply, is just equal to the amount of national output purchased, or **aggregate demand**. We then have an economy in a period of prosperity without economic instability. But market economies experience the fluctuations of the business cycle, the ups and downs in the level of economic activity. There are four phases: **boom** (period of prosperity), **recession** (a period of declining GDP and rising unemployment), **trough** (the low point of the recession), and **recovery** (a period of lessening unemployment and rising prices). There are no rules pertaining to the duration or severity of any of the phases. The phases result in periods of unemployment and periods of inflation. Inflation results from too much spending in the economy. Buyers want to buy more than sellers can produce and bid up prices for the available output. Unemployment occurs when there is not enough spending in the economy.

Sellers that produce more output than buyers are buying result in a surplus situation. Firms faced with surplus merchandise lower their production levels and layoff workers and there is unemployment. These are situations that require government policy actions.

A deficiency in aggregate spending results in **unemployment**. There is not enough aggregate demand in the economy to cause producers to produce enough output that requires the full labor force to be employed. Unemployment is measured by the unemployment rate, a percentage of the labor force that is unemployed. The labor force consists of people aged sixteen or older who are working or who want to work and are actively seeking employment. It does not include people who cannot work because they are too young or are institutionalized or those who do not want to work, such as the retired population or the parent that stays home with the children. There are certain situations that cause these figures to be inaccurate. First, the figures do not account for underemployment or for people who are working part-time while looking for full-time employment. They just ask if the person is employed; it doesn't matter if it is full-time employment or part-time employment. This practice tends to understate the unemployment rate. The figures also do not account for the discouraged worker. This is the worker who has given up trying to find employment. The figures treat him as being out of the labor force because he is not actively looking for employment. This practice also understates the published unemployment figures.

The last problem is people who give false information. People may claim to be actively seeking employment when they really aren't, just to collect unemployment compensation. This tends to overstate the published figures.

Unemployment tends to strike certain groups in society harder than other groups. Blue-collar workers are usually more likely to be laid off in a recession than are white-collar workers. Teenagers are more likely to be unemployed than adults are. They have fewer job skills and higher quit rates than do adults. The black population usually has higher unemployment rates than the white population. This is due to discrimination, more blacks in blue-collar jobs, and living in areas where employment opportunities are not that good. Unemployment is not just an individual problem.

Skill 5.2c   Demonstrate understanding of inflation and its causes and consequences

The overall macroeconomic instability problems of inflation and unemployment are, for the most part, caused by the inequality of aggregate demand and aggregate supply. They are referred to as the twin evils of capitalism. Inflation results from excess aggregate demand; buyers want to buy a larger quantity of national output at a given price level than sellers can produce and sell.

An economy that is growing too rapidly and has too high a level of spending has inflation, a period of rises in the price level as buyers bid up prices to obtain the given supply of goods and services. Inflation results in a dollar with less purchasing power. When there is, say, five percent inflation, this means the $100 that bought $100 of goods last year buys just $95 of goods this year. Goods and services are more expensive.

The inflation rate is computed from index numbers. The formula is very simple.

$$\text{Price Index} = \frac{\text{Price in any year}}{\text{Price in base year}} \times 100$$

Any year in the series can be selected as the base year, and it is then used to compute the index number for the rest of the years, as given in the above formula.

The index numbers are then used to compute the inflation rate using the formula below:

$$\text{Inflation Rate} = \frac{[\text{This year's index \# - Last year's index \#}]}{\text{Last year's index \#}}$$

Inflation affects different people in different ways. Some people are affected more than others are. People on fixed incomes feel the effects of inflation more than people who have flexible incomes. Social security benefits are an example of a fixed income. The recipients cannot request a raise like working people can. They lose purchasing power during periods of inflation. The value of tangible assets increases during inflation. If you own assets, such as a house, you experience an increase in your net worth because of inflation. On the other hand, the amount of your savings account is fixed and has less purchasing power because of inflation. How inflation affects people depends on the individual position.

Inflation is caused by the economy expanding too quickly. There is excess aggregate demand that is fueling the inflation. This is a situation where the appropriate governmental action is to slow down the economy. The government will implement policies that result in less spending in the economy to end the inflation. These will be **contractionary** monetary and fiscal policy. Contractionary monetary policy will result in the banking system having less money available for loans. Aspects of contractionary monetary policy consist of raising the reserve ratio, raising the discount rate and selling bonds. Contractionary fiscal policy consists of raising taxes and/or decreasing government spending. If there is less money to spend in the economy, it takes the pressure off prices because there is a decrease in aggregate demand, which slows down the economy and stops the rising price level.

COMPETENCY 5.3   MACROECONOMICS II

Skill 5.3a   Demonstrate understanding of national income determination using aggregate demand and supply analysis

Macroeconomics is concerned with a study of the economy's overall economic performance, or what is called the Gross Domestic Product or GDP. The GDP is a monetary measure of the economy's output during a specified time period and is used by all nations to measure and compare national production. Tabulating the economy's output can be measured in two ways, both of which give the same result: the expenditures approach and the incomes approach. Basically, what is spent on the national output by each sector of the economy is equal to what is earned producing the national output by each of the factors of production. The two methods have to be equal.

The macro economy consists of four broad sectors: consumers, businesses, government, and the foreign sector. In the expenditures approach, GDP is determined by the amount of spending in each sector. GDP is equal to the consumption expenditures of consumers plus the investment expenditures of businesses plus spending of all three levels of government plus the net export spending in the foreign sector.

$$GDP = C + I + G + (X-M)$$

The above formula is called the GDP identity. The computation of GDP includes only final goods and services, not the value of intermediate goods. An intermediate good is a good that is used in the production of other goods. It is an input, and its value is included in the price of the final good. If the value of intermediate goods is included, there would be double counting and GDP would be overstated.

This can be shown in terms of the aggregate demand-aggregate supply model. The aggregate demand curve represents the different quantities of national output that the people in the economy are willing and able to purchase at different price levels during a given period of time. The aggregate supply curve represents the different quantities of the national output that producers are willing and able to supply at different price levels during a given period of time. Where the aggregate demand and aggregate supply curves intersect determines the price level in the economy and the equilibrium level of output, income, and employment in the economy. The quantity of output is the monetary value of all final goods and services produced by the economy during a given time period, which is the definition of the Gross Domestic Product, shown in the above GDP identity. The intersection of aggregate demand and aggregate supply shows the level of employment because there is a certain level of employment required to produce that dollar amount of output. A lower level of output requires fewer workers; a higher level of output requires more workers.

The figure derived from computing GDP by summing its components in the GDP identity is the same figure that is derived by taking a graphical approach and looking at the intersection of aggregate demand and aggregate supply. Both are giving the monetary value of the output level.

Skill 5.3 b Demonstrate understanding of fiscal policy and its instruments

Fiscal policy consists of changing the level of taxes and government spending to influence the level of economic activity. Contractionary fiscal policy consists of decreasing government spending and/or raising taxes and is intended to slow down a rapidly expanding economy and to curb inflation. Expansionary fiscal policy consists of lowering taxes and raising government spending to stimulate a sluggish economy and generate higher levels of employment. Changes take place in government revenues and expenditures when fiscal policy is used.

The **federal budget** is a statement showing government expenditures and revenues for the fiscal year. The government's budget does not have to balance. When government expenditures are equal to revenues, the budget is balanced. When government expenditures are greater than revenues, the government has a budget deficit, and when expenditures are less than revenues, the government has a budget surplus. Whenever there is a budget deficit the budget deficit has to be financed. The government can finance its deficit by borrowing or by the process of money creation. When government borrows, it sells bonds and uses the funds acquired by the bond sales to finance its deficit. Money creation refers to increasing the reserves in the banking system. Expansionary fiscal policy—lowering taxes and increasing government spending—puts the budget in a deficit position where government is spending more than it is taking in.

If we add all of the deficits that have occurred over time and subtract from it the figures for all of the surpluses, we have the figure for the national debt.

National debt = Total Surpluses – Total Deficits

The figure for the national debt represents the amount of money that government owes to the holders of U.S. government debt obligations. These are basically Treasury bonds, notes, and bills. Every time you buy a U.S. savings bond, you are helping to finance the national debt because you are loaning money to the government. Every year that the federal government has a budget deficit that is financed by borrowing, the size of the national debt increases and so do the interest payments on the debt. Whenever the government implements contractionary fiscal policy to stimulate the economy and this fiscal policy results in a budget deficit, then the size of the national debt increases.

Skill 5.3c   Demonstrate understanding of the Federal Reserve System and monetary policy

Nations need a smoothly functioning banking system in order to experience economic growth. The **Federal Reserve System** (Fed) provides the framework for the monetary system in the United States. The Fed implements monetary policy through the banking system, and it is a tool used to promote economic stability at the macro level of the economy. There are three components of monetary policy: the **reserve ratio**, the **discount rate**, and **open market operations**. Changes in any of these three components affect the amount of money in the banking system and, thus, the level of spending in the economy.

The reserve ratio refers to the portion of deposits that banks are required to hold as vault cash or on deposit with the Fed. The purpose of this reserve ratio is to give the Fed a way to control the money supply. These funds can't be used for any other purpose. When the Fed changes the reserve ratio, it changes the money creation and lending ability of the banking system. When the Fed wants to expand the money supply, it lowers the reserve ratio, leaving banks with more money to loan. This is one aspect of expansionary monetary policy. When the reserve ratio is increased, this results in banks having less money to make loans with, which is a form of contractionary monetary policy, which leads to a lower level of spending in the economy.

Another way in which monetary policy is implemented is by changing the discount rate. When banks have temporary cash shortages, they can borrow from the Fed. The interest rate on the funds they borrow is called the **discount rate**. Raising and lowering the discount rate is a way of controlling the money supply. Lowering the discount rate encourages banks to borrow from the Fed, instead of restricting their lending to deal with the temporary cash shortage. By encouraging banks to borrow, their lending ability is increased and this results in a higher level of spending in the economy. Lowering the discount rate is a form of expansionary monetary policy. Discouraging bank lending by raising the discount rate, then, is a form of contractionary monetary policy.

The final tool of monetary policy is called open market operations. This consists of the Fed buying or selling government securities with the public or with the banking system. When the Fed sells bonds, it is taking money out of the banking system. The public and the banks pay for the bonds, thus resulting in fewer dollars in the economy and a lower level of spending. The sale of bonds is a form of contractionary monetary policy that leads to a lower level of spending in the economy. The Fed is expanding the money supply when it buys bonds from the public or the banking system because it is paying for those bonds with dollars that enter the income-expenditures stream. The result of the Fed buying bonds is to increase the level of spending in the economy.

Skill 5.3d   Demonstrate understanding of the major concepts in international finance and investment

All nations have records of their international transactions. A nation's international transactions are recorded in the Balance of Payments. The Balance of Payment consists of two major accounts: the Current Account, which gives the figures for the exchange of goods, services and unilateral transfers; and the Capital Account, which provides the figures for capital flows resulting from the exchange of real and financial assets. The Current Account contains the Balance of Trade, which equals a nation's merchandise imports minus its merchandise exports. If the nation's exports are greater than its imports, it has a trade surplus. If its imports are greater than its exports, it has a trade deficit. Adding in the category of exports and imports of services gives the Balance on Goods and Services. Adding unilateral transfers, military expenditures and other miscellaneous items yields the Balance on Current Account. The Capital Accounts consists of strictly financial items in various categories. The last category is Statistical Discrepancies, which is a balancing entry so that the overall Balance of Payments always balances. This has to do with floating exchange rate regimes. It is the trade account that is watched closely today.

The exchange rates of most currencies today are determined in a floating exchange rate regime. In a clean float, supply and demand factors for each currency in terms of another are what determine the equilibrium price or the exchange rate. A clean float is a market functioning without any government interference, purely on the basis of demand and supply. Sometimes nations will intervene in the market to affect the value of their currency vis-à-vis the other currency. This situation is referred to as a managed or dirty float. A government is not required to intervene to maintain a currency value, as they were under a regime of fixed exchange rates. A government that intervenes in the currency market now does so because it wants to, not because it is required to intervene to maintain a certain exchange rate value. For example, if the U.S. government thinks the dollar is depreciating too much against the Canadian dollar, the U.S. government will buy U.S. dollars in the open market and pay for them with Canadian dollars. This increases the demand for U.S. dollars and increases the supply of Canadian dollars. The U.S. dollar appreciates, or increases in value, and the Canadian dollar depreciates, or decreases in value, in response to the government intervention. A stronger U.S. dollar means Canadian goods are cheaper for Americans and American goods are more expensive for Canadians.

In the international economy, capital flows where it earns the highest rate of return, regardless of national borders. If the interest rate is higher in London than it is in New York, dollars will be converted into pounds, which results in dollar depreciation and pound appreciation, as capital flows into London in response to the higher interest rate.

The weaker dollar means that U.S. exports are more attractive to foreigners. It also means that U.S. citizens pay a higher price for imports. Markets today are truly international when it comes to capital flows.

Skill 5.3e Demonstrate understanding of the determinants of long run economic growth

Economic growth can be defined as increases in real output over time. The growth rate is computed as the difference between the growth rate in two periods divided by the growth rate in the first period. Obviously, nations want to see their growth rates increase. Nations experience economic growth when there is an increase in the supply of resources or when they use their existing resources more efficiently. Total output will increase whenever there is an increase in labor and a corresponding increase in productivity. There are many factors that enter into this.

Supply factors are factors that affect the physical capabilities of the economy. They involve the quantity and quality of resources. The first factor is natural resources, and this involves the quantity and quality of natural resources that a country has. Human resources are the second factor, and this involves the quantity and quality of the labor force. The quality of the labor force has to do with productivity or how much output they are producing. Factors affecting productivity have to do with education and training, health, nutrition, government policies in health and safety and environment, and the amount and quality of capital such as equipment and machinery available for the worker to work with. This last one is determined by the level of investment and is called the Stock of Capital, which is the third factor. Here the capital-labor ratio is important because this shows the amount of capital a worker has to work with. If a nation has a growing labor force, it needs growth in its capital stock in order to experience growth. Higher levels of investment lead to higher growth rates. At the same time, the economy needs public investment in order to improve and expand the infrastructure. The last factor is technological progress. Technological progress results in new and better ways of doing things, new and more productive production processes. These supply factors determine the economy's ability to grow.

The other side of the growth rate has to do with the demand side of the economy. There must be sufficient demand in the economy to generate economic growth. Aggregate demand has to grow steadily to absorb the increased output that comes with growth. The economy must have full employment and full production in order to experience growth. Not only must all factors be employed; they must be employed in their most productive capacity.

The above discussion is illustrated as an outward shift of the Production Possibility Curve. This is the curve that shows the maximum amount of output that an economy can achieve given its supply of resource and its technology.

Technological progress and increases in the quality of labor result in economic growth, or outward shifts of the curve.

Skill 5.3f   Demonstrate understanding of current national and international issues and controversies

Current national and international issues and controversies involve employment and trade issues. In today's world, markets are international. Nations are all part of a global economy. No nation exists in isolationism or is totally independent of other nations. **Isolationism** is referred to as autarky or a closed economy. No one nation has all of the resources needed to be totally self-sufficient in everything it produces and consumes. Even a nation with such a well-diversified resource base as the United States has to import such items as coffee, tea, and other staples. The United States is not as dependent on trade as are other nations, but we still need to trade for goods and items that we either can't produce domestically or that we can't produce as cheaply as other nations can.

Membership in a global economy means that what one nation does affects other nations because economies are linked through international trade, commerce, and finance. They all have open economies. International transactions affect the levels of income, employment and prices in each of the trading economies. The relative importance of trade is based on what percentage of Gross Domestic Product trade constitutes. In a country like the United States, trade represents only a few percent of GDP. In other nations, trade may represent more than fifty percent of GDP. For those countries changes in international transactions can cause many economic fluctuations and problems.

Trade barriers are a way economic problems are caused in other countries. Suppose the domestic government is confronted with rising unemployment in the domestic industry due to cheaper foreign imports. Consumers are buying the cheaper foreign import instead of the higher priced domestic good. In order to protect domestic labor, government imposes a tariff, thus raising the price of the more efficiently produced foreign good. The result of the tariff is that consumers buy more of the domestic good and less of the foreign good. The problem is that the foreign good is the product of the foreign nation's labor. A decrease in the demand for the foreign good means foreign producers don't need as much labor, so they lay off workers in the foreign country. The result of the trade barrier is that unemployment has been exported from the domestic country to the foreign country. Treaties such as the North American Free Trade Agreement (NAFTA) are a way of lowering or eliminating trade barriers on a regional basis. As trade barriers are lowered or eliminated, this causes changes in labor and output markets. Some grow; some shrink. These adjustments are taking place now for Canada, the United States, and Mexico. Membership in a global economy adds another dimension to economics, in terms of aiding developing countries and in terms of national policies that are implemented.

COMPETENCY 6.0   SOCIALIZATION

Skill 6.0a   Demonstrate understanding of the role of socialization in society and of positive and negative sanctions in the socialization process

Socialization is the process by which humans learn the expectations their society has for their behavior, in order that they might successfully function within that society.

Socialization takes place primarily in children as they learn and are taught the rules and norms of their culture. Children grow up eating the common foods of a culture and develop a "taste" for these foods, for example. By observing adults and older children, they learn about gender roles, and appropriate ways to interact.

Socialization also takes place among adults who change their environment and are expected to adopt new behaviors. Joining the military, for example, requires a different type of dress and behavior than civilian culture. Taking a new job or going to a new school are other examples of situations where adults must re-socialize.

Two primary ways that socialization occurs are through positive and negative sanctions. Positive sanctions are rewards for appropriate or desirable behavior, and negative sanctions are punishments for inappropriate behavior. Recognition from peers and praise from a parent are examples of positive sanctions that reinforce expected social behaviors. Negative sanctions might include teasing by peers for unusual behavior or punishment by a parent.

Sanctions can be either formal or informal. Public awards and prizes are ways a society formally reinforces positive behaviors. Laws that provide for punishment of specific infractions are formal negative sanctions.

COMPETENCY 6.1 PATTERNS OF SOCIAL ORGANIZATION

Skill 6.1a **Demonstrate knowledge of folkways, mores, laws, beliefs, and values**

Sociologists have identified three main types of norms that cultures define behavioral expectations. Each are associated with different consequences if they are violated. These norms are called folkways, mores, and laws.

Folkways are the informal rules of etiquette and behaviors that a society follows in day-to-day practice. Forming a line at a shop counter or holding a door open for an elderly person are examples of folkways in many societies. Someone who violates a folkway— by pushing to the front of a line, for instance—might be seen as rude, but is not thought to have done anything immoral or illegal.

Mores are stronger than folkways in the consequences they carry for not observing them. Examples of mores might include honesty and integrity. Cheating on a test or lying might violate a social more, and a person who does so may be considered immoral.

Laws are formal adoptions of norms by a society with formal punishment for their violation. Laws are usually based on the mores of a society. The more that it is wrong to kill is codified in a law against murder, for example. Laws are the most formal types of social norm, as their enforcement is specifically provided for. Folkways and mores, on the other hand, are primarily enforced informally by the fellow members of a society.

The folkways, mores, and laws of a society are based on the prevailing beliefs and values of that society. Beliefs and values are similar and interrelated systems.

Beliefs are those things that are thought to be true. Beliefs are often associated with religion, but beliefs can also be based on political or ideological philosophies. "All men are created equal" is an example of an ideological belief.

Values are what a society thinks are right and wrong and are often based on and shaped by beliefs. The value that every member of the society has a right to participate in his government might be considered to be based on the belief that "All mean are created equal," for instance.

Skill 6.1b   Demonstrate understanding of social stratification

Social Stratification is the division of a society into different levels based on factors such as race, religion, economic standing or family heritage. Various types of social stratification may be closely related. For instance, stratification by race may result in people of one race being relegated to a certain economic class as well.

The pioneering sociologist Max Weber theorized that there are three components of social stratification: class, status, and political.

Social class, as Weber defined it, is based on economics and a person's relationship to the economic market. For example, a factory worker is of a different social class than a factory owner. Social status is based on non-economic factors such as honor or religion. Political status is based on the relationships and influence one has in the political domain.

The economic revolutionary Karl Marx identified social stratification as the source of exploitation of one level of society by another and based his theory of revolution and economic reform on this belief.

Mobility between social strata may differ between societies. In some societies, a person may move up or down in social class because of changes in one's personal economic fortunes. Political status can change when prevailing political thought shifts. Some systems of stratification are quite formal, however, as in the former caste system in India. In these systems, lines between strata are more rigid, with employment, marriage, and other social activities tightly defined by one's position.

COMPETENCY 6.2   SOCIAL INSTITUTIONS

Skill 6.2a   Demonstrate understanding of the roles of the following social institutions and of their interactions: the family, education, government, religion, and the economy

Sociologists have identified five different types of institutions around which societies are structured: family, education, government, religion, and economy. These institutions provide a framework for members of a society to learn about and participate in a society and also allow for a society to perpetuate its beliefs and values to succeeding generations.

The **family** is the primary social unit in most societies. It is through the family that children learn the most essential skills for functioning in their society such as language and appropriate forms of interaction. The size of the family unit varies among cultures, with some including grandparents, aunts, uncles, and cousins as part of the basic family, who may all live together. The family is also related to a society's economic institutions, as families often purchase and consume goods as a unit. A family that works to produce its own food and clothing, as was the case historically in many societies, is also a unit of economic production.

Education is an important institution in a society because it allows for the formal passing on of a culture's collected knowledge. The institution of education is connected to the family because that is where a child's earliest education takes place. Educational traditions within a society are also closely associated with economic institutions because some levels of employment require specific academic achievement.

A society's **governmental** institutions often embody its beliefs and values. Laws, for instance, reflect a society's values by enforcing its ideas of right and wrong. The structure of a society's government can reflect that society's ideals about the role of an individual in his society. A democracy may emphasize that an individual's rights are more important than the needs of the larger society, while a socialist governmental institution may place the needs of the whole group first in importance.

Religion is frequently the institution from which spring a society's primary beliefs and values and can be closely related to other social institutions. Many religions have definite teachings on the structure and importance of the family, for instance. In some societies, the head of the government is also the head of the predominant religion, or the government may be operated on religious principles. Historically, formal educational institutions in many societies were primarily religious, and all religions include an educational aspect to teach their beliefs.

A society's **economic** institutions define how an individual can contribute and receive economic reward from his society. Economic institutions are usually closely tied to governmental institutions, each informing and regulating the other. They are linked to family institutions, as workers are often supporting more than one person with their wages. A society's economic institutions might affect its educational goals by creating a demand for certain skills and knowledge.

COMPETENCY 6.3   THE STUDY OF POPULATIONS

Skill 6.3a   Demonstrate knowledge of populations, including the impact on society of changes in population growth and distribution, migration, and immigration

A **population** is a group of people living within a certain geographic area. Populations are usually measured on a regular basis by census, which also measures age, economic, ethnic, and other data. Populations change over time because of many factors, and these changes can have significant impact on cultures.

When a population grows in size, it becomes necessary for it to either expand its geographic boundaries to make room for new people or to increase its density. Population density is simply the number of people in a population divided by the geographic area in which they live. Cultures with a high population density are likely to have different ways of interacting with one another than those with low density, as people live in closer proximity to one another.

As a population grows, its economics need to change. More basic needs are required, and more workers are needed to produce them. If a population's production or purchasing power does not keep pace with its growth, its economy can be adversely affected. The age distribution of a population can impact the economy as well, if the number of young and old people who are not working is disproportionate to those who are.

Growth in some areas may spur migration to other parts of a population's geographic region that are less densely populated. This redistribution of population also places demands on the economy, since infrastructure is needed to connect these new areas to older population centers and land is put to new use.

Populations can grow naturally, when the rate of birth is higher than the rate of death, or by adding new people from other populations through immigration. Immigration is often a source of societal change as people from other cultures bring their institutions and language to a new area. Immigration also impacts a population's educational and economic institutions as immigrants enter the workforce and place their children in schools.

Populations can also decline in number. Two factors are when the death rate exceeds the birth rate or when people migrate to another area. War, famine, disease, and natural disasters can also dramatically reduce a population. The economic problems from population decline can be similar to those from overpopulation because economic demands may be higher than can be met. In extreme cases, a population may decline to the point where it can no longer perpetuate itself and its members and their culture either disappear or are absorbed into another population.

COMPETENCY 6.4   MULTICULTURAL DIVERSITY

Skill 6.4a   Define the concepts of ethnocentrism and cultural relativity

Ethnocentrism and **cultural relativity** are terms used by sociologists to describe two ways of thinking about other cultures in relation to one's own culture. These terms have been expanded to describe two general ways that cultures view themselves and other cultures.

Ethnocentrism is the belief that one's own culture to be the central and usually superior culture and views all other cultures in terms of how they are different. An ethnocentric view usually considers these different practices in other cultures as inferior or even "savage."

Psychologists have suggested that ethnocentrism is a naturally occurring attitude. For the large part, people are most comfortable among other people who share their same upbringing, language, and cultural background and are likely to judge other cultural behaviors as alien or foreign.

In the objective study of other cultures, however, ethnocentrism can skew the way the behaviors of other cultures are interpreted. Current thinking is that the study of another culture should not be made in terms of the observer's own culture, but only in relation to that culture's other attributes. This is called cultural relativity. Cultural relativity aims to remove the biases and prejudices inherent in ethnocentrism to produce a clearer and more complete picture of other cultures.

Skill 6.4b   Demonstrate knowledge of variation in race, ethnicity, and religion

Race is a term most generally used to describe a population of people from a common geographic area that share certain common physical traits. Skin color and facial features have traditionally been used to categorize individuals by race. The term has generated some controversy among sociologists, anthropologists, and biologists as to what, race and racial variation mean. Biologically speaking, a race of people shares a common genetic lineage. Socially, race can be more complicated to define, with many people identifying themselves as part of a racial group that others might not. This self-perception of race, and the perception of race by others, is perhaps more crucial than any genetic variation when trying to understand the social implications of variations in race.

An **ethnic group** is a group of people who identify themselves as having a common social background and set of behaviors and who perpetuate their culture by traditions of marriage within their own group. Ethnic groups will often share a common language and ancestral background and frequently exist within larger populations with which they interact. Ethnicity and race are sometimes interlinked but differ in that many ethnic groups can exist within a population of people thought to be of the same race. Ethnicity is based more on common cultural behaviors and institutions than common physical traits.

Religion can be closely tied to ethnicity, as it is frequently one of the common social institutions shared by an ethnic group. Like ethnicity, religion varies in practices and beliefs even within the large major religions. Some religions and religious sects link their beliefs closely to their ancestry and so are closely linked to the concept of race.

Variations in race, ethnicity, and religion—both real and perceived—are primary ways in which cultures and cultural groups are defined. They are useful in understanding cultures but can also be the source of cultural biases and prejudices.

Eight common religions are practiced today. Interestingly, all of these religions have divisions or smaller sects within them. Not one of them is totally completely unified.

Judaism: the oldest of the eight major religions and was the first to teach and practice the belief in monotheism. Judaism puts an emphasis on learning and law. The Jewish bible consist of the Old Testament, including the Ten Commandments.

Christianity: grew out of Judaism, and spread in the first century CE throughout the Roman Empire, despite persecution. A later schism resulted in the Western (Roman Catholic) and Eastern (Orthodox) parts. Protestant sects developed as part of the Protestant Revolution.

The name "Christian" means one who is a follower of Jesus Christ, who started Christianity. Christians follow his teachings and examples, living by the laws and principles of the Bible.

Islam: founded in Arabia by Mohammed, who preached about God, Allah. Islam spread through trade, travel, and conquest. Followers of Islam, called Muslims, live by the teachings of the Quran, their holy book, and of their prophets.

Hinduism: begun by people called Aryans around 1500 BCE and spread into India. The Aryans blended their culture with the culture of the Dravidians, natives they conquered. Today, it has many sects, promotes worship of hundreds of gods and goddesses and belief in reincarnation. Though forbidden today by law, a prominent feature of Hinduism in the past was a rigid adherence to and practice of the caste system.

Buddhism: developed in India from the teachings of Prince Gautama and spread to most of Asia. Its beliefs opposed the worship of numerous deities, the Hindu caste system and the supernatural. Worshippers must be free of attachment to all things worldly and devote themselves to finding release from life's suffering.

Confucianism: is a Chinese philosophy based on the teachings of the Chinese philosopher Confucius. There is no clergy and no belief in a deity or in life after death. It emphasizes political and moral ideas with respect for authority and ancestors. Rulers were expected to govern according to high moral standards.

Daoism: a native Chinese belief system with veneration for many deities and natural phenomena. It teaches all followers to make the effort to achieve the two goals of happiness and immortality. Practices and rituals include meditation, prayer, magic, reciting scriptures, special diets, breath control, beliefs in geomancy, fortune telling, astrology, and communicating with the spirits of the dead.

Shinto: the native religion of Japan developed from native folk beliefs worshipping spirits and demons in animals, trees, and mountains. According to its mythology, deities created Japan and its people, which resulted in worshipping the emperor as a god. Shinto never had strong doctrines on salvation or life after death.

Skill 6.4c   Demonstrate understanding of the prevalence and consequences of discrimination and prejudice

Prejudice is of pre-judging something or someone without firsthand experience. It often involves making judgments based on stereotypes, or the automatic rejection of a behavior or practice that seems unusual or foreign.

Discrimination takes place when a person or group acts out of prejudice to harm or deny privileges to another. Discrimination takes place between all races and ethnic groups and between men and women at all levels. It can occur between individuals or groups.

In some cases, discrimination based on prejudice is official government policy and is reflected in the laws of a society. The United States has a history of official racial discrimination. The enslavement of black people was legal and common until the end of the Civil War in the mid-nineteenth century. However, once blacks were freed, dominant prejudicial thinking at the time was that they did not possess the intelligence or moral ability to participate equally in society. As a result, various laws were passed that discriminated against blacks' voting rights, property ownership and education. These "Jim Crow" laws also regulated how and where blacks could participate in commerce. Jim Crow laws remained in effect in many areas of the U.S. until the mid 1960s.

These racial prejudices also led to a two-tiered educational system in many parts of the country, with black children segregated into black schools. While these schools were supposed to receive the same support as other schools, in practice they were often poorly maintained, understaffed, and did not always have current teaching materials.

While official discrimination toward anyone on the basis of race is no longer legal in the U.S., it is still common and widespread. Unofficial and de jure discrimination can be equally damaging. In competitive situations such as applying for a job, racial or gender prejudices of the person making the decision of whom to hire may result in one or more candidates being discriminated against. A similar scenario may play out when a landlord is deciding to whom an apartment will be rented. This kind of discrimination, when it occurs systematically has the consequence of relegating groups of people to a lower economic level.

Skill 6.4d   Demonstrate understanding of the concept of pluralism

Cultural pluralism is the simultaneous existence of several cultures and ethnic groups, with each afforded the protection and ability to observe their cultural institutions. It is also sometimes called multiculturalism.

The concept of cultural pluralism calls for mutual respect between ethnic groups and cultures, allowing them to exist together and perpetuate their cultures. As an ideal, multiculturalism aims to provide equal access and status to all cultures and so is often described in terms of civil rights, especially in reference to minority ethnic groups. Multiculturalism calls for official support of these ideals in the form of legislation and encourages this approach in school curricula.

Proponents of **multiculturalism** believe it also leads to the interchange of ideas, art, music, and other cultural features between groups. This interchange, it is thought, furthers the understanding and acceptance of a culturally pluralistic society, reducing prejudice and discrimination.

Multiculturalism can be controversial in some societies, especially those experiencing high rates of immigration. In some of these societies, there are a significant number of people who feel that newcomers should aim to assimilate into the dominant culture as much as possible and that multiculturalism should not receive official support or endorsement. As a result of this counter-movement, some groups have passed official language laws and other regulations intended to encourage or require a certain amount of assimilation by immigrants.

COMPETENCY 6.5   SOCIAL PROBLEMS

Skill 6.5a   **Demonstrate understanding of major contemporary social problems, including causes, consequences, and proposed solutions**

The list of major social problems facing the world is long, with each culture approaching them based on their own values and beliefs. Four broad areas where social problems are affecting the world are the global economy, the environment, education, and health.

Economic—The world is becoming more global in its economy, requiring societies to adapt their production and economic strategies to suit these changing conditions. As some countries are able to capitalize on the emergence of new markets, the gap between poor countries that cannot participate is widening. Economic forces are also attracting immigrants from poorer countries to those with job opportunities, creating social stresses.

International organizations such as the United Nations and the World Bank have programs to assist developing nations with loans and education so they might join the international economy. Many countries are taking steps to regulate immigration.

Environmental—The impact a growing world population is having on the world environment is a subject of great concern and some controversy. Increased demand for food and fuel are creating environmental stresses that may have worldwide consequences.

The use of fossil fuels such as coal and natural gas, for instance, are widely thought to be contributing to the gradual warming of the planet by creating "greenhouse gases." The effects of this warming may include the rising of world sea levels and adverse changes in climate. Because oil and gas are non-renewable resources, continual exploration must take place to identify new sources. This drilling itself impacts the environment and presents potential pollution danger from pipelines and oil spills.

The international community has attempted to place limits on the production of greenhouse gases, but not all developed countries have agreed to these protocols. Many countries have placed limits on emissions from factories and automobiles in an effort to reduce the amount of pollution that enters the atmosphere. Alternative, "clean" energy resources are being researched.

Education—As the world's economy changes, educational needs change to provide a skilled workforce, and a society's ability to educate its people is crucial to participating in this economy. Likewise, educational institutions contribute to the artistic, cultural, and academic advancement of a nation.

Disparity in educational opportunities within and between nations can contribute to social and economic disparities. Failure to keep pace with international demands for certain fields of education can leave a country at a disadvantage.

Health—In most developed countries, the population is living longer and placing a higher demand on health care systems. This in turn places a burden on the larger society as taxes used to support the healthcare system rise, in the case of socialized medicine, or health insurance costs increase, as in private systems. In the U.S., people who are unemployed or otherwise unable to obtain health insurance are sometimes unable to meet the high costs of health care.

Diseases such as AIDS and other viruses are rampant in some parts of the world. Treatments can be difficult to come by either because of their high costs, or lack of organization to distribute them. International aid organizations exist to provide treatment to disease victims and to assist local governments in developing plans to reduce disease transmission.

COMPETENCY 6.6   HOW CULTURES CHANGE

Skill 6.6a   Demonstrate understanding of how cultures change

Innovation is the introduction of new ways of performing work or organizing societies. It can spur drastic changes in a culture. Prior to the innovation of agriculture, for instance, human cultures were largely nomadic and survived by hunting and gathering their food. Agriculture led directly to the development of permanent settlements and a radical change in social organization. Likewise, technological innovations in the Industrial Revolution of the nineteenth century changed the way work was performed and transformed the economic institutions of western cultures. Recent innovations in communications are changing the way cultures interact today.

Cultural diffusion is the movement of cultural ideas or materials between populations independent of the movement of those populations. Cultural diffusion can take place when two populations are close to one another, through direct interaction, or across great distances, through mass media and other routes. American movies are popular all over the world, for instance. Hockey, a traditional Canadian pastime, has become a popular sport in the United States. These are both examples of cultural diffusion.

Adaptation is the process that individuals and societies go through in changing their behavior and organization to cope with social, economic and environmental pressures.

Acculturation is an exchange or adoption of cultural features when two cultures come into regular direct contact. An example of acculturation is the adoption of Christianity and western dress by many Native Americans in the United States.

Assimilation is the process of a minority ethnic group largely adopting the culture of the larger group it exists within. These groups are typically immigrants moving to a new country, as with the European immigrants who traveled to the United States at the beginning of the twentieth century who assimilated to American culture.

Extinction is the complete disappearance of a culture. Extinction can occur suddenly, from disease, famine or war when the people of a culture are completely destroyed, or slowly over time as a culture adapt, acculturate or assimilate to the point where their original features are lost.

Bibliography

Adams, James Truslow. (2006). "The March of Democracy," Vol 1. "The Rise of the Union". New York: Charles Scribner's Sons, Publisher.

Barbini, John & Warshaw, Steven. (2006). "The World Past and Present." New York: Harcourt, Brace, Jovanovich, Publishers.

Berthon, Simon & Robinson, Andrew. (2006. "The Shape of the World." Chicago: Rand McNally, Publisher.

Bice, David A. (2006). "A Panorama of Florida II". (Second Edition). Marceline, Missouri: Walsworth Publishing Co., Inc.

Bram, Leon (Vice-President and Editorial Director). (2006). "Funk and Wagnalls New Encyclopedia." United States of America.

Burns, Edward McNall & Ralph, Philip Lee. (2006. "World Civilizations Their History and Culture" (5th ed.). New York: W.W. Norton & Company, Inc., Publishers.

Dauben, Joseph W. (2006). "The World Book Encyclopedia." Chicago: World Book, Inc. A Scott Fetzer Company, Publisher.

De Blij, H.J. & Muller, Peter O. (2006). "Geography Regions and Concepts" (Sixth Edition). New York: John Wiley & Sons, Inc., Publisher.

Encyclopedia Americana. (2006). Danbury, Connecticut: Grolier Incorporated, Publisher.

Heigh, Christopher (Editor). (2006). "The Cambridge Historical Encyclopedia of Great Britain and Ireland." Cambridge: Cambridge University Press, Publisher.

Hunkins, Francis P. & Armstrong, David G. (2006). "World Geography People and Places." Columbus, Ohio: Charles E. Merrill Publishing Co. A Bell & Howell Company, Publishers.

Jarolimek, John; Anderson, J. Hubert & Durand, Loyal, Jr. (2006). "World Neighbors." New York: Macmillan Publishing Company. London: Collier Macmillan Publishers.

McConnell, Campbell R. (2006). "Economics—Principles, Problems, and Policies" (Tenth Edition). New York: McGraw-Hill Book Company, Publisher.

Millard, Dr. Anne & Vanags, Patricia. (2006). "The Usborne Book of World History." London: Usborne Publishing Ltd., Publisher.

Novosad, Charles (Executive Editor). (2006). "The Nystrom Desk Atlas." Chicago: Nystrom Division of Herff Jones, Inc., Publisher.

Patton, Clyde P.; Rengert, Arlene C.; Saveland, Robert N.; Cooper, Kenneth S. & Cam, Patricia T. (2006). "A World View." Morristown, New Jersey: Silver Burdette Companion, Publisher.

Schwartz, Melvin & O'Connor, John R. (2006). "Exploring A Changing World." New York: Globe Book Company, Publisher.

"The Annals of America: Selected Readings on Great Issues in American History 1620-1968." (2006). United States of America: William Benton, Publisher.

Tindall, George Brown & Shi, David E. (2006). "America—A Narrative History" (Fourth Edition). New York: W.W. Norton & Company, Publisher.

Todd, Lewis Paul & Curti, Merle. (2006). "Rise of the American Nation" (Third Edition). New York: Harcourt, Brace, Jovanovich, Inc., Publishers.

Tyler, Jenny; Watts, Lisa; Bowyer, Carol; Trundle, Roma & Warrender, Annabelle (2006) "The Usbome Book of World Geography." London: Usbome Publishing Ltd., Publisher.

Willson, David H. (2006). "A History of England." Hinsdale, Illinois: The Dryder Press, Inc. Publisher.

Sample Test

1. The continent of North America includes all but which of the following countries: *(Easy) (Skill 1.1a)*

   A) Canada

   B) Mexico

   C) Cuba

   D) Ecuador

2. Which river is the longest in the United States: *(Average) (Skill 1.1a)*

   A . Rio Grande

   B. St. Lawrence

   C. Mississippi

   D. Colorado

3. The Mediterranean type climate is characterized by: *(Average) (Skill 1.1b)*

   A. Hot, dry summers and mild, relatively wet winters

   B. Cool, relatively wet summers and cold winters

   C. Mild summers and winters, with moisture throughout the year

   D. Hot, wet summers and cool, dry winters

4. Which location may be found in Canada? *(Rigorous) (Skill 1.1b)*

   A. 27 N 93 W

   B. 41 N 93 E

   C. 50 N 111 W

   D. 18 N 120 W

5. The climate of Southern Florida is the _____ type. *(Rigorous) (Skill 1.1b)*

   A. Humid subtropical

   B. Marine West Coast

   C. Humid continental

   D. Tropical wet-dry

6. Apartments built out of cliff faces; shared government by adult citizens; absence of aggression toward other groups and perhaps the oldest representative government in the world. These factors characterize the Native American group known as: *(Average) (Skill 1.2b)*

   A. Pueblos

   B. Comanches

   C. Seminoles

   D. Sioux

7. **The Native Americans of the Eastern Woodlands lived on:** *(Rigorous) (Skill 1.2b)*

   A. Buffalo and crops such as corn, beans, and sunflowers

   B. Chiefly farming of squash, beans, and corn

   C. A variety of game (deer, bear, moose) and crops (squash, pumpkins, corn)

   D. Wolves, foxes, polar bears, walruses, and fish

8. **One tribe of Indians formed a representative government referred to as the _____ Confederacy.** *(Average) (Skill 1.2b)*

   A. Cherokee

   B. Seminole

   C. Wampanoag

   D. Iroquois

9. **Columbus first reached Western Hemisphere lands in what is now:** *(Easy) (Skill 1.3a)*

   A. Florida

   B. Bermuda

   C. Puerto Rico

   D. Bahamas

10. **Which one of the following is not a reason why Europeans came to the New World?** *(Average) (Skill 1.3c)*

    A. To find resources in order to increase wealth

    B. To establish trade

    C. To increase a ruler's power and importance

    D. To spread Christianity

11. **After 1783, the largest "land owner" in the Americas was:** *(Average) (Skill 1.3c)*

    A. Britain

    B. Spain

    C. France

    D. United States

12. **During the early years of colonization in New France, what commodity was the livelihood for many people, both in New France and in France?** *(Average) (Skill 1.3c)*

    A. Wampum

    B. Fish

    C. Gold

    D. Fur

13. The Middle Colonies of the Americas were: *(Average) (Skill 1.3d)*

A. Maryland, Virginia, North Carolina

B. New York, New Jersey, Pennsylvania, Delaware

C. Rhode Island, Connecticut, New York, New Jersey

D. Vermont and New Hampshire

14. The year 1619 was a memorable year for the colony of Virginia. Three important events occurred resulting in lasting effects on US history. Which one of the following was not one of the events? *(Rigorous) (Skill 1.3d)*

A. Twenty African slaves arrived.

B. The London Company granted the colony a charter making it independent.

C. The colonists were given the right by the London Company to govern themselves through representative government in the Virginia House of Burgesses

D. The London Company sent to the colony 60 women who were quickly married, establishing families and stability in the colony.

15. Slavery arose in the Southern Colonies partly as a perceived economical way to: *(Average) (Skill 1.3d)*

A. Increase the owner's wealth through human beings used as a source of exchange

B. Cultivate large plantations of cotton, tobacco, rice, indigo, and other crops

C. Provide Africans with humanitarian aid, such as health care, Christianity, and literacy

D. Keep ships' holds full of cargo on two out of three legs of the "triangular trade" voyage

16. France decided in 1777 to help the American colonies in their war against Britain. This decision was based on: *(Average) (Skill 1.4a)*

A. The naval victory of John Paul Jones over the British ship Serapis

B. The survival of the terrible winter at Valley Forge

C. The success of colonial guerilla fighters in the South

D. The defeat of the British at Saratoga

17. **"These are the times that try men's souls" were words penned by:** *(Average) (Skill 1.4b)*

    A. Thomas Jefferson

    B. Samuel Adams

    C. Benjamin Franklin

    D. Thomas Paine

18. **Which concept is not embodied as a right in the First Amendment to the U.S. Constitution?** *(Average) (Skill 1.4d)*

    A. Peaceable assembly

    B. Protection against unreasonable search and seizure

    C. Freedom of speech

    D. Petition for redress of grievances

19. **The Bill of Rights was mostly written by:** *(Rigorous) (Skill 1.4b)*

    A. Thomas Jefferson

    B. James Madison

    C. George Washington

    D. Alexander Hamilton

20. **The area of the United States was effectively doubled through purchase of the Louisiana Territory under which President?** *(Average) (Skill 1.5b)*

    A. John Adams

    B. Thomas Jefferson

    C. James Madison

    D. James Monroe

21. **Which one of the following was not a reason why the United States went to war with Great Britain in 1812?** *(Rigorous) (Skill 1.5b)*

    A. Resentment by Spain over the sale, exploration, and settlement of the Louisiana Territory

    B. The westward movement of farmers because of the need for more land

    C. Canadian fur traders were agitating the northwestern Indians to fight American expansion

    D. Britain continued to seize American ships on the high seas and force American seamen to serve aboard British ships

22. **Under the brand new Constitution, the most urgent of the many problems facing the new federal government was that of:** *(Average) (Skill 1.5c)*

    A. Maintaining a strong army and navy

    B. Establishing a strong foreign policy

    C. Raising money to pay salaries and war debts

    D. Setting up courts, passing federal laws, and providing for law enforcement officers

23.. **What was a major source of contention between American settlers in Texas and the Mexican government in the 1830s and 1840s?** *(Rigorous) (Skill 1.6a)*

    A. The Americans wished to retain slavery, which had been outlawed in Mexico

    B. The Americans had agreed to learn Spanish and become Roman Catholic, but failed to do so

    C. The Americans retained ties to the United States, and Santa Ana feared the power of the U.S.

    D. All of the above were contentious issues between American settlers and the Mexican government

24. **The belief that the United States should control all of North America was called:** *(Easy) (Skill 1.6b)*

    A. Westward Expansion

    B. Pan Americanism

    C. Manifest Destiny

    D. Nationalism

25. **The "Trail of Tears" relates to:** *(Average) (Skill 1.6b)*

    A. The removal of the Cherokees from their native lands to Oklahoma Territory

    B. The revolt and subsequent migration of the Massachusetts Pilgrims under pressure from the Iroquois

    C. The journey of the Nez Perce under Chief Joseph before their capture by the U.S. Army

    D. The 1973 standoff between federal marshals and Native Americans at Wounded Knee, S.D.

26. **Abraham Lincoln won re-election in 1864 chiefly through:** *(Rigorous) (Skill 1.7a)*

    A. His overwhelming force of personality and appeal to all segments of the electorate

    B. His reputation as the Great Emancipator

    C. The fact that people felt sorry for him because of his difficulties

    D. His shrewd political manipulation, clever use of patronage jobs, and wide-appeal selection of cabinet members

27. **According to the Constitution any amendment must be ratified by _____ of the states to become a part of the Constitution:** *(Easy) (Skill 1.7a)*

    A. Three-fourths

    B. Two-thirds

    C. Three-fifths

    D. Five-sixths

28. **Which President helped postpone a civil war by supporting the Compromise of 1850?** *(Rigorous) (Skill 1.7c)*

    A. Henry Clay

    B. Franklin Pierce

    C. Millard Fillmore

    D. James Buchanan

29. **Of the following groups of states, which were slave states?** *(Rigorous) (Skill 1.7a)*

    A. Delaware, Maryland, Missouri

    B. California, Texas, Florida

    C. Kansas, Missouri, Kentucky

    D. Virginia, West Virginia, Indiana

30. **In the American Civil War, who was the first commander of the forces of the United States?** *(Average) (Skill 1.7d)*

    A. Gen. Ulysses S. Grant

    B. Gen. Robert E. Lee

    C. Gen. Irwin McDowell

    D. Gen. George Meade

31. **Which of the following most closely characterizes the Supreme Court's decision in <u>Brown v. Board of Education?</u> *(Rigorous) (Skill 1.7e)***

    A. Chief Justice Warren had to cast the deciding vote in a sharply divided Court

    B. The decision was rendered along sectional lines, with northerners voting for integration and southerners voting for continued segregation

    C. The decision was 7-2, with dissenting justices not even preparing a written dissent

    D. Chief Justice Warren was able to persuade the Court to render a unanimous decision

32. **What event sparked a great migration of people from all over the world to California? *(Easy) (Skill 1.8a)***

    A. The birth of Labor Unions

    B. California statehood

    C. The invention of the automobile

    D. The gold rush

33. **The American labor union movement started gaining new momentum: *(Average) (Skill 1.8b)***

    A. During the building of the railroads

    B. After 1865 with the growth of cities

    C. With the rise of industrial giants such as Carnegie and Vanderbilt

    D. During the war years of 1861-1865

34. **Which of the following was NOT a factor in the United States' entry into World War I? *(Average) (Skill 1.9b)***

    A. The closeness of the Presidential election of 1916

    B. The German threat to sink all allied ships, including merchant ships

    C. The desire to preserve democracy as practiced in Britain and France as compared to the totalitarianism of Germany

    D. The sinking of the <u>Lusitania</u> and the <u>Sussex</u>

35. **Concerning the present political map of Africa, which statement most closely applies?** *(Rigorous) (Skill 1.9b)*

   A. The modern states reflect an effort to establish political units based on ethnic groupings

   B. The international community allowed for a period of elasticity with regard to boundaries, so that a condition of relative equilibrium could develop

   C. Africans were given the task of delineating the modern states, using whatever criteria they chose

   D. The modern states reflect imposed boundaries, without regard to ethnic groupings or other indigenous considerations

36. **President Truman suspended**

Gen. Douglas MacArthur from command of Allied forces in Korea because of: *(Average) (Skill 1.10a)*

   A. MacArthur's inability to make any progress against North Korea

   B. MacArthur's criticism of Truman, claiming that the President would not allow him to pursue aggressive tactics against the Communists

   C. The harsh treatment MacArthur exhibited toward the Japanese after World War II

   D. The ability of the U.S. Navy to continue the conflict without the presence of MacArthur

37. **The international organization established to work for world peace at the end of the First World War is the:** *(Average) (Skill 1.10a)*

   A. League of Nations

   B. United Federation of Nations

   C. United Nations

   D. United World League

38. In issuing an ultimatum for Soviet ships not to enter Cuban waters in October, 1962, President John F. Kennedy, as part of his decision, used the provisions of the: *(Rigorous) (Skill 1.11a, 1.10b)*

A. Monroe Doctrine

B. Declaration of the Rights of Man

C. Geneva Convention

D. Truman Doctrine

39. The economic practices under President Ronald Reagan ("Reaganomics") were characterized by: *(Rigorous) (Skill 1.11b)*

A. Low inflation, high unemployment, high interest rates, high national debt

B. High inflation, low unemployment, low interest rates, low national debt

C. Low inflation, high unemployment, low interest rates, depletion of national debt

D. High inflation, low unemployment, high interest rates, low national debt

40. Which of the following developments is most closely associated with the Neolithic Age? *(Average) (Skill 2.1a)*

A. Human use of fire

B. First use of stone chipping instruments

C. Domestication of plants

D. Development of metallurgical alloys

41. The Tigris-Euphrates Valley was the site of which two primary ancient civilizations? *(Average) (Skill 2.1b)*

A. Babylonian and Assyrian

B. Sumerian and Egyptian

C. Hyksos and Hurrian

D. Persian and Phoenician

S. The politics of classical Athens is best described by which of the following? *(Average) (Skill 2.1c)*

A. Limited democracy, including both slaves and free men

B. One man dictatorial rule

C. Universal democracy among free owners of property

D. Oligarchy with a few families controlling all decisions

43. The first ancient civilization to introduce and practice monotheism was: *(Easy) (Skill 2.1c)*

    A. Sumerians

    B. Hebrews

    C. Phoenicians

    D. Minoans

44. The principle of zero in mathematics is the discovery of the ancient civilization found in: *(Average) (Skill 2.1c)*

    A. Egypt

    B. Persia

    C. India

    D. Babylon

45. An early cultural group was so skillful in navigating on the seas that they were able to sail at night guided by stars. They were the: *(Average) (Skill 2.1c)*

    A. Greeks

    B. Persians

    C. Minoans

    D. Phoenicians

46. A historian might compare the governmental systems of the Roman Empire and the twentieth century United States with regard to which of the following commonalities? *(Average) (Skill 2.1c)*

    A. Totalitarianism

    B. Technological development

    C. Constitutional similarities

    D. Federalism

47. Development of a solar calendar, invention of the decimal system, and contributions to the development of geometry and astronomy are all the legacy of: *(Average) (Skill 2.1c)*

    A. The Babylonians

    B. The Persians

    C. The Sumerians

    D. The Egyptians

48. **Which ancient civilization is credited with being the first to develop irrigation techniques through the use of canals, dikes, and devices for raising water?** *(Average) (Skill 2.1c)*

   A. The Sumerians

   B. The Egyptians

   C. The Babylonians

   D. The Akkadians

49. **Chinese civilization is generally credited with the original development of which of the following sets of technologies:** *(Average) (Skill 2.1c, 2.1d)*

   A. Movable type and mass production of goods

   B. Wool processing and domestication of the horse

   C. Paper and gunpowder manufacture

   D. Leather processing and modern timekeeping

50. **The Age of Exploration begun in the 1400s was led by:** *(Average) (Skill 2.2a)*

   A. The Portuguese

   B. The Spanish

   C. The English

   D. The Dutch

51. **The painter of the Sistine Ceiling was:** *(Easy) (Skill 2.2a)*

   A. Raphael

   B. Michelangelo

   C. Leonardo da Vinci

   D. Titian

52. **The ideas and innovations of the period of the Renaissance were spread throughout Europe mainly because of:** *(Average) (Skill 2.2a)*

   A. Extensive exploration

   B. Craft workers and their guilds

   C. The invention of the printing press

   D. Increased travel and trade

53. **The first explorer to reach India by sailing around the southern tip of Africa was:** *(Average) (Skill 2.2a)*

   A. Amerigo Vespucci

   B. Vasco da Gama

   C. Ferdinand Magellan

   D. John Cabot

54. Luther issued strong objection to all but which of the following practices of the 15th century Roman Catholic Church? *(Average) (Skill 2.2a)*

A. The sacrament of baptism

B. Absolution of sins through the intermediation of a priest and through ceremony

C. The sale of indulgences, whereby the buyer may purchase purgation of sins

D. Imposed church control over the individual conscience

55. Who is considered to be the most important figure in the spread of Protestantism across Switzerland? *(Average) (Skill 2.2a)*

A. Calvin

B. Zwingli

C. Munzer

D. Leyden

56. Bartholomeu Diaz, in seeking a route around the tip of Africa, was forced to turn back. Nevertheless, the cape he discovered near the southern tip of Africa became known as: *(Average) (Skill 2.2a)*

A. Cape Horn

B. Cabo Bojador

C. Cape of Good Hope

D. Cape Hatteras

57. India's greatest ruler is considered to be: *(Easy) (Skill 2.2a)*

A. Akbar

B. Asoka

C. Babur

D. Jahan

58. China's last imperial ruling dynasty was one of its most stable and successful and, under its rule, Chinese culture made an outstanding impression on Western nations. This dynasty was: *(Average) (Skill 2.2a)*

A. Min

B. Manchu

C. Han

D. Chou

59. Extensive exports of gold and copper; elaborate court and constitution; trade links on both the Atlantic and Indian Oceans; use of heavy stone architecture; these most closely characterize the civilization of: *(Average) (Skill 2.2a)*

A. Mwene Mutapa

B. Chichen Itza

C. Great Zimbabwe

D. Muscat and Oman

60. In Western Europe, the achievements of the Renaissance were unsurpassed and made these countries outstanding cultural centers on the continent. All of the following were accomplishments except: *(Average) (Skill 2.2)*

A. Invention of the printing press

B. A rekindling of interest in the learning of classical Greece & Rome

C. Growth in literature, philosophy, and art

D. Better military tactics

61. The years 1793-94 in France, characterized by numerous trials and executions of supposed enemies of the Revolutionary Convention, were known as the: *(Rigorous) (Skill 2.2b)*

A. Reign of Terror

B. Dark Ages

C. French Inquisition

D. Glorious Revolution

62. Colonial expansion by Western European powers in the 18th and 19th centuries was due primarily to: *(Average) (Skill 2.2b)*

A. Building and opening the Suez Canal

B. The Industrial Revolution

C. Marked improvements in transportation

D. Complete independence of all the Americas and loss of European domination and influence

63. **Great Britain became the center of technological and industrial development during the nineteenth century chiefly on the basis of:** *(Average) (Skill 2.2b)*

   A. Central location relative to the population centers of Europe

   B. Colonial conquests and military victories over European powers

   C. Reliance on exterior sources of financing

   D. Resources of coal and production of steel

64. **It can be reasonably stated that the change in the United States from primarily an agricultural country into an industrial power was due to all of the following except:** *(Average) (Skill 2.2b)*

   A. Tariffs on foreign imports

   B. Millions of hardworking immigrants

   C. An increase in technological developments

   D. The change from steam to electricity for powering industrial machinery

65. **In the <u>first</u> aggression of World War II outside the Orient, identify the aggressor nation and the nation which was invaded**: *(Rigorous) (Skill 2.3a)*

   A. Germany; Sudetenland

   B. Italy; Abyssinia

   C. Germany; Poland

   D. Italy; Yugoslavia

66. **Of all the major causes of both World Wars I and II, the most significant one is considered to be:** *(Average) (Skill 2.3a)*

   A. Extreme nationalism

   B. Military buildup and aggression

   C. Political unrest

   D. Agreements and alliances

67. **Which of the following most closely characterizes the geopolitical events of the USSR in 1991-92:** *(Rigorous) (Skill 2.3b)*

   A. The USSR established greater military and economic control over the fifteen Soviet republics

   B. The Baltic States (Estonia, Latvia, Lithuania) declared independence, while the remainder of the USSR remained intact.

   C. Fourteen of fifteen Soviet republics declared some degree of autonomy; the USSR was officially dissolved; the Supreme Soviet rescinded the Soviet Treaty of 1922

   D. All fifteen Soviet republics simultaneously declared immediate and full independence from the USSR, with no provisions for a transitional form of government

68. **Which of the following is most reasonably studied under the social sciences?** *(Easy) (Skill 3.0a)*

   A. Political science

   B. Geometry

   C. Physics

   D. Grammar

69. **Who wrote the book *"The Social Contract"?*** *(Average) (Skill 3.0b)*

   A. Jean-Jacques Rousseau

   B. Thomas Hobbes

   C. Niccolo Machiavelli

   D. William Shakespeare

70. **Public administration, such as public officials in the areas of budgets, accounting, distribution of public funds, and personnel management would be a part of the field of:** *(Easy) (Skill 3.0b)*

   A. Anthropology

   B. Sociology

   C. Law and Taxation

   D. Political Science and Economics

71. **A political scientist might use all of the following except:** *(Average) (Skill 3.0b)*

   A. An investigation of government documents

   B. A geological timeline

   C. Voting patterns

   D. Polling data

72. **Political science is primarily concerned with _____.**
(Rigorous) (Skill 3.0b)

A. Elections

B. Economic Systems

C. Boundaries

D. Public Policy

73. **Which one of the following is not a function or responsibility of the US political parties?**
(Average) (Skill 3.0d, 3.1d)

A. Conducting elections or the voting process

B. Obtaining funds needed for election campaigns

C. Choosing candidates to run for public office

D. Making voters aware of issues and other public affairs information

74. **In the United States, checks and balances refers to:**
(Average) (Skill 3.1a)

A. The ability of each branch of government to "check" or limit the actions of others

B. Balance of payments

C. International law

D. The federal deficit

75. **In the Constitutional system of checks and balances, a primary "check" which accrues to the President is the power of:**
(Average) (Skill 3.1a)

A. Executive privilege

B. Approval of judges nominated by the Senate

C. Veto of Congressional legislation

D. Approval of judged nominated by the House of Representatives

76. **In the United States, if a person is accused of a crime and cannot afford a lawyer:**
(Average) (Skill 3.1a)

A. The person cannot be tried

B. A court will appoint a lawyer, but the person must pay the lawyer back when able to do so

C. The person must be tried without legal representation

D. A court will appoint a lawyer for the person free of charge

77. The term that best describes how the Supreme Court can block laws that may be unconstitutional from being enacted is: *(Average) (Skill 3.1a)*

   A. Jurisprudence

   B. Judicial Review

   C. Exclusionary Rule

   D. Right of Petition

78. Only one amendment has been repealed. Which amendment was repealed? *(Average) (Skill 3.1a)*

   A. 21st

   B. 18th

   C. 17th

   D. 22nd

79. An amendment is: *(Average) (Skill 3.1a)*

   A. A change or addition to the United States Constitution

   B. The right of a state to secede from the Union

   C. To add a state to the Union

   D. The right of the Supreme Court to check actions of Congress and the President

80. Collectively, the first ten Amendments to the Constitution are known as the: *(Easy) (Skill 3.1a)*

   A. Articles of Confederation

   B. Mayflower Compact

   C. Bill of Rights

   D. Declaration of the Rights of Man

81. Why is the system of government in the United States referred to as a federal system? *(Rigorous) (Skill 3.1b)*

   A. There are different levels of government

   B. There is one central authority in which all governmental power is vested

   C. The national government cannot operate except with the consent of the governed

   D. Elections are held at stated periodic times, rather than as called by the head of the government

82. **Which branch is responsible for carrying out the laws of the country?** *(Average) (Skill 3.1b)*

A. Judicial

B. Executive

C. Legislative

D. Supreme Court

83. **Which branch established the power of the Supreme Court?** *(Average) (Skill 3.1b)*

A. Judicial

B. Executive

C. Legislative

D. House of Representatives

84. **The _____ branch of government is made up of House of Representatives and the Senate.** *(Average) (Skill 3.1b)*

A. Judicial

B. Executive

C. Legislative

D. Supreme Court

85. **What were the first political parties in the United States?** *(Rigorous) (Skill 3.1c)*

A. Democrats and Whigs

B. Whigs and Federalists

C. Federalists and Democratic-Republicans

D. Democrats and Republicans

86. **In the United States government, the power of coining money is:** *(Rigorous) (Skill 3.1d)*

A. Implied or suggested

B. Concurrent or shared

C. Delegated or expressed

D. Reserved

87. **Which of the following are NOT local governments in the United States?** *(Easy) (Skill 3.1e)*

A. Cities

B. Townships

C. School boards

D. All of these are forms of local government

88. How are major party candidates chosen to run for President in the United States? *(Average) (Skill 3.1e)*

A. Caucuses of major party officeholders meet to select a state's choice for the party, and the candidate selected by the most states becomes the nominee

B. Potential Presidential nominees seek pledges from each state party's chair and co-chair, and the candidate with the most pledges becomes the nominee

C. Nationwide primaries are held by each party, to select delegates to a national nominating convention

D. Each state party decides how to select delegates to a nominating convention; these selection processes may be caucuses, primaries, or any other method chosen by the state party

89. _____ is the effort to create, by dictatorial means, a viable national society in which competing interests were to be adjusted to each other by being entirely subordinated to the service of the state although it will tolerate some private ownership of the means of production. *(Average) (Skill 3.2a)*

A. Dictatorship

B. Parliamentary System

C. Anarchism

D. Fascism

90. Which of the following is not generally considered to be a discipline within the social sciences? *(Easy) (Domain IV VI)*

A. Geometry

B. Anthropology

C. Geography

D. Sociology

91. The end to hunting, gathering, and fishing of prehistoric people was due to: *(Rigorous)* *(Skill 4.0d)*

A. Domestication of animals

B. Building crude huts and houses

C. Development of agriculture

D. Organized government in villages

92. Relief maps can be depicted in different ways. One way is the use of: *(Easy)* *(Skill 4.1a)*

A. Great Circle Route

B. Opisometer

C. Meridians

D. Contour Lines

93. Maps as a rule are: *(Average)* *(Skill 4.1a)*

A. All subject to some sort of distortion

B. Always entirely accurate

C. Not very useful in political science studies

D. Difficult usually to understand

94. Meridians, or lines of longitude, not only help in pinpointing locations, but are also used for: *(Rigorous)* *(Skill 4.1b)*

A. Measuring distance form the Poles

B. Determining direction of ocean currents

C. Determining the time around the world

D. Measuring distance to the Equator

95. The study of "spatial relationships and interaction" would be used by people in the field of:
(Easy) *(Skill 4.1c)*

A. Political Science

B. Anthropology

C. Geography

D. Sociology

96. Physical geographer would be concerned with which of the following groups of terms? *(Average)* *(Skill 4.2a)*

A. Landform, biome, precipitation

B. Scarcity, goods, services

C. Nation, state, administrative subdivision

D. Cause and effect, innovation, Exploration

97. A result of the Industrial Revolution was the increase in mobility. Which of the following is NOT a result of increased mobility? *(Average)* *(Skill 4.3a)*

A. A rapid diffusion of knowledge and ideas

B. Wide-scale immigration to industrialized countries

C. Cultures clashed and cultures melded

D. Rise in religious tolerance

98. What landforms rise to an elevation of about 500 to 2000 feet and are found everywhere on earth including Antarctica, where they are covered by ice. *(Easy)* *(Skill 4.4a)*

A. Valleys

B. Mountains

C. Hills

D. Canyons

99. How many oceans cover the earth? *(Easy)* *(Skill 4.4a)*
A. 3

B. 4

C. 5

D. 6

100. Which of the following is not a river? *(Easy)* *(Skill 4.4a)*

A. Yangtze

B. Rio Grande

C. Artic

D. Ganges

101. This subject is a study of how a society allocates its scarce resources to satisfy what are basically unlimited and competing wants. *(Easy)* *(Skill 5.0a)*

A. Geometry

B. Statistics

C. Cultural Geography

D. Economics

102. Economics is best described as: *(Average)* *(Skill 5.0b)*

A. The study of how money is used in different societies

B. The study of how different political systems produce goods and services

C. The study of how human beings use limited resources to supply their necessities and wants

D. The study of how human beings have developed trading practices through the years

103. In order to achieve efficiency, two conditions must be fulfilled: *(Average) (Skill 5.0c)*

A. Low unemployment and low inflation

B. Full-employment and full-production

C. Full-employment and stable monetary supply

D. Access to resources and full-production

104. Capitalism and communism are alike in that they are both: *(Easy) (Skill 5.0d)*

A. Organic systems

B. Political systems

C. Centrally planned systems

D. Economic systems

105. Which best describes the economic system of the United States? *(Average) (Skill 5.0d)*

A. Most decisions are the result of open markets, with little or no government modification or regulation

B. Most decisions are made by the government, but there is some input by open market forces

C. Most decisions are made by open market factors, with important regulatory functions and other market modifications the result of government activity

D. There is joint decision making by government and private forces, with final decisions resting with the government

106. In a command economy: *(Average) (Skill 5.0d)*

A. The open market determines how much of a good is produced and distributed

B. The government determines how much of a good is produced and distributed

C. Individuals produce and consume a specified good as commanded by their needs

D. The open market determines the demand for a good, and then the government produces and distributes the good

107. One method of trade restriction used by some nations is: *(Easy) (Skill 5.0e)*

A. Limited treaties

B. Floating exchange rate

C. Bill of exchange

D. Import quotas

108. If the price of Good G increases, what is likely to happen with regard to comparable Good H? *(Rigorous) (Skill 5.0g)*

A. The demand for Good G will stay the same

B. The demand for Good G will increase

C. The demand for Good H will increase

D. The demand for Good H will decrease

109. What is a major difference between monopolistic competition and perfect competition? *(Rigorous) (Skill 5.1a)*

A. Perfect competition has many consumers and suppliers, while monopolistic competition does not

B. Perfect competition provides identical products, while monopolistic competition provides similar but not identical products

C. Entry to perfect competition is difficult, while entry to monopolistic competition is relatively easy

D. Monopolistic competition has many consumers and suppliers, while perfect competition does not

110. Of the following, the best example of an oligopoly in the United States is: *(Average) (Skill 5.1a)*

A. Automobile industry

B. Electric power provision

C. Telephone service

D. Clothing manufacturing

111. Inflation is the result of the economy _____? *(Average) (Skill 5.2c)*

A. Expanding too slowly

B. Remaining stable

C. Expanding too quickly

D. Expanding in conjunction with the unemployment rate

112. The _____ is a monetary measure of the economy's output during a specified time period and is used by all nations to measure and compare national production. *(Average) (Skill 5.2a)*

A. Float Rate

B. Gross Domestic Product (GDP)

C. Unemployment Rate

D. National Output

113. An economist might engage in which of the following activities? *(Rigorous) (Domain V, Skill 5.3c, 5.3d)*

A. An observation of the historical effects of a nation's banking practices

B. The application of a statistical test to a series of data

C. Introduction of an experimental factor into a specified population to measure the effect of the factor

D. An economist might engage in all of these

114. The advancement of understanding in dealing with human beings has led to a number of interdisciplinary areas. Which of the following interdisciplinary studies would NOT be considered under the social sciences? *(Rigorous) (Skill 6.0a)*

A. Molecular biophysics

B. Peace studies

C. African-American studies

D. Cartographic information Systems

115. As a sociologist, you would be most likely to observe: *(Average) (Skill 6.0a)*

    A. The effects of an earthquake on farmland

    B. The behavior of rats in sensory-deprivation experiments

    C. The change over time in Babylonian obelisk styles

    D. The behavior of human beings in television focus groups

116. Which of the following is NOT considered to be an economic need: *(Average) (Skill 6.2a)*

    A. Food

    B. Transportation

    C. Shelter

    D. Clothing

117. A teacher and a group of students take a field trip to an Indian mound to examine artifacts. This activity most closely fits under which branch of the social sciences? *(Average) (Skill 6.2a)*

    A. Anthropology

    B. Sociology

    C. Psychology

    D. Political Science

118. An economist investigates the spending patterns of low-income individuals. Which of the following would yield the most pertinent information? *(Average) (Skill 6.3a)*

    A. Prime lending rates of neighborhood banks

    B. The federal discount rate

    C. City-wide wholesale distribution figures

    D. Census data and retail sales figures

119. Populations are usually measured by all of the following EXCEPT: *(Easy) (Skill 6.3a)*

    A. Height

    B. Economic data

    C. Ethnicity

    D. Age

120. Describe the naturally occurring attitude that people, for the most part are most comfortable with others like themselves. *(Average) (Skill 6.4a)*

    A. Pluralism

    B. Discrimination

    C. Ethnocentrism

    D. Racial Bias

121. The native metaphysical outlook of Japan, usually characterized as a religion, is: *(Rigorous) (Skill 6.4b)*

   A. Tao

   B. Shinto

   C. Nichiren Shoju

   D. Shaolin

122. The world religion which includes a caste system is: *(Easy) (Skill 6.4b)*

   A. Buddhism

   B. Hinduism

   C. Sikhism

   D. Jainism

123. _____ toward anyone on the basis of race is no longer legal in the U.S., however it is still common and widespread. *(Easy) (Skill 6.4c)*

   A. Sexual discrimination

   B. Racial discrimination

   C. Age discrimination

   D. Religious discrimination

124. What concept calls for mutual respect between ethnic groups and cultures, allowing them to exist together and perpetuate their cultures? *(Average) (Skill 6.4d)*

   A. Syllogism

   B. Conformance

   C. Discrimination

   D. Cultural pluralism

125. Which of the following is not one of the four broad areas where social problems are affecting? *(Average) (Skill 6.5a)*

   A. Desertification

   B. The environment

   C. Education

   D. Health

Answer Key

1.	D	34.	A	67.	C	100.	C
2.	C	35.	B	68.	A	101.	D
3	A	36.	B	69.	A	102.	C
4.	C	37.	A	70.	D	103.	B
5.	A	38.	A	71.	B	104.	D
6.	A	39.	A	72.	D	105.	C
7.	C	40.	C	73.	A	106.	B
8.	D	41.	A	74.	A	107.	D
9.	D	42.	C	75.	C	108.	C
10.	B	43.	B	76.	D	109.	B
11.	B	44.	C	77.	B	110.	A
12.	D	45.	D	78.	B	111.	C
13.	B	46.	D	79.	A	112.	B
14.	B	47.	D	80.	C	113.	D
15.	B	48.	A	81.	A	114.	A
16.	D	49.	C	82.	B	115.	D
17.	D	50.	A	83.	A	116.	B
18.	B	51.	B	84.	C	117.	A
19.	B	52.	C	85.	C	118.	D
20.	B	53.	B	86.	C	119.	A
21.	A	54.	A	87.	D	120.	C
22.	C	55.	A	88.	D	121.	B
23.	D	56.	C	89.	D	122.	B
24.	C	57.	A	90.	A	123.	B
25.	A	58.	B	91.	C	124.	D
26.	D	59.	C	92.	D	125.	A
27.	A	60.	D	93.	A		
28.	C	61.	A	94.	C		
29.	A	62.	B	95.	C		
30.	C	63.	D	96.	A		
31.	D	64.	A	97.	D		
32.	D	65.	B	98.	C		
33.	B	66.	A	99.	B		

Rigor Table

	Easy %20	Average Rigor %40	Rigorous %40
Question #	1, 9 24, 27, 32, 43, 51, 57, 68, 70, 80, 87, 90, 92, 95, 98, 99, 100, 101, 104, 107, 199 122, 123	2, 3, 6, 8, 10, 11, 12, 13, 15, 16, 17, 18, 20 ,22, 25, 30, 33, 34, 36, 37, 40, 41, 42, 44, 45, 46, 47 ,48, 49, 50, 52, 53, 54, 55, 56, 58, 59, 60, 62, 63, 64, 66, 69, 71, 73, 74, 75, 76, 77, 78, 79, 82, 83, 84, 88, 89, 93, 96. 97, 102, 103, 105, 106, 110, 111, 112, 115, 116, 117, 118, 120, 124, 125	4, 5, 7, 14, 19, 21, 23, 26, 28, 29, 31, 35, 38, 39, 61, 65, 67, 72, 81, 85, 86, 91, 94, 108, 109, 113, 114, 121

Rationales with Sample Questions

1. The continent of North America includes all but which of the following countries: *(Easy) (Skill 1.1a)*

A) Canada

B) Mexico

C) Cuba

D) Ecuador

Answer: D. Ecuador

North America consists of (A) Canada; the United States of America; (B) Mexico; the Caribbean island nations of the West Indies including (C) Cuba, Jamaica, Haiti and the Dominican Republic; and the "land bridge" of Middle America, including Panama, Honduras, El Salvador, Nicaragua, Guatemala, and others. (D) Ecuador is a part of South America.

2. Which river is the longest in the United States: *(Average) (Skill 1.1a)*

A . Rio Grande

B. St. Lawrence

C. Mississippi

D. Colorado

Answer: C. Mississippi

The (C) Mississippi River is the longest river in the United States, extending from the U.S.-Canada border to the Gulf of Mexico, draining the Ohio River from the east and the Missouri River to the west. It is 2,320 miles long. Other significant rivers are the (B) St. Lawrence at 744 miles, which connects Lake Erie to the Atlantic Ocean, and the (A) Rio Grande, (1885 miles) forming most of the border between Mexico and the United States. The (D) Colorado River is in the southwestern United States and northwestern Mexico approximately 1,450 miles long.

3. The Mediterranean type climate is characterized by:

A. Hot, dry summers and mild, relatively wet winters

B. Cool, relatively wet summers and cold winters

C. Mild summers and winters, with moisture throughout the year

D. Hot, wet summers and cool, dry winters

Answer: A Hot, dry summers and mild, relatively wet winters

Westerly winds and nearby bodies of water create stable weather patterns along the west coasts of several continents and along the coast of the Mediterranean Sea, after which this type of climate is named. Temperatures rarely fall below the freezing point and have a mean between 70 and 80 degrees F in the summer. Stable conditions make for little rain during the summer months.

4. Which location may be found in Canada?

A. 27 N 93 W

B. 41 N 93 E

C. 50 N 111 W

D. 18 N 120 W

Answer: C 50 N 111 W

(A) 27 North latitude, 93 West longitude is located in the Gulf of Mexico. (B) 41 N 93 E is located in northwest China. (D) 18 N 120 W is in the Pacific Ocean, off the coast of Mexico. (C) 50 N 111 W is located near the town of Medicine Hat in the province of Alberta, in Canada.

5. **The climate of Southern Florida is the** _____ **type.** *(Rigorous) (Skill 1.1b)*

   A. Humid subtropical

   B. Marine West Coast

   C. Humid continental

   D. Tropical wet-dry

Answer: A Humid subtropical

The (B) marine west coast climate is found on the western coasts of continents. Florida is on the eastern side of North America. The (C) humid continental climate is found over large land masses, such as Europe and the American Midwest, not along coasts such as where Florida is situated. The (D) tropical wet-dry climate occurs within about 15 degrees of the equator, in the tropics. Florida is sub-tropical. Florida is in a (A) humid subtropical climate, which extends along the East Coast of the United States to about Maryland, and along the gulf coast to northeastern Texas.

6. **Apartments built out of cliff faces; shared government by adult citizens; absence of aggression toward other groups; and perhaps the oldest representative government in the world. These factors characterize the Native American group known as:** *(Average) (Skill 1.2b)*

   A. Pueblos

   B. Comanches

   C. Seminoles

   D. Sioux

Answer: A Pueblos

The famous (A) **Pueblo** in houses that bear their tribe's name. They wore clothes made of wool and woven cotton, farmed crops in the middle of desert land, created exquisite pottery and Kachina dolls, and had one of the most complex religions of all the tribes. They are perhaps best known for the challenging vista-based villages that they constructed from the sheer faces of cliffs and rocks and for their **adobes**, mud-brick buildings that housed their living and meeting quarters. The Pueblos chose their own chiefs. This was perhaps one of the oldest representative governments in the world.

7. **The Native Americans of the Eastern Woodlands lived on:** *(Rigorous)* *(Skill 1.2b)*

    A. Buffalo and crops such as corn, beans, and sunflowers

    B. Chiefly farming of squash, beans, and corn

    C. A variety of game (deer, bear, moose) and crops (squash, pumpkins, corn)

    D. Wolves, foxes, polar bears, walruses, and fish

Answer: C A variety of game (deer, bear, moose) and crops (squash, pumpkins, corn)

(A) Buffalo live in the plains habitat found in Western and Midwestern North America. (B) & (C) While the Native Americans did farm the "Three Sisters" of corn, squash and beans, the woods of the East also meant that a variety of game (deer, bear, moose) were widely available for them to hunt. (D) However, wolves, foxes, walruses, polar bears, and fish are found together only within the Arctic Circle, not in eastern woodlands.

8. **One tribe of Indians formed a representative government referred to as the _____ Confederacy.** *(Average)* *(Skill 1.2b)*

    A. Cherokee

    B. Seminole

    C. Wampanoag

    D. Iroquois

Answer: D Iroquois

Five of the (D) Iroquois tribes formed a Confederacy, a shared form of government. Living in the Southeast were the (B) Seminoles and Creeks, a huge collection of people who are best known, however, for their struggle against Spanish and English settlers, especially led by the great Osceola. The (A) Cherokee also lived in the Southeast. They were one of the most advanced tribes, living in domed houses and wearing deerskin and rabbit fur. Accomplished hunters, farmers, and fishermen, the Cherokee were known the continent over for their intricate and beautiful basketry and clay pottery. They also played a game called lacrosse, which survives to this day in countries around the world. The (C) Wampanoag tribe was found mainly in Massachusetts.

9. Columbus first reached Western Hemisphere lands in what is now: *(Easy) (Skill 1.3a)*

   A. Florida

   B. Bermuda

   C. Puerto Rico

   D. Bahamas

Answer: D. Bahamas

Christopher Columbus (1451-1506) visited the Bahamas in 1492 and Puerto Rico in 1493 but never landed on either (B) Bermuda or (A) Florida.

10. Which one of the following is not a reason why Europeans came to the New World? *(Average) (Skill 1.3c)*

   A. To find resources in order to increase wealth

   B. To establish trade

   C. To increase a ruler's power and importance

   D. To spread Christianity

Answer: B. To establish trade

The Europeans came to the New World for a number of reasons; often they came to find new natural resources to extract for manufacturing. The Portuguese, Spanish and English were sent over to increase the monarch's power and spread influences such as religion (Christianity) and culture. Therefore, the only reason given that Europeans didn't come to the New World was to establish trade.

11. **After 1783, the largest "land owner" in the Americas was:**
   (Average) (Skill 1.3c)

   A. Britain

   B. Spain

   C. France

   D. United States

Answer: B. Spain

Despite the emergence of the (D) United States as an independent nation in control of the colonies over the (A) British, and the (C) French control of Canada, (B) Spain remained the largest "land owner" in the Americas controlling much of the southwest as well as much of Central and South America.

12. **During the early years of colonization in New France, what commodity was the livelihood for many people, both in New France and in France? (Average) (Skill 1.3c)**

   A. Wampum

   B. Fish

   C. Gold

   D. Fur

Answer: D Fur

French fur traders made friends with the friendly tribes of Indians, spending the winters with them getting the furs needed for trade. Most of the wealth for New France and its "Mother Country" was from the (D) fur trade, which provided a livelihood for many, many people. Manufacturers and workmen back in France, ship-owners and merchants, as well as the fur traders and their Indian allies all benefited.

13. The Middle Colonies of the Americas were: *(Average) (Skill 1.3d)*

A. Maryland, Virginia, North Carolina

B. New York, New Jersey, Pennsylvania, Delaware

C. Rhode Island, Connecticut, New York, New Jersey

D. Vermont and New Hampshire

Answer: B New York, New Jersey, Pennsylvania, Delaware

(A), (C) & (D). Maryland, Virginia, and North Carolina were Southern colonies, Rhode Island, Connecticut and New Hampshire were New England colonies and Vermont was not one of the 13 original colonies.

14. The year 1619 was a memorable year for the colony of Virginia. Three important events occurred resulting in lasting effects on US history. Which one of the following was not one of the events? *(Rigorous) (Skill 1.3d)*

A. Twenty African slaves arrived.

B. The London Company granted the colony a charter making it independent.

C. The colonists were given the right by the London Company to govern themselves through representative government in the Virginia House of Burgesses

D. The London Company sent to the colony 60 women who were quickly married, establishing families and stability in the colony.

Answer: B. The London Company granted the colony a charter making it independent.

In the year 1619, the Southern colony of Virginia had an eventful year including the first arrival of twenty African slaves, the right to self-governance through representative government in the Virginia House of Burgesses (their own legislative body), and the arrival of sixty women sent to marry and establish families in the colony. The London Company did not, however, grant the colony a charter in 1619.

15. **Slavery arose in the Southern Colonies partly as a perceived economical way to:** *(Average) (Skill 1.3d)*

    A. Increase the owner's wealth through human beings used as a source of exchange

    B. Cultivate large plantations of cotton, tobacco, rice, indigo, and other crops

    C. Provide Africans with humanitarian aid, such as health care, Christianity, and literacy

    D. Keep ships' holds full of cargo on two out of three legs of the "triangular trade" voyage

Answer: B Cultivate large plantations of cotton, tobacco, rice, indigo, and other crops.

The Southern states, with their smaller populations, were heavily dependent on slave labor as a means of being able to fulfill their role and remain competitive in the greater U.S. economy. (A) When slaves arrived in the South, the vast majority would become permanent fixtures on plantations, intended for work, not as a source of exchange. (C) While some slave owners instructed their slaves in Christianity, provided health care or some level of education, such attention was not their primary reason for owning slaves – a cheap and ready labor force was. (D) Whether or not ships' holds were full on two or three legs of the triangular journey was not the concern of Southerners as the final purchasers of slaves. Such details would have concerned the slave traders.

16. **France decided in 1777 to help the American colonies in their war against Britain. This decision was based on:**
(Average) (Skill 1.4a)

    A. The naval victory of John Paul Jones over the British ship Serapis"

    B. The survival of the terrible winter at Valley Forge

    C. The success of colonial guerilla fighters in the South

    D. The defeat of the British at Saratoga

Answer: D The defeat of the British at Saratoga

The turning point in the Americans' favor occurred in 1777 with the (D) American victory at Saratoga. This victory decided for the French to align themselves with the Americans against the British. With the aid of French warships blocking the entrance to Chesapeake Bay, British General Cornwallis trapped at Yorktown, Virginia, surrendered in 1781 and the war was over.

17. **"These are the times that try men's souls" were words penned by:**
(Average) (Skill 1.4b)

    A. Thomas Jefferson

    B. Samuel Adams

    C. Benjamin Franklin

    D. Thomas Paine

Answer: D. Thomas Paine

Thomas Paine (1737-1809), the great American political theorist, wrote "these are the times that try men's souls" in his 16 part pamphlet *The Crisis*. Paine's authoring of Common Sense was an important step in spreading information to the American colonists about their need for independence from Great Britain. (A) Thomas Jefferson and (C) Benjamin Franklin were some of the authors of the Declaration of Independence.

18. Which concept is not embodied as a right in the First Amendment to the U.S. Constitution? *(Average) (Skill 1.4d)*

    A. Peaceable assembly

    B. Protection against unreasonable search and seizure

    C. Freedom of speech

    D. Petition for redress of grievances

Answer: B

B.   Protection against unreasonable search and seizure

The first amendment to the Constitution reads, "Congress shall make no law respecting an establishment of religion, or prohibiting the free exercise thereof; or abridging the (C) freedom of speech, or of the press; or the right of the people (A) peaceably to assemble, and to (D) petition the government for a redress of grievances." The protection against (B) unreasonable search and seizure is a constitutional right, however it is found in the fourth amendment, not the first.

19. The Bill of Rights was mostly written by: *(Rigorous) (Skill 1.4b)*

    A. Thomas Jefferson

    B. James Madison

    C. George Washington

    D. Alexander Hamilton

Answer: B. James Madison

The Bill of Rights, along with the majority of the Constitution, was mostly written by James Madison. Thomas Jefferson wrote the Declaration of Independence. Washington and Hamilton were present at the Constitutional Convention of 1787 in Philadelphia and they were advocates of federalism or increasing the power of the federal government.

20. **The area of the United States was effectively doubled through purchase of the Louisiana Territory under which President?** *(Average) (Skill 1.5b)*

    A. John Adams

    B. Thomas Jefferson

    C. James Madison

    D. James Monroe

Answer: B Thomas Jefferson

(B) The Louisiana Purchase, an acquisition of territory from France, in 1803 occurred under Thomas Jefferson. (A) John Adams (1735-1826) was president from 1797-1801, before the purchase, and (C) James Madison, (1751-1836) after the Purchase (1809-1817). (D) James Monroe (1758-1831) was actually a signatory on the Purchase but also did not become President until 1817.

21. **Which one of the following was not a reason why the United States went to war with Great Britain in 1812?** *(Rigorous) (Skill 1.5b)*

    A. Resentment by Spain over the sale, exploration, and settlement of the Louisiana Territory

    B. The westward movement of farmers because of the need for more land

    C. Canadian fur traders were agitating the northwestern Indians to fight American expansion

    D. Britain continued to seize American ships on the high seas and force American seamen to serve aboard British ships

Answer: A. Resentment by Spain over the sale, exploration, and settlement of the Louisiana Territory

The United States went to war with Great Britain in 1812 for a number of reasons including the expansion of settlers westward and the need for more land, the agitation of Indians by Canadian fur traders in eastern Canada, and the continued seizures of American ships by the British on the high seas. Therefore, the only statement given that was not a reason for the War of 1812 was the resentment by Spain over the sale, exploration and settlement of the Louisiana Territory. In fact, the Spanish continually held more hostility towards the British than towards the United States. The War of 1812 is often considered to be the second American war for independence.

22. **Under the brand new Constitution, the most urgent of the many problems facing the new federal government was that of:** *(Average)* *(Skill 1.5c)*

   A. Maintaining a strong army
      and navy

   B. Establishing a strong
      foreign policy

   C. Raising money to pay
      salaries and war debts

   D. Setting up courts, passing federal laws, and providing for law
      enforcement officers

Answer: C. Raising money to pay salaries and war debts

Maintaining strong military forces, establishment of a strong foreign policy, and setting up a justice system were important problems facing the United States under the newly ratified Constitution. However, the most important and pressing issue was how to raise money to pay salaries and war debts from the Revolutionary War. Alexander Hamilton (1755-1804) then Secretary of the Treasury proposed increased tariffs and taxes on products such as liquor. This money would be used to pay off war debts and to pay for internal programs. Hamilton also proposed the idea of a National Bank.

23. What was a major source of contention between American settlers in Texas and the Mexican government in the 1830s and 1840s? *(Rigorous)* *(Skill 1.6a)*

   A. The Americans wished to retain slavery, which had been outlawed in Mexico

   B. The Americans had agreed to learn Spanish and become Roman Catholic, but failed to do so

   C. The Americans retained ties to the United States, and Santa Anna feared the power of the U.S.

   D. All of the above were contentious issues between American settlers and the Mexican government

Answer: D All of the above were contentious issues between American settlers and the Mexican government.

The American settlers simply were not willing to assimilate into Mexican society but maintained their prior commitments to slave holding, the English language, Protestantism, and the United States government.

24. The belief that the United States should control all of North America was called: *(Easy)* *(Skill 1.6b)*

   A. Westward Expansion

   B. Pan Americanism

   C. Manifest Destiny

   D. Nationalism

Answer: C. Manifest Destiny

The belief that the United States should control all of North America was called (B) Manifest Destiny. This idea fueled much of the violence and aggression towards those already occupying the lands such as the Native Americans. Manifest Destiny was certainly driven by sentiments of (D) nationalism and gave rise to (A) westward expansion.

25. The "Trail of Tears" relates to: *(Average) (Skill 1.6b)*

A. The removal of the Cherokees from their native lands to Oklahoma Territory

B. The revolt and subsequent migration of the Massachusetts Pilgrims under pressure from the Iroquois

C. The journey of the Nez Perce under Chief Joseph before their capture by the U.S. Army

D. The 1973 standoff between federal marshals and Native Americans at Wounded Knee, S.D.

Answer: A The removal of the Cherokees from their native lands to Oklahoma Territory (1838-39).

(B) There never was a revolt and migration of the Massachusetts Pilgrims under pressure from the Iroquois. (C) The 1877 journey of the Nez Perce under Chief Joseph was a strategically impressive attempt to retreat from an oncoming U.S. Army into Canada. (D) The 1973 Wounded Knee incident was the occupation of the town of Wounded Knee, South Dakota, by the American Indian Movement to call attention to issues of Native American civil rights. Their action led to a 71-day standoff with U.S. Marshals, which was eventually resolved peacefully.

26. Abraham Lincoln won re-election in 1864 chiefly through: *(Rigorous)* *(Skill 1.7a)*

    A. His overwhelming force of personality and appeal to all segments of the electorate

    B. His reputation as the Great Emancipator

    C. The fact that people felt sorry for him because of his difficulties

    D. His shrewd political manipulation, clever use of patronage jobs, and wide-appeal selection of cabinet members

Answer: D His shrewd political manipulation, clever use of patronage jobs, and wide-appeal selection of cabinet members

President Lincoln in his own lifetime was a hugely divisive figure, even in the North. He did not appeal to all segments of the electorate, his reputation as the Great Emancipator really developed after the war, and few felt sorry for him for his personal and political difficulties. Rather, Lincoln constantly maneuvered to maintain the advantage, using all the powers of the Presidency to win re-election despite his own unpopularity.

27. According to the Constitution any amendment must be ratified by _____ of the states to become a part of the Constitution: *(Easy) (Skill 1.7a)*

    A. Three-fourths

    B. Two-thirds

    C. Three-fifths

    D. Five-sixths

Answer: A Three-fourths

Article V of the Constitution spells out how the document may be ratified. First, an amendment must be proposed by a two-thirds majority of both houses of Congress. Then it is passed to the state legislatures. If (A) three-fourths of the states pass the amendment, it is adopted as part of the constitution. The constitution currently has 27 amendments.

28. Which President helped postpone a civil war by supporting the Compromise of 1850?

A. Henry Clay

B. Franklin Pierce

C. Millard Fillmore

D. James Buchanan

Answer: C

C.   Millard Fillmore

Millard Fillmore was the President who signed the Compromise of 1850. Henry Clay was instrumental in negotiating the compromise but was never President. Presidents Franklin Pierce and James Buchanan were later involved in the 1854 Kansas-Nebraska Act, which undid this Compromise.

29. Of the following groups of states, which were slave states? *(Rigorous)* *(Skill 1.7a)*

A. Delaware, Maryland, Missouri

B. California, Texas, Florida

C. Kansas, Missouri, Kentucky

D. Virginia, West Virginia, Indiana

Answer: A   Delaware, Maryland, Missouri.

(A) Delaware, Maryland and Missouri were all slave states at the time of the Civil War. (B) Florida and Texas were slave states, while California was a free state. (C) Kansas, Missouri, and Kentucky were all originally slave territories, and Missouri and Kentucky were admitted to the Union as such. However, Kansas' petition to join the union in 1858 was blocked in order to preserve the balance between slave and free states. Kansas was admitted as a free state in 1861. (D) Indiana was a free state.

30. **In the American Civil War, who was the first commander of the forces of the United States?**

    A. Gen. Ulysses S. Grant

    B. Gen. Robert E. Lee

    C. Gen. Irwin McDowell

    D. Gen. George Meade

Answer: C

C.   General Irwin McDowell

(A) Gen. Ulysses S. Grant was the final commander of the Union army during the Civil War. (B) Gen. Robert E. Lee was the commander of the Confederate army. (D) Gen. George Meade was the Union commander at the Battle of Gettysburg in 1863.

31. **Which of the following most closely characterizes the Supreme Court's decision in <u>Brown v. Board of Education?</u>**

    A. Chief Justice Warren had to cast the deciding vote in a sharply divided Court

    B. The decision was rendered along sectional lines, with northerners voting for integration and southerners voting for continued segregation

    C. The decision was 7-2, with dissenting justices not even preparing a written dissent

    D. Chief Justice Warren was able to persuade the Court to render a unanimous decision

Answer: D Chief Justice Warren was able to persuade the Court to render a unanimous decision. The Supreme Court decided 9-0 against segregated educational facilities.

32. **What event sparked a great migration of people from all over the world to California?** *(Easy) (Skill 1.8a)*

    A. The birth of Labor Unions

    B. California statehood

    C. The invention of the automobile

    D. The gold rush

Answer: D The gold rush

The discovery of gold in California created a lust for gold that quickly brought immigrants from the eastern United States and many parts of the world. To be sure, there were struggles and conflicts, as well as the rise of nativism. Yet this vast migration of people from all parts of the world began the process that has created California's uniquely diverse culture.

33. **The American labor union movement started gaining new momentum:** *(Average) (Skill 1.8b)*

    A. During the building of the railroads

    B. After 1865 with the growth of cities

    C. With the rise of industrial giants such as Carnegie and Vanderbilt

    D. During the war years of 1861-1865

Answer: B After 1865 with the growth of cities

The American Labor Union movement had been around since the late eighteenth and early nineteenth centuries. The Labor movement began to first experience persecution by employers in the early 1800s. The American Labor Movement remained relatively ineffective until after the Civil War. In 1866, the National Labor Union was formed, pushing such issues as the eight-hour workday and new policies of immigration. This gave rise to the Knights of Labor and eventually the American Federation of Labor (AFL) in the 1890s and the Industrial Workers of the World (1905). Therefore, it was the (B) period following the Civil War that empowered the labor movement in terms of numbers, militancy, and effectiveness.

34. **Which of the following was NOT a factor in the United States' entry into World War I?** *(Average) (Skill 1.9b)*

    A. The closeness of the Presidential Election of 1916

    B. The German threat to sink all allied ships, including merchant ships

    C. The desire to preserve democracy as practiced in Britain and France as compared to the totalitarianism of Germany

    D. The sinking of the <u>Lusitania</u> and the <u>Sussex</u>

Answer: A The closeness of the Presidential Election of 1916

President Woodrow Wilson was narrowly re-elected in 1916, but this was not a factor in the United State's entry into World War I. All the other answers were indeed factors.

35. **Concerning the present political map of Africa, which statement most closely applies?** *(Rigorous) (Skill 1.9b)*

    A. The modern states reflect an effort to establish political units based on ethnic groupings

    B. The international community allowed for a period of elasticity with regard to boundaries, so that a condition of relative equilibrium could develop

    C. Africans were given the task of delineating the modern states, using whatever criteria they chose

    D. The modern states reflect imposed boundaries, without regard to ethnic groupings or other indigenous considerations

Answer: B The international community allowed for a period of elasticity with regard to boundaries, so that a condition of relative equilibrium could develop.

Many African states were originally colonized by other countries and had borders drawn up (D) without regard to ethnic groupings or other indigenous considerations. With the relatively recent independence of colonial states, border disputes have arisen, but no complete delineation has taken place along ethnic or any other grounds, as described in answers (A) and (C). The international community has been involved individually and jointly, as members of the United Nations, providing diplomacy and refugee aid in some of the recent border disputes, as in that between Eritrea and Ethiopia, but has largely taken the stance that these issues should be worked out between the nations involved.

36. **President Truman suspended Gen. Douglas MacArthur from command of Allied forces in Korea because of:** *(Average) (Skill 1.10a)*

    A. MacArthur's inability to make any progress against North Korea

    B. MacArthur's criticism of Truman, claiming that the President would not allow him to pursue aggressive tactics against the Communists

    C. The harsh treatment MacArthur exhibited toward the Japanese after World War II

    D. The ability of the U.S. Navy to continue the conflict without the presence of MacArthur

Answer: B MacArthur's criticism of Truman, claiming that the President would not allow him to pursue aggressive tactics against the Communists

Truman suspended MacArthur because of clear insubordination: MacArthur had publicly criticized the President, his Commander in Chief, and had openly undermined his policy of negotiating a settlement with the Communists. MacArthur was a general of proven effectiveness; so, (A) cannot be correct. MacArthur was actually rather lenient to the Japanese after World War II, and he was a general, not an admiral of the Navy.

37. **The international organization established to work for world peace at the end of the First World War is the:** *(Average) (Skill 1.10a)*

    A. League of Nations

    B. United Federation of Nations

    C. United Nations

    D. United World League

Answer: A League of Nations

The international organization established to work for world peace at the end of the Second World War was the (C) United Nations. From the ashes of the failed League of Nations (A), established following World War I, the United Nations continues to be a major player in world affairs today.

38. **In issuing an ultimatum for Soviet ships not to enter Cuban waters in October 1962, President John F. Kennedy, as part of his decision, used the provisions of the:** *(Rigorous) (Skill 1.11a, 1.10b)*

    A. Monroe Doctrine

    B. Declaration of the Rights of Man

    C. Geneva Convention

    D. Truman Doctrine

Answer: A

A.   Monroe Doctrine

(A) The Monroe Doctrine, initially formulated by Presidents James Monroe (1758-1831) and John Quincy Adams (1767-1848) and later enhanced by President Theodore Roosevelt (1858-1915), opposed European colonization or interference in the Americas, perceived any such attempts as a threat to US security, and promised U.S. neutrality in conflicts between European powers and/or their already established colonies. (B) The Declaration of the Rights of Man, widely adapted in future declarations about international human rights, was formulated in France during the French Revolution and adopted by the National Constituent Assembly in 1789 as the premise of any future French constitution. (C) The Geneva Conventions (1864, 1929, and 1949, with later additions and amendments) established humanitarian and ethical standards for conduct during times of war and has been widely accepted as international law. (D) The Truman Doctrine (1947), formulated by President Harry Truman (1884-1972), provided for the support of Greece and Turkey as a means of protecting them from Soviet influence. It thereby began the Cold War (1947-1991), a period in which the U.S. sought to contain the Soviet Union by limiting its influence in other countries.

39. The economic practices under President Ronald Reagan ("Reaganomics") were characterized by: *(Rigorous) (Skill 1.11b)*

   A. Low inflation, high unemployment, high interest rates, high national debt

   B. High inflation, low unemployment, low interest rates, low national debt

   C. Low inflation, high unemployment, low interest rates, depletion of national debt

   D. High inflation, low unemployment, high interest rates, low national debt

Answer: A

A.   High inflation, low unemployment, high interest rates, high national debt.

President Reagan was an advocate of "trickle-down" economics, which espoused cutting social programs to save money and decrease the tax burden on the wealthy and corporations, believing that largesse for the top tier of the population would eventually trickle down to the lower income strata of workers. Ronald Reagan was a strong supporter of de-regulation, insisting that private sector corporations could do oversight and self-policing better, which was contradicted by the high level of corporate abuse for safety, health and environmental concerns. Although the Reagan Era (Reaganomics) was a period of great wealth and financial boom times, the unprecedented level of military spending increased the national debt to its highest levels to date during peacetime.

40. Which of the following developments is most closely associated with the Neolithic Age? *(Average) (Skill 2.1)*

   A. Human use of fire

   B. First use of stone chipping instruments

   C. Domestication of plants

   D. Development of metallurgical alloys

Answer: C

C.   Domestication of plants

The Neolithic or "New Stone" Age, as its name implies, is characterized by the use of stone implements, but the first use of stone chipping instruments appears in the Paleolithic period. Human use of fire may go back still farther and certainly predates the Neolithic era. The Neolithic period is distinguished by the domestication of plants. The development of metallurgical alloys marks the conclusion of the Neolithic Age.

41. **The Tigris-Euphrates Valley was the site of which two primary ancient civilizations?** *(Average) (Skill 2.1b)*

    A. Babylonian and Assyrian

    B. Sumerian and Egyptian

    C. Hyksos and Hurrian

    D. Persian and Phoenician

Answer: A

A.   Babylonian and Assyrian

(B) While the Sumerians also lived in the southern Tigris-Euphrates valley, Egyptian civilization grew up in the Nile delta (3500BC-30 BC). (C) The Hyksos were an Asiatic people who controlled the Nile Delta during the 15th and 16th Dynasties (1674BC-1548BC). The Hurrians (2500BC-1000BC) came from the Khabur River Valley in northern Mesopotamia, where they spread out to establish various small kingdoms in the region. (D) The Persians (648BC- early 19th century AD) had a succession of empires based in the area known as modern-day Iran. The Phoenicians were a seafaring people who dominated the Mediterranean during the first century BC.

42. **The politics of classical Athens is best described by which of the following?** *(Average) (Skill 2.1c)*

    A. Limited democracy, including both slaves and free men

    B. One man dictatorial rule

    C. Universal democracy among free owners of property

    D. Oligarchy with a few families controlling all decisions

Answer: C

C.   Universal democracy among free owners of property.

A citizen of Athens was a free man who owned property. Each had an equal vote in the governance of the city. All the other answers are thereby excluded by definition.

43. **The first ancient civilization to introduce and practice monotheism was the:** *(Easy) (Skill 2.1c)*

    A. Sumerians

    B. Hebrews

    C. Phoenicians

    D. Minoans

Answer: B. Hebrews

The (A) Sumerians and (C) Phoenicians both practiced religions in which many gods and goddesses were worshipped. Often these Gods/Goddesses were based on a feature of nature such as a sun, moon, weather, rocks, water, etc. The (D) Minoan culture shared many religious practices with the Ancient Egyptians. It seems that the king was somewhat of a god figure and the queen, a goddess. Much of the Minoan art points to the worship of multiple gods. Therefore, only the (B) Hebrews introduced and fully practiced monotheism, or the belief in one god.

44. **The principle of zero in mathematics is the discovery of the ancient civilization found in:** *(Average) (Skill 2.1c)*

    A. Egypt

    B. Persia

    C. India

    D. Babylon

Answer: C. India

Although the (A) Egyptians practiced algebra and geometry, the (B) Persians developed an alphabet, and the (D) Babylonians developed Hammurabi's Code, which would come to be considered among the most important contributions of the Mesopotamian civilization, it was the (C) Indians that created the idea of zero in mathematics changing drastically our ideas about numbers.

45. An early cultural group was so skillful in navigating on the seas that they were able to sail at night guided by stars. They were the: *(Average) (Skill 2.1c)*

    A. Greeks

    B. Persians

    C. Minoans

    D. Phoenicians

Answer: D Phoenicians

Although the (A) Greeks were quite able sailors and developed a strong navy in their defeat of the (B) Persians at sea in the Battle of Marathon, it was the Eastern Mediterranean culture of the (D) Phoenicians that had first developed the astronomical skill of sailing at night with the stars as their guide. The (C) Minoans were an advanced early civilization off the Greek coast on Crete more noted for their innovations in terms of sewage systems, toilets, and running water.

46. A historian might compare the governmental systems of the Roman Empire and the twentieth century United States with regard to which of the following commonalities? ? *(Average) (Skill 2.1c)*

    A. Totalitarianism

    B. Technological development

    C. Constitutional similarities

    D. Federalism

Answer: D Federalism

(A) Totalitarianism is a form of government where citizens are completely subservient to the state. While this was sometimes the case during the reign of the Roman Empire, it was not common to 20th century America. (B) Technological development does not necessarily address similarities in governmental systems. (C) The Roman constitution applied to the republic of Rome but not directly to the empire as a whole. (D) Federalism is a type of governmental system where several separate states join under a common government. This describes both the United States and the Roman Empire and is the best answer.

47. **Development of a solar calendar, invention of the decimal system, and contributions to the development of geometry and astronomy are all the legacy of:** *(Average) (Skill 2.1c)*

   A. The Babylonians

   B. The Persians

   C. The Sumerians

   D. The Egyptians

Answer: D. The Egyptians

The (A) Babylonians of ancient Mesopotamia flourished for a time under their great contribution of organized law and code, called Hammurabi's Code (1750 B.C.), after the ruler Hammurabi. The fall of the Babylonians to the Persians in 539 B.C. made way for the warrior-driver Persian Empire that expanded from Pakistan to the Mediterranean Sea until the conquest of Alexander the Great in 331 B.C. The Sumerians of ancient Mesopotamia were most noted for their early advancements as one of the first civilizations and their contributions towards written language known as cuneiform. It was the (D) Egyptians who were the first true developers of a solar calendar, the decimal system, and made significant contributions to the development of geometry and astronomy

48. **Which ancient civilization is credited with being the first to develop irrigation techniques through the use of canals, dikes, and devices for raising water?** *(Average) (Skill 2.1c)*

   A. The Sumerians

   B. The Egyptians

   C. The Babylonians

   D. The Akkadians

Answer: A. The Sumerians

The ancient (A) Sumerians of the Fertile Crescent of Mesopotamia are credited with being the first to develop irrigation techniques through the use of canals, dikes, and devices for raising water. The (B) Egyptians also practiced controlled irrigation but that was primarily through the use of the Nile's predictable flooding schedule. The (C) Babylonians were more noted for their revolutionary systems of law than their irrigation systems.

49. Chinese civilization is generally credited with the original development of which of the following sets of technologies: *(Average) (Skill 2.1c, 2.1d)*

A. Movable type and mass production of goods

B. Wool processing and domestication of the horse

C. Paper and gunpowder manufacture

D. Leather processing and modern timekeeping

Answer: C

C.   Paper and gunpowder manufacture

(A) While China's Bi Sheng (d. 1052) is credited with the earliest forms of movable type (1041-48), mass production was spearheaded by America's Henry Ford (1863-1947) in his campaign to create the first truly affordable automobile, the Model T Ford. (B) While wool has been processed in many ways in many cultures, production on a scale beyond cottage industries was not possible without the many advances made in England during the Industrial Revolution (18th century). Various theories exist about the domestication of the horse, with estimates ranging from 4600 BC to 2000 BC in Eurasia. Recent DNA evidence suggests that the horse may actually have been domesticated in different cultures at independent points. (C) The earliest mention of gunpowder appears in ninth century Chinese documents. The earliest examples of paper made of wood pulp come from China and have been dated as early as the second century BC. (D) Leather processing and timekeeping have likewise seen different developments in different places at different times.

50. The Age of Exploration begun in the 1400s was led by: *(Average) (Skill 2.2a)*

    A. The Portuguese

    B. The Spanish

    C. The English

    D. The Dutch

Answer: A. The Portuguese

Although the Age of Exploration had many important players among them, the Dutch, Spanish and English, it was the Portuguese who sent the first explorers to the New World.

51. The painter of the Sistine Ceiling was: *(Easy) (Skill 2.2a)*

    A. Raphael

    B. Michelangelo

    C. Leonardo da Vinci

    D. Titian

Answer: B Michaelangelo

(A) Raphael (1483-1520 AD), (B) Michelangelo (1475-1564 AD), (C) Leonardo da Vinci (1452-1519 AD) and (D) Titian (1488-1576 AD) were all contemporary Italian Renaissance masters, but only Michelangelo painted the Sistine Chapel ceiling (1508-1512 AD).

52. The ideas and innovations of the period of the Renaissance were spread throughout Europe mainly because of: *(Average) (Skill 2.2a)*

A. Extensive exploration

B. Craft workers and their guilds

C. The invention of the printing press

D. Increased travel and trade

Answer: C. The invention of the printing press

The ideas and innovations of the Renaissance were spread throughout Europe for a number of reasons. While exploration, increased travel, and spread of craft may have aided the spread of the Renaissance to small degrees, nothing was as important to the spread of ideas as Gutenberg's invention of the printing press in Germany.

53. The first explorer to reach India by sailing around the southern tip of Africa was: *(Average) (Skill 2.2a)*

A. Amerigo Vespucci

B. Vasco da Gama

C. Ferdinand Magellan

D. John Cabot

Answer: B

B. Vasco da Gama

(A) Amerigo Vespucci (1454-1512) was the Italian explorer to first assert that the lands to the west of Africa and Europe were actually part of a new continent and thus the name "America" was derived from his own "Amerigo." (B) Portuguese Vasco da Gama (1469-1524) built on the discoveries of previous explorers to finally round Africa's Cape of Good Hope and open a sea route for European trade with the east and the eventual Portuguese colonization of India. (C) Portuguese explorer Ferdinand Magellan (1480-1521), working for the Spanish crown, led the first successful expedition to circumnavigate the globe (1519-1522). Magellan himself actually died before the voyage was over, but his ship and 18 crewmembers did return safely to Spain. (D) John Cabot (1450-1499) was an Italian explorer working for the English crown and is thought to have been the first European to discover North America (1497) since the Vikings.

54. Luther issued strong objection to all but which of the following practices of the 15th century Roman Catholic Church? *(Average) (Skill 2.2a)*

A. The sacrament of baptism

B. Absolution of sins through the intermediation of a priest and through ceremony

C. The sale of indulgences, whereby the buyer may purchase purgation of sins

D. Imposed church control over the individual conscience

Answer: A

A. The sacrament of baptism

Absolution of sins by priests, the sale of indulgences and imposed church control over individual consciences were all practices which Martin Luther (1483-1546) and subsequent Protestants objected to on the basis that they required the Church to act as an intermediary between God and the individual believer. The sacrament of baptism, however, continues to be practiced in some form in most Protestant denominations, as the rite of initiation into the Christian community.

55. Who is considered to be the most important figure in the spread of Protestantism across Switzerland? *(Average) (Skill 2.2a)*

   A. Calvin

   B. Zwingli

   C. Munzer

   D. Leyden

Answer: A. Calvin

While (B) Huldreich Zwingli (1484-1531) was the first to spread the Protestant Reformation in Switzerland around 1519, it was (A) John Calvin (1509-1564), whose less radical approach to Protestantism who really made the most impact in Switzerland. Calvin's ideas separated from the Lutherans over the "Lord's Supper" debate over the sacrament, and his branch of Protestants became known as Calvinism. Calvin certainly built on Zwingli's early influence but really made the religion widespread throughout Switzerland. (C) Thomas Munzer (1489-1525) was a German Protestant reformer whose radical and revolutionary ideas about God's will to overthrow the ruling classes and his siding with the peasantry got him beheaded. Munzer has since been studied and admired by Marxists for his views on class. Leyden (or Leiden) was a founder of the University of Leyden, a Protestant place for study in the Netherlands.

56. Bartholomeu Diaz, in seeking a route around the tip of Africa, was forced to turn back. Nevertheless, the cape he discovered near the southern tip of Africa became known as: *(Average) (Skill 2.2a)*

   A. Cape Horn

   B. Cabo Bojador

   C. Cape of Good Hope

   D. Cape Hatteras

Answer: C Cape of Good Hope

(A) Cape Horn is located at the southern tip of Chile, South America. It was discovered by Sir Francis Drake as he sailed around the globe in 1578. (B) Cajo Bojador, on the Western coast of northern Africa, was first successfully navigated by a European, Portuguese Gil Eanes, in 1434. (D) Cape Hatteras is located on the U.S. Atlantic coast, at North Carolina.

57. **India's greatest ruler is considered to be:** *(Easy) (Skill 2.2a)*

    A. Akbar

    B. Asoka

    C. Babur

    D. Jahan

Answer: A Akbar

Akbar (1556-1605) is considered to be India's greatest ruler. He combined a drive for conquest with a magnetic personality and went so far as to invent his own religion, Dinillahi, a combination of Islam, Christianity, Zoroastrianism, and Hinduism. Asoka (273 B.C.-232 B.C.) was also an important ruler as he was the first to bring together a fully united India. Babur (1483-1540) was both considered to be a failure as he struggled to maintain any power early in his reign, but later to be somewhat successful in his quest to reunite Northern India. Jahan's (1592-1666) rule of India is considered to be the golden age of art and literature in the region.

58. **China's last imperial ruling dynasty was one of its most stable and successful and, under its rule, Chinese culture made an outstanding impression on Western nations. This dynasty was:**
    (Average) (Skill 2.2a)

    A. Min

    B. Manchu

    C. Han

    D. Chou

Answer: B Manchu

The (A) Ming Dynasty lasted from 1368-1644 and was among the more successful dynasties but focused attention towards foreign trade and encouraged growth in the arts. Therefore, it was the (B) Manchu Dynasty, the last imperial ruling dynasty, which came to power in the 1600s and expanded China's power in Asia greatly that was and still is considered to be among the most important, most stable, and most successful of the Chinese dynasties. The (C) Han and (D) Chou Dynasties were part of the "ancient" dynasties of China and while important in Chinese History, their influence did not hold impression on Western nations as

59. Extensive exports of gold and copper; elaborate court and constitution; trade links on both the Atlantic and Indian Oceans; use of heavy stone architecture; these most closely characterize the civilization of: *(Average) (Skill 2.2a)*

   A. Mwene Mutapa

   B. Chichen Itza

   C. Great Zimbabwe

   D. Muscat and Oman

Answer: C. Great Zimbabwe

The medieval kingdom of (C) Great Zimbabwe left the largest ruins in Africa from which archeologists have been able to discern the nature of their civilization. (B) Chichen Itza is a Mayan temple complex complete with other supporting buildings which has been excavated in Yucatan, Mexico, and is thought to date from 987 AD. (D) Muscat and Oman was an empire that dominated the southern Persian Gulf and Saudi peninsula and parts of the East African coast and Iranian Plateau. Its main export, however, was slaves.

60. In Western Europe, the achievements of the Renaissance were unsurpassed and made these countries outstanding cultural centers on the continent. All of the following were accomplishments except: *(Average) (Skill 2.2)*

   A. Invention of the printing press

   B. A rekindling of interest in the learning of classical Greece & Rome

   C. Growth in literature, philosophy, and art

   D Better military tactics

Answer: D. Better military tactics

Some of the most important developments during the Renaissance were Gutenberg's invention of the printing press in Germany and a reexamination of the ideas and philosophies of (B) classical Greece and Rome that eventually helped Renaissance thinkers to approach more modern ideas. Also important during the Renaissance was the (C) growth in literature (Petrarch, Boccaccio, Erasmus), philosophy (Machiavelli, More, Bacon) and art (Van Eyck, Giotto, da Vinci). Therefore, (D) improved military tactics is the only possible answer as it was clearly not a characteristic of the Renaissance in Western Europe.

61. The years 1793-94 in France, characterized by numerous trials and executions of supposed enemies of the Revolutionary Convention, were known as the: *(Rigorous) (Skill 2.2b)*

A. Reign of Terror

B. Dark Ages

C. French Inquisition

D. Glorious Revolution

Answer: A

A.   Reign of Terror

(A) The period of the French Revolution known as the Reign of Terror (1793-94) is estimated to have led to the deaths of up to 40,000 people: aristocrats, clergy, political activists, and anyone else denounced as an enemy of the Revolutionary Convention, many falsely so. (B) The Dark Ages is the term commonly used for the Early Middle Ages in Europe, from the fall of Rome in 476 to 1000. (C) The French Inquisition was the Roman Catholic Church's attempts to codify into ecclesiastical and secular law the prosecution of heretics, most notably at the time, the Albigensians, in the 13th century. (D) The Glorious Revolution (1688-1689) is the title given to the overthrow of the last Catholic British monarch, James II, in favor of his Protestant daughter Mary and her husband, the Dutch prince William of Orange.

62. **Colonial expansion by Western European powers in the 18th and 19th centuries was due primarily to:** *(Average) (Skill 2.2b)*

    A. Building and opening the Suez Canal

    B. The Industrial Revolution

    C. Marked improvements in transportation

    D. Complete independence of all the Americas and loss of European domination and influence

Answer: B. The Industrial Revolution

Colonial expansion by Western European powers in the late 18th and 19th centuries was due primarily to the Industrial Revolution in Great Britain that spread across Europe and needed new natural resources and therefore, new locations from which to extract the raw materials needed to feed the new industries.

63. **Great Britain became the center of technological and industrial development during the nineteenth century chiefly on the basis of:** *(Average) (Skill 2.2b)*

   A. Central location relative to the population centers of Europe

   B. Colonial conquests and military victories over European powers

   C. Reliance on exterior sources of financing

   D. Resources of coal and production of steel

Answer: D

D.   Resources of coal and production of steel

Great Britain possessed a unique set of advantages in the 18th and 19th centuries, making it the perfect candidate for the technological advances of the Industrial Revolution. (A) Relative isolation from the population centers in Europe meant little to Great Britain, which benefited from its own relatively unified and large domestic market, enabling it to avoid the tariffs and inefficiencies of trading on the diverse (and complicated) continent. (B) Colonial conquests and military victories over European powers were fueled by Great Britain's industrial advances in transportation and weaponry, rather than being causes of them. (C) Reliance on exterior sources of funding – while Great Britain would enjoy an increasing influx of goods and capital from its colonies, the efficiency of its own domestic market consistently generated an impressive amount of capital for investment in the new technologies and industries of the age. (D) Great Britain's rich natural resources of coal and ore enabled steel production and, set alongside new factories in a Britain's landscape, allowed the production of goods quickly and efficiently.

64. It can be reasonably stated that the change in the United States from primarily an agricultural country into an industrial power was due to all of the following except: *(Average) (Skill 2.2b)*

   A. Tariffs on foreign imports

   B. Millions of hardworking immigrants

   C. An increase in technological developments

   D. The change from steam to electricity for powering industrial machinery

Answer: A. Tariffs on foreign imports

It can be reasonably stated that the change in the United States from primarily an agricultural country into an industrial power was due to a great degree of three of the reasons listed above. It was a combination of millions of hard-working immigrants, an increase in technological developments, and the change from steam to electricity for powering industrial machinery. The only reason given that really had little effect was the tariffs on foreign imports.

65. In the <u>first</u> aggression of World War II outside the Orient, identify the aggressor nation and the nation which was invaded: *(Rigorous) (Skill 2.3a)*

   A. Germany; Sudetenland

   B. Italy; Abyssinia

   C. Germany; Poland

   D. Italy; Yugoslavia

Answer: B

B.   Italy; Abyssinia

(A) The Sudetenland (part of Czechoslovakia) was ceded to Nazi Germany in 1938 by the Munich Agreement of France, Britain, Italy, and Germany. The pretense for the annexation was the mistreatment of resident Germans by the Czechs. (B) Italy's invasion and annexation of Abyssinia in 1935-36 was condemned by the League of Nations but left unchallenged until the East African Campaign of World War II in 1941. Nazi Germany invaded Poland in 1939 and would occupy it until 1945. (D) After attempts to convince the Yugoslavians to join the Axis powers, Germany and Italy invaded Yugoslavia in 1941 and established the Independent State of Croatia.

66. **Of all the major causes of both World Wars I and II, the most significant one is considered to be:** *(Average Rigor) (Skill 2.3a)*

   A. Extreme nationalism

   B. Military buildup and aggression

   C. Political unrest

   D. Agreements and alliances

Answer:

A. Extreme nationalism

Although military buildup and aggression, political unrest, and agreements and alliances were all characteristic of the world climate before and during World War I and World War II, the most significant cause of both wars was extreme nationalism. Nationalism is the idea that the interests and needs of a particular nation are of the utmost and primary importance above all else. Some nationalist movements could be liberation movements while others were oppressive regimes, much depends on their degree of nationalism. The nationalism that sparked WWI included a rejection of German, Austro-Hungarian, and Ottoman imperialism by Serbs, Slavs and others culminating in the assassination of Archduke Ferdinand by a Serb nationalist in 1914. Following WWI and the Treaty of Versailles, many Germans and others in the Central Alliance Nations, malcontent at the concessions and reparations of the treaty started a new form of nationalism. Adolf Hitler and the Nazi regime led this extreme nationalism. Hitler's ideas were an example of extreme, oppressive nationalism combined with political, social and economic scapegoating and were the primary cause of WWII.

67. **Which of the following most closely characterizes the geopolitical events of the USSR in 1991-92:** *(Rigorous) (Skill 2.3b)*

    A. The USSR established greater military and economic control over the fifteen Soviet republics

    B. The Baltic States (Estonia, Latvia, Lithuania) declared independence, while the remainder of the USSR remained intact.

    C. Fourteen of fifteen Soviet republics declared some degree of autonomy; the USSR was officially dissolved; the Supreme Soviet rescinded the Soviet Treaty of 1922

    D. All fifteen Soviet republics simultaneously declared immediate and full independence from the USSR, with no provisions for a transitional form of government

Answer: C Fourteen of fifteen Soviet republics declared some degree of autonomy; the USSR was officially dissolved; the Supreme Soviet rescinded the Soviet Treaty of 1922.

The unraveling of the USSR in 1991-92 and the establishment of independent republics in its wake was a complex if relatively peaceful end to its existence. After a succession of declarations of autonomy by constituent states forced the dissolution of the central government, the Baltic States of Latvia, Lithuania, and Estonia immediately declared their independence. Other republics took longer to reconfigure their relationships to one another. There was no serious attempt by the central government to resist these changes militarily or economically.

68. **Which of the following is most reasonably studied under the social sciences?** *(Easy) (Skill 3.0a)*

    A. Political science

    B. Geometry

    C. Physics

    D. Grammar

Answer: A

(B) Geometry is one of the oldest sciences and is a part of the study of mathematics concerned with questions of size, shape and relative position of figures and with properties of space. (C) Physics is the science of matter and motion that deals with concepts such as force, energy, mass and charge, for example. (D) Grammar is the study of rules that governs the use of language. (A) Political science is primarily concerned with the political and governmental activities of societies.

69. Who wrote the book *"The Social Contract"?* (Average) (Skill 3.0b)

A. Jean-Jacques Rousseau

B. John Locke

C. Niccolo Machiavelli

D. Thomas Hobbes

Answer: A

(A) In his work of 1762, "The Social Contract," Jean Jacques Rousseau described the "general will" leading to Socialism. Niccolo Machiavelli (C) was the famous politician from Florence who disregarded the ideals of Christianity in favor of realistic power politics. Thomas Hobbes (D) whose most famous work was "Leviathan" believed that a person's life was a constant unceasing search for power and believed in the state's supremacy to combat this.

(B) John Locke (1632-1704), whose book *Two Treatises of Government* has long been considered a founding document on the rights of people to rebel against an unjust government, was an important figure in the founding of the US Constitution and on general politics of the American Colonies.

70. Public administration, such as public officials in the areas of budgets, accounting, distribution of public funds, and personnel management would be a part of the field of: (Easy) (Skill 3.0b)

A. Anthropology

B. Sociology

C. Law and Taxation

D. Political Science and Economics

Answer: D. Political Science and Economics

Public administration, such as public officials in the areas of budgets, accounting, distribution of public funds, and personnel management, would be parts of the fields of Economics and Political Science. While political scientists would be concerned with public administration, economists would also be concerned with the distribution of public funds, budgets, and accounting and their effects on the economy.

71. **A political scientist might use all of the following except:** *(Average)*
(Skill 3.0b)

   A. An investigation of government documents

   B. A geological timeline

   C. Voting patterns

   D. Polling data

Answer: B A geological timeline

Political science is primarily concerned with the political and governmental activities of societies. (A) Government documents can provide information about the organization and activities of a government. (C) Voting patterns reveal the political behavior of individuals and groups. (D) Polling data can provide insight into the predominant political views of a group of people. (B) A geological timeline describes the changes in the physical features of the earth over time and would not be useful to a political scientist.

72. **Political science is primarily concerned with _____.**
(Rigorous) (Skill 3.0b)

   A. Elections

   B. Economic Systems

   C. Boundaries

   D. Public Policy

Answer: D Public policy

Political science studies the actions and policies of the government of a society. (D) Public policy is the official stance of a government on an issue and is a primary source for studying a society's dominant political beliefs. (A) Elections are also an interest of political scientists but are not a primary field of study. (B) Economic systems are of interest to an economist and (C) boundaries to a geographer.

73. Which one of the following is not a function or responsibility of the US political parties? *(Average) (Skill 3.0d, 3.1d)*

A. Conducting elections or the voting process

B. Obtaining funds needed for election campaigns

C. Choosing candidates to run for public office

D. Making voters aware of issues and other public affairs information

Answer: A. Conducting elections or the voting process

The US political parties have numerous functions and responsibilities. Among them are obtaining funds needed for election campaigns, choosing the candidates to run for office, and making voters aware of the issues. The political parties, however, do not conduct elections or the voting process, as that would be an obvious conflict of interest.

74. In the United States, checks and balances refers to: *(Average) (Skill 3.1a)*

A. The ability of each branch of government to "check" or limit the actions of others

B. Balance of payments

C. International law

D. The federal deficit

Answer: A. The ability of each branch of government to "check" or limit the actions of the others

In the United States, checks and balances refers to the ability of each branch of government (Executive, Legislative, and Judicial) to "check" or limit the actions of the others. Examples of checks and balances are: The Executive branch limits the Legislature by power of veto over bills and appointments in the court system. The Judicial branch limits the power of the Legislature by judicial review and the ability to rule laws unconstitutional and may also determine executive orders unconstitutional. The Legislature checks the Executive by power of impeachment

75. In the Constitutional system of checks and balances, a primary "check" which accrues to the President is the power of: *(Average) (Skill 3.1a)*

A. Executive privilege

B. Approval of judges nominated by the Senate

C. Veto of Congressional legislation

D. Approval of judged nominated by the House of Representatives

Answer: C Veto of Congressional legislation

The power to (C) veto congressional legislation is granted to the U.S. President in Article I of the Constitution, which states that all legislation passed by both houses of the Congress must be given to the president for approval. This is a primary check on the power of the Congress by the President. The Congress may override a presidential veto by a two-thirds majority vote of both houses, however. (A) Executive privilege refers to the privilege of the president to keep certain documents private. Answers (B) and (D) are incorrect, as Congress does not nominate judges. This is a presidential

76. In the United States, if a person is accused of a crime and cannot afford a lawyer: : *(Average) (Skill 3.1a)*

A. The person cannot be tried

B. A court will appoint a lawyer, but the person must pay the lawyer back when able to do so

C. The person must be tried without legal representation

D. A court will appoint a lawyer for the person free of charge

Answer: D A court will appoint a lawyer for the person free of charge

The sixth amendment to the Constitution grants the right to a speedy and public jury trial in a criminal prosecution, as well as the right to "the assistance of counsel for his defense." This has been interpreted as the right to receive legal assistance at no charge if a defendant cannot afford one. (D) A court will appoint a lawyer for the person free of charge, is the correct answer.

77. **The term that best describes how the Supreme Court can block laws that may be unconstitutional from being enacted is:** *(Average) (Skill 3.1a)*

    A. Jurisprudence

    B. Judicial Review

    C. Exclusionary Rule

    D. Right of Petition

Answer: B. Judicial Review

(A) Jurisprudence is the study of the development and origin of law. (B) Judicial review is the term that best describes how the Supreme Court can block laws that they deem as unconstitutional as set forth in Marbury vs Madison. The (C) "exclusionary rule" is a reference to the Fourth Amendment of the Constitution and says that evidence gathered in an illegal manner or search must be thrown out and excluded from evidence. There is nothing called the (D) "Right of Petition", however the Petition of Right is a reference to a statement of civil liberties sent by the English Parliament to Charles I in 1628.

78. **Only one amendment has been repealed. Which amendment was repealed?** *(Average) (Skill 3.1a)*

    A. 21st

    B. 18th

    C. 17th

    D. 22nd

Answer: B

To date there are only 27 amendments to the Constitution that have passed. An amendment may be used to cancel out a previous one, such as the (B) 18th Amendment (1919) known as Prohibition, canceled by the 21st Amendment (1933). Amending the United States Constitution is an extremely difficult thing to do.

79. An amendment is: *(Average) (Skill 3.1a)*

    A. A change or addition to the United States Constitution

    B. The right of a state to secede from the Union

    C. To add a state to the Union

    D. The right of the Supreme Court to check actions of Congress and the President

Answer: A. A change or addition to the United States Constitution

An amendment is a change or addition to the United States Constitution. No amendment refers to states' abilities to succeed or be annexed or the right of the Supreme Court to check actions of Congress and the President.

80. Collectively, the first ten Amendments to the Constitution are known as the: *(Easy) (Skill 3.1a)*

    A. Articles of Confederation

    B. Mayflower Compact

    C. Bill of Rights

    D. Declaration of the Rights of Man

Answer: C Bill of Rights

The (A) Articles of Confederation was the document under which the thirteen colonies of the American Revolution came together and was the first governing document of the United States. The (B) Mayflower Compact was an agreement signed by several of the pilgrims aboard the Mayflower before establishing their colony at Plymouth in 1620. The (D) Declaration of the Rights of Man was the French document adopted after the French Revolution in 1789. The first ten amendments of the US Constitution, spelling out the limitations of the federal government, are referred to as (C) the Bill of Rights.

81. **Why is the system of government in the United States referred to as a federal system?** *(Rigorous) (Skill 3.1b)*

   A. There are different levels of government

   B. There is one central authority in which all governmental power is vested

   C. The national government cannot operate except with the consent of the governed

   D. Elections are held at stated periodic times, rather than as called by the head of the government

Answer: A

A. There are different levels of government

(A) The United States is composed of fifty states, each responsible for its own affairs but united under a federal government. (B) A centralized system is the opposite of a federal system. (C) That national government cannot operate except with the consent of the governed is a founding principle of American politics. It is not a political system like federalism. A centralized democracy could still be consensual but would not be federal. (D) This is a description of electoral procedure, not a political system like federalism

82. Which branch is responsible for carrying out the laws of the country? *(Average) (Skill 3.1b)*

    A. Judicial

    B. Executive

    C. Legislative

    D. Supreme Court

Answer: B. Executive

In the United States, the three branches of the federal government mentioned earlier, the **Executive**, the **Legislative**, and the **Judicial**, divide up their powers thus:

Article 2 of the Constitution created the (B) Executive branch of the government, headed by the President, who leads the country, recommends new laws, and can veto bills passed by the legislative branch. As the chief of state, the President is responsible for carrying out the laws of the country and the treaties and declarations of war passed by the legislative branch.

84. Which branch established the power of the Supreme Court? *(Average) (Skill 3.1b)*

    A. Judicial

    B. Executive

    C. Legislative

    D. House of Representatives

Answer: A. Judicial

In the United States, the three branches of the federal government mentioned earlier, the **Executive**, the **Legislative**, and the **Judicial**, divide up their powers thus:

Article 3 of the Constitution established the (A) judicial branch of government headed by the Supreme Court. The Supreme Court has the power to rule that a law passed by the legislature or an act of the Executive branch is illegal and unconstitutional.

84. The _____ branch of government is made up of House of Representatives and the Senate. *(Average) (Skill 3.1b)*

    A. Judicial

    B. Executive

    C. Legislative

    D. Supreme Court

Answer: C Legislative

In the United States, the three branches of the federal government mentioned earlier, the **Executive**, the **Legislative**, and the **Judicial**, divide up their powers thus:

Article 1 of the Constitution established the (C) legislative, or law-making branch of the government called the Congress. It is made up of two houses, the House of Representatives and the Senate.

85. **What were the first political parties in the United States?** *(Rigorous) (Skill 3.1c)*

    A. Democrats and Whigs

    B. Whigs and Federalists

    C. Federalists and Democratic-Republicans

    D. Democrats and Republicans

Answer: C Federalists and Democratic-Republicans

Jefferson's supporters called themselves (C) Democratic-Republicans. Hamilton and his supporters were known as Federalists, because they favored a strong federal government. By the late 1820s, new political parties had grown up. The **Democratic-Republican** Party, or simply the **Republican** Party, had been the major party for many years, but differences within it about the direction the country was headed in caused a split after 1824. Those who favored strong national growth took the name (B) **Whigs** after a similar party in Great Britain and united around then President John Quincy Adams

86. **In the United States government, the power of coining money is:** *(Rigorous) (Skill 3.1d)*

   A. Implied or suggested

   B. Concurrent or shared

   C. Delegated or expressed

   D. Reserved

Answer: C. Delegated or expressed

In the United States government, the power of coining money is delegated or expressed. Therefore, only the United States government may coin money, the states may not coin money for themselves.

87. **Which of the following are NOT local governments in the United States?** *(Easy) (Skill 3.1e)*

   A. Cities

   B. Townships

   C. School boards

   D. All of these are forms of local government

Answer: D

D. All of these are forms of local government

A local government is a body with the authority to make policy and enforce decisions on behalf of a local community. Cities and townships are by definition local, not statewide or federal, governments. A more central authority might make school policy in other countries, but, in the United States, school boards are local authorities. [However, according to the 2002 Census, several states run certain school districts themselves, without a local school board.]

88. **How are major party candidates chosen to run for President in the United States?** *(Average) (Skill 3.1e)*

   A. Caucuses of major party officeholders meet to select a state's choice for the party, and the candidate selected by the most states becomes the nominee

   B. Potential Presidential nominees seek pledges from each state party's chair and co-chair, and the candidate with the most pledges becomes the nominee

   C. Nationwide primaries are held by each party, to select delegates to a national nominating convention

   D. Each state party decides how to select delegates to a nominating convention; these selection processes may be caucuses, primaries, or any other method chosen by the state party

Answer: D

D. Each state party decides how to select delegates to a nominating convention; these selection processes may be caucuses, primaries, or any other method chosen by the state party.

A nominating convention selects each party nominee, and the delegates from each state are chosen as the state party sees fit. Caucuses are only one possible method. Pledges or nationwide primaries have never been a way of determining the nominee.

89. _____ is the effort to create, by dictatorial means, a viable national society in which competing interests were to be adjusted to each other by being entirely subordinated to the service of the state although it will tolerate some private ownership of the means of production. *(Average)* *(Skill 3.2a)*

A. Dictatorship

B. Parliamentary System

C. Anarchism

D. Fascism

Answer: D Fascism

(A) Dictatorship is the rule by an individual or small group of individuals (Oligarchy) that centralizes all political control in itself and enforces its will with a terrorist police force. (B) Parliamentary System - A system of government with a legislature, usually involving a multiplicity of political parties and often coalition politics. There is division between the head of state and head of government. Head of government is usually known as a Prime Minister who is also usually the head of the largest party. The head of government and cabinet usually both sit and vote in the parliament. (C) Anarchism is a political movement believing in the elimination of all government and its replacement by a cooperative community of individuals. Sometimes it has involved political violence such as assassinations of important political or governmental figures. The historical banner of the movement is a black flag. But (D) fascism is a belief as well as a political system, opposed ideologically to Communism, though similar in basic structure, with a one party state, centralized political control and a repressive police system. It however tolerates private ownership of the means of production, though it maintains tight overall control. Central to its belief is the idolization of the Leader, a "Cult of the Personality," and most often an expansionist ideology. Examples have been German Nazism and Italian Fascism

90. **Which of the following is not generally considered a discipline within the social sciences?** *(Easy) (Domain IV VI)*

    A. Geometry

    B. Anthropology

    C. Geography

    D. Sociology

Answer: A

A.   Geometry

(B) Anthropology studies the culture of groups of people. (C) Geography examines the relationship between societies and the physical place on earth where they live. (D) Sociology studies the predominant attitudes, beliefs and behaviors of a society. All three of these fields are related to the social interactions of humans, and so are considered social sciences. (A) Geometry is a field of mathematics and does not relate to the social interactions of people, so it is not considered a social science.

91. **The end to hunting, gathering, and fishing of prehistoric people was due to:** *(Rigorous) (Skill 4.0d)*

    A. Domestication of animals

    B. Building crude huts and houses

    C. Development of agriculture

    D. Organized government in villages

Answer: C. Development of agriculture

Although the (A) domestication of animals, (B) the building of huts and houses and the (D) first organized governments were all very important steps made by early civilizations, it was the development of agriculture that ended the once dominant practices of hunting, gathering, and fishing among prehistoric people. The development of agriculture provided a more efficient use of time and for the first time a surplus of food. This greatly improved the quality of life and contributed to early population growth.

92. Relief maps can be depicted in different ways. One way is the use of: *(Easy) (Skill 4.1a)*

    A. Great-Circle Route

    B. Opisometer

    C. Meridians

    D. Contour Lines

Answer: D Contour Lines

A (A) Great-Circle is any circle that cuts a sphere, such as the globe, into two equal parts. Because of distortion, most maps do not show great-circle routes as straight lines. A method for measuring curvilinear map distances is to use a mechanical device called an (B) opisometer. This device uses a small rotating wheel that records the distance traveled. The recorded distance is measured by this device either in centimeters or inches. (C) Meridians, or lines of longitude, are the determining factor in separating time zones and determining time around the world. (D) The way to show relief is by using contour lines. These lines connect all points of a land surface which are the same height surrounding the particular area of land.

93. Maps as a rule are: *(Average) (Skill 4.1a)*

    A. All subject to some sort of distortion

    B. Always entirely accurate

    C. Not very useful in political science studies

    D. Difficult usually to understand

Answer: A. All subject to some sort of distortion

Maps as a rule are all subject to some sort of distortion. Since they are representing a three-dimensional world in a two-dimensional representation, it will never be completely accurate. Even maps that are specifically designed to limit distortion still will lack total accuracy. Maps are still very helpful in most social science disciplines and generally designed to be understood easily using keys and symbols.

94. **Meridians, or lines of longitude, not only help in pinpointing locations, but are also used for:** *(Rigorous) (Skill 4.1b)*

    A. Measuring distance from the Poles

    B. Determining direction of ocean currents

    C. Determining the time around the world

    D. Measuring distance to the Equator

Answer: C. Determining the time around the world

Meridians, or lines of longitude, are the determining factor in separating time zones and determining time around the world.

95. **The study of "spatial relationships and interaction" would be used by people in the field of:** *(Easy) (Skill 4.1c)*

    A. Political Science

    B. Anthropology

    C. Geography

    D. Sociology

Answer: C. Geography

(C) Geography is the discipline within Social Science that most concerns itself with the study of "spatial relationships and interaction". (B) Anthropology is the study of human culture and the way in which people of different cultures live. The artifacts created by people of a certain culture can provide information about the behaviors and beliefs of that culture, making anthropology the best-fitting field of study for this field trip. (D) Sociology, and (A) political science are more likely to study behaviors and institutions directly than through individual artifacts created by a specific culture.

96. **A physical geographer would be concerned with which of the following groups of terms?** *(Average) (Skill 4.2a)*

   A. Landform, biome, precipitation

   B. Scarcity, goods, services

   C. Nation, state, administrative subdivision

   D. Cause and effect, innovation, exploration

Answer: A

A.   Landform, biome, precipitation.

(A) Landform, biome, and precipitation are all terms used in the study of geography. A landform is a physical feature of the earth, such as a hill or valley. A biome is a large community of plants or animals, such as a forest. Precipitation is the moisture that falls to earth as rain or snow. (B) Scarcity, goods, and services are terms encountered in economics. (C) Nation, state, and administrative subdivision are terms used in political science. (D) Cause and effect, innovation, and exploration are terms in developmental psychology.

98. **A result of the Industrial Revolution was the increase in mobility. Which of the following is NOT a result of increased mobility?** *(Average) (Skill 4.3a)*

   A. A rapid diffusion of knowledge and ideas

   B. Wide-scale immigration to industrialized countries

   C. Cultures clashed and cultures melded

   D. Rise in religious tolerance

Answer: D Rise in religious tolerance

The social results of the Industrial Revolution were many but actually caused a decline of religion. Increased mobility produced (A) a rapid diffusion of knowledge and ideas. Increased mobility also resulted in (B) wide-scale immigration to industrialized countries. (C) Cultures clashed and cultures melded.

98. **What landforms rise to an elevation of about 500 to 2000 feet and are found everywhere on earth including Antarctica, where they are covered by ice.** *(Easy) (Skill 4.4a)*

   A. Valleys

   B. Mountains

   C. Hills

   D. Canyons

Answer: C Hills

(A) Mountains are landforms with rather steep slopes at least 2,000 feet or more above sea level. Mountains are found in groups called mountain chains or mountain ranges. (C) Hills are elevated landforms rising to an elevation of about 500 to 2000 feet. They are found everywhere on earth including Antarctica, where they are covered by ice. (A) Valleys are land areas found between hills and mountains. Some have gentle slopes containing trees and plants; others have steep walls and are referred to as (D) canyons. One example is Arizona's Grand Canyon of the Colorado River.

99. **How many oceans cover the earth?** *(Easy) (Skill 4.4a)*

   A. 3

   B. 4

   C. 5

   D. 6

Answer: B. 4

Oceans are the largest bodies of water on the planet. The four oceans of the earth are the **Atlantic Ocean**, one-half the size of the Pacific and separating North and South America from Africa and Europe; the **Pacific Ocean**, covering almost one-third of the entire surface of the earth and separating North and South America from Asia and Australia; the **Indian Ocean**, touching Africa, Asia, and Australia; and the ice-filled **Arctic Ocean,** extending from North America and Europe to the North Pole. The waters of the Atlantic, Pacific, and Indian Oceans also touch the shores of Antarctica

100. Which of the following is not a river? *(Easy) (Skill 4.4a)*

  A. Yangtze

  B. Rio Grande

  C. Artic

  D. Ganges

Answer: C Artic

Examples of important rivers for the people and countries affected by and/or dependent on them include the Nile, Niger, and Zaire Rivers of Africa; the Rhine, Danube, and Thames Rivers of Europe; (A) the Yangtze, (D) Ganges, Mekong, Hwang He, and Irrawaddy Rivers of Asia; the Murray-Darling in Australia; and the Orinoco in South America. River systems are made up of large rivers and numerous smaller rivers or tributaries flowing into them. Examples include the vast Amazon Rivers system in South America and the Mississippi River system in the United States. The (C) Artic is an ocean.

101. This subject is a study of how a society allocates its scarce resources to satisfy what are basically unlimited and competing wants. *(Easy) (Skill 5.0a)*

  A. Geometry

  B. Statistics

  C. Cultural Geography

  D. Economics

Answer: D. Economic

(D) Economics is a study of how a society allocates its scarce resources to satisfy what are basically unlimited and competing wants. Or economics can be defined as the study of the production, distribution and consumption of goods and resources subject to the constraint of scarce resources. (B) Geometry is a branch of mathematics. (C) Cultural Geography examines social results. For example, the social results of the Industrial Revolution include: Increase of population, especially in industrial centers; Advances in science applied to agriculture, sanitation and medicine; Growth of great cities and Disappearance of the difference between city dwellers and farmers. (B) Statistics is the mathematical science pertaining to the collection, analysis and interpretation and explanation of presentation of data.

102. Economics is best described as:

    A. The study of how money is used in different societies

    B. The study of how different political systems produces goods and services

    C. The study of how human beings use limited resources to supply their necessities and wants

    D. The study of how human beings have developed trading practices through the years

Answer: C

C.   The study of how human beings use limited resources to supply their necessities and wants

(A) How money is used in different societies might be of interest to a sociologist or anthropologist. (B) The study of how different political systems produce goods and services is a topic of study that could be included under the field of political science. (D) The study of historical trading practices could fall under the study of history. Only (C) is the best general description of the social science of economics as a whole.

103. In order to achieve efficiency, two conditions must be fulfilled: *(Average) (Skill 5.0c)*

    A. Low unemployment and low inflation

    B. Full-employment and full-production

    C. Full-employment and stable monetary supply

    D. Access to resources and full-production

Answer: B Full-employment and full-production

In order to achieve efficiency, two conditions must be fulfilled: full-employment and full-production. **Full-employment** refers to having all resources employed. Idle resources result in lower levels of output. The other condition, **full-production**, means that resources should be employed in their most productive capacity.

104. Capitalism and communism are alike in that they are both: *(Easy)* *(Skill 5.0d)*

   A. Organic systems

   B. Political systems

   C. Centrally planned systems

   D. Economic systems

Answer: D Economic systems

While economic and (B) political systems are often closely connected, capitalism and communism are primarily (D) economic systems. Capitalism is a system of economics that allows the open market to determine the relative value of goods and services. Communism is an economic system where the market is planned by a central state. While communism is a (C) centrally planned system, this is not true of capitalism. (A) Organic systems are studied in biology, a natural science.

105. **Which best describes the economic system of the United States? ?**
    (Average) (Skill 5.0d)

    A. Most decisions are the result of open markets, with little or no government modification or regulation

    B. Most decisions are made by the government, but there is some input by open market forces

    C. Most decisions are made by open market factors, with important regulatory functions and other market modifications the result of government activity

    D. There is joint decision making by government and private forces, with final decisions resting with the government

Answer: C Most decisions are made by open market factors, with important regulatory functions and other market modifications the result of government activity.

The United States does not have a planned economy, as described in answers (B) and (D) where the government makes major market decisions. Neither is the U.S. market completely free of regulation, as described in answer (A). Products are regulated for safety, and many services are regulated by certification requirements, for example. The best description of the U.S. economic system is therefore (C) Most decisions are made by open market factors, with important regulatory functions and other market modifications the result of government activity.

106. In a command economy: *(Average) (Skill 5.0d)*

   A. The open market determines how much of a good is produced and distributed

   B. The government determines how much of a good is produced and distributed

   C. Individuals produce and consume a specified good as commanded by their needs

   D. The open market determines the demand for a good, and then the government produces and distributes the good

Answer: B

B.   The government determines how much of a good is produced and distributed.

A command economy is where (B) the government determines how much of a good is produced and distributed, as was the case in the Soviet Union and is still the case in Cuba and North Korea. A command economy is the opposite of a market economy, where (A) the open market determines how much of a good is produced and distributed.

107. One method of trade restriction used by some nations is: *(Easy) (Skill 5.0e)*

   A. Limited treaties

   B. Floating exchange rate

   C. Bill of exchange

   D. Import quotas

Answer: D Import quotas

One method of trade restriction used by some nations is (D) import quotas. The amounts of goods imported are regulated in an effort to protect domestic enterprise and limit foreign competition. Both the United States and Japan, two of the world's most industrialized nations have import quotas to protect domestic industries.

108. If the price of Good G increases, what is likely to happen with regard to comparable Good H? *(Rigorous) (Skill 5.0g)*

A. The demand for Good G will stay the same

B. The demand for Good G will increase

C. The demand for Good H will increase

D. The demand for Good H will decrease

Answer: C The demand for Good H will increase.

If Good G and Good H are viewed by consumers as equal in value but then the cost of Good G increases, it follows that consumers will now choose Good H at a higher rate, increasing the demand.

109. What is a major difference between monopolistic competition and perfect competition? *(Rigorous) (Skill 5.1a)*

A. Perfect competition has many consumers and suppliers, while monopolistic competition does not

B. Perfect competition provides identical products, while monopolistic competition provides similar but not identical products

C. Entry to perfect competition is difficult, while entry to monopolistic competition is relatively easy

D. Monopolistic competition has many consumers and suppliers, while perfect competition does not

Answer: B Perfect competition provides identical products, while monopolistic competition provides similar but not identical products.

A perfect market is a hypothetical market used in economics to discuss the underlying effects of supply and demand. To control for differences between products, it is assumed in perfect competition that all products are identical, with no differences, and the prices for these products will rise and fall based on a small number of factors. Monopolistic competition takes place in a market where each producer can act monopolistically and raise or lower the cost of its product, or change its product to make different from similar products. This is the primary difference between these two models; (B) perfect competition provides identical products, while monopolistic competition provides similar but not identical products.

110. **Of the following, the best example of an oligopoly in the United States is:** *(Average) (Skill 5.1a)*

    A. Automobile industry

    B. Electric power provision

    C. Telephone service

    D. Clothing manufacturing

Answer: A Automobile industry

An oligopoly exists when a small group of companies controls an industry. In the United States at present, there are hundreds of (B) electric power providers, (C) telephone service providers and (D) clothing manufacturers. There are currently still just three major automobile manufacturers, however, making the (A) automobile industry an oligopoly.

111. **Inflation is the result of the economy _____?** *(Average) (Skill 5.2c)*

    A. Expanding too slowly

    B. Remaining stable

    C. Expanding too quickly

    D. Expanding in conjunction with the unemployment rate

Answer: C. Expanding too quickly

Inflation is caused by the economy expanding too quickly. There is excess aggregate demand that is fueling the inflation. This is a situation where the appropriate governmental action is to slow down the economy. The government will implement policies that result in less spending in the economy to end the inflation. These will be **contractionary** monetary and fiscal policy.

112. The _____ is a monetary measure of the economy's output during a specified time period and is used by all nations to measure and compare national production. *(Average) (Skill 5.2a)*

    A. Float Rate

    B. Gross Domestic Product (GDP)

    C. Unemployment Rate

    D. National Output

Answer: B Gross Domestic Product (GDP)

The GDP is a monetary measure of the economy's output during a specified time period and is used by all nations to measure and compare national production. Tabulating the economy's output can be measured in two ways, both of which give the same result: the expenditures approach and the incomes approach. Basically, what is spent on the national output by each sector of the economy is equal to what is earned producing the national output by each of the factors of production. The two methods have to be equal.

113. **An economist might engage in which of the following activities?** *(Rigorous) (Domain V, Skill 5.3c, 5.3d)*

    A. An observation of the historical effects of a nation's banking practices

    B. The application of a statistical test to a series of data

    C. Introduction of an experimental factor into a specified population to measure the effect of the factor

    D. An economist might engage in all of these

Answer: D An economist might engage in all of these

Economists use statistical analysis of economic data, controlled experimentation as well as historical research in their field of social science.

114. **The advancement of understanding in dealing with human beings has led to a number of interdisciplinary areas. Which of the following interdisciplinary studies would NOT be considered under the social sciences?** *(Rigorous) (Skill 6.0a)*

    A. Molecular biophysics

    B. Peace studies

    C. African-American studies

    D. Cartographic information Systems

Answer: A Molecular biophysics

(A) Molecular biophysics is an interdisciplinary field combining the fields of biology, chemistry, and physics. These are all natural sciences and not social sciences

115. **As a sociologist, you would be most likely to observe:** *(Average) (Skill 6.0a)*

    A. The effects of an earthquake on farmland

    B. The behavior of rats in sensory-deprivation experiments

    C. The change over time in Babylonian obelisk styles

    D. The behavior of human beings in television focus groups

Answer: D The behavior of human beings in television focus groups.

Predominant beliefs and attitudes within human society are studied in the field of sociology. (A) The effects of an earthquake on farmland might be studied by a geographer. (B) The behavior of rats in an experiment falls under the field of behavioral psychology. (C) Changes in Babylonian obelisk styles might interest a historian. None of these answers fits easily within the definition of sociology. (D) A focus group, where people are asked to discuss their reactions to a certain product or topic, would be the most likely method for a sociologist of observing and discovering attitudes among a selected group.

116. **Which of the following is NOT considered to be an economic need:** *(Average) (Skill 6.2a)*

    A. Food

    B. Transportation

    C. Shelter

    D. Clothing

Answer: B Transportation

An economic need is something that a person absolutely must have to survive. (A) Food, (C) shelter and (D) clothing are examples of these needs. While an individual may also require (B) transportation to participate in an economy, it is not considered an absolute need.

117. **A teacher and a group of students take a field trip to an Indian mound to examine artifacts. This activity most closely fits under which branch of the social sciences?** *(Average) (Skill 6.2a)*

    A. Anthropology

    B. Sociology

    C. Psychology

    D. Political Science

Answer: A

A.   Anthropology

(A) Anthropology is the study of human culture and the way in which people of different cultures live. The artifacts created by people of a certain culture can provide information about the behaviors and beliefs of that culture, making anthropology the best-fitting field of study for this field trip. (B) Sociology, (C) psychology and (D) political science are more likely to study behaviors and institutions directly than through individual artifacts created by a specific culture.

118. **An economist investigates the spending patterns of low-income individuals. Which of the following would yield the most pertinent information?***(Average) (Skill 6.3a)*

    A. Prime lending rates of neighborhood banks

    B. The federal discount rate

    C. City-wide wholesale distribution figures

    D. Census data and retail sales figures

Answer: D

D.   Census data and retail sales figures

(A) Local lending rates and (B) the federal discount rate might provide information on borrowing habits, but not necessarily spending habits, and give no information on income levels. (C) Citywide wholesale distribution figures would provide information on the business activity of a city, but tell nothing about consumer activities. (D) Census data records the income levels of households within a certain area, and retail sales figures for that area would give an economist data on spending, which can be compared to income levels, making this the most pertinent source.

119. **Populations are usually measured by all of the following EXCEPT:** *(Easy) (Skill 6.3a)*

    A. Height

    B. Economic data

    C. Ethnicity

    D. Age

Answer: A Height

A **population** is a group of people living within a certain geographic area. Populations are usually measured on a regular basis by census, which also measures (D) age, (B) economic, (C) ethnic, and other data. Populations change over time because of many factors, and these changes can have significant impact on cultures.   (A)Height is usually not a measurement of populations.

120. **Describe the naturally occurring attitude that people, for the most part are most comfortable with others like themselves.** *(Average) (Skill 6.4a)*

   A. Pluralism

   B. Discrimination

   C. Ethnocentrism

   D. Racial Bias

Answer: C Ethnocentrism

Psychologists have suggested that (C) ethnocentrism is a naturally occurring attitude. For the large part, people are most comfortable among other people who share their same upbringing, language, and cultural background and are likely to judge other cultural behaviors as alien or foreign. (A) Cultural pluralism is the simultaneous existence of several cultures and ethnic groups, with each afforded the protection and ability to observe their cultural institutions. It is also sometimes called multiculturalism. (B) Prejudice or racial bias is the act of pre-judging something or someone without firsthand experience. It often involves making judgments based on stereotypes, or the automatic rejection of a behavior or practice that seems unusual or foreign. (B) Discrimination takes place when a person or group acts out of prejudice to harm or deny privileges to another.

121. **The native metaphysical outlook of Japan, usually characterized as a religion, is:** *(Rigorous) (Skill 6.4b)*

   A. Tao

   B. Shinto

   C. Nichiren Shoju

   D. Shaolin

Answer: B Shinto

(A) Tao is the Chinese philosophical work that inspired Taoism, the religious tradition sourced in China. (B) Shinto is the system of rituals and beliefs honoring the deities and spirits believed to be native to the landscape and inhabitants of Japan. (C) Nichiren Shoju is a strand of Nichiren Buddhism, a tradition started by a Japanese Buddhist monk, Nichiren (1222-1282). (D) The Shaolin temple (originally built in 497 AD) is the Chinese Buddhist monastery considered to be the source of Zen Buddhism and its subsequent martial arts.

122. **The world religion which includes a caste system is:** *(Easy) (Skill 6.4b)*

    A. Buddhism

    B. Hinduism

    C. Sikhism

    D. Jainism

Answer: B. Hinduism

(A) Buddhism, (C) Sikhism, and (D) Jainism all rose out of protest against Hinduism and its practices of sacrifice and the caste system. The caste system, in which people were born into castes, would determine their class for life including who they could marry, what jobs they could perform, and their overall quality of life.

123. **_____ toward anyone on the basis of race is no longer legal in the U.S., however it is still common and widespread.** *(Easy) (Skill 6.4c)*

    A. Sexual discrimination

    B. Racial discrimination

    C. Age discrimination

    D. Religious discrimination

Answer: B. Racial discrimination

While official discrimination toward anyone on the basis of race is no longer legal in the U.S., it is still common and widespread. Unofficial discrimination can be equally damaging. In competitive situations such as applying for a job, racial or gender prejudices of the person making the decision of whom to hire may result in one or more candidates being discriminated against. A similar scenario may play out when a landlord is deciding to whom an apartment will be rented. This kind of discrimination, when it occurs systematically has the consequence of relegating groups of people to a lower economic level.

124.What concept calls for mutual respect between ethnic groups and cultures, allowing them to exist together and perpetuate their cultures? *(Average) (Skill 6.4d)*

A. Syllogism

B. Conformance

C. Discrimination

D. Cultural pluralism

Answer: D. Cultural pluralism

(C) Discrimination takes place when a person or group acts out of prejudice to harm or deny privileges to another. Discrimination takes place between all races and ethnic groups and between men and women at all levels. It can occur between individuals or groups. (D) Cultural pluralism is the simultaneous existence of several cultures and ethnic groups, with each afforded the protection and ability to observe their cultural institutions. It is also sometimes called multiculturalism.

125. Which of the following is not one of the four broad areas where social problems are affecting? *(Average) (Skill 6.5a)*

A. Desertification

B. The environment

C. Education

D. Health

Answer: A Desertification

The list of major social problems facing the world is long, with each culture approaching them based on their own values and beliefs. Four broad areas where social problems are affecting the world are the global economy, the environment, education, and health. While (A) desertification is a growing problem the world over, it falls under the category of the environment.

XAMonline, INC. 21 Orient Ave. Melrose, MA 02176

Toll Free number 800-509-4128

TO ORDER Fax 781-662-9268 OR www.XAMonline.com
PRAXIS SERIES   - PRAXIS - 2009

Address:

City, State Zip

 Credit card number_____-_____-_____-_____   expiration_____

 EMAIL _____

 PHONE   FAX

13# ISBN 2009	TITLE	Qty	Retail	Total
978-1-60787-043-2	Art Sample Test 10133			
978-1-60787-031-9	Biology 20231, 20232, 20235			
978-1-58197-691-5	Chemistry 20241 20242, 20245			
978-1-60787-046-3	Earth and Space Sciences 20571			
978-1-60787-033-3	Special Education: Knowledge-Based Core Principles 20351			
978-1-60787-037-1	Special Education: Teaching Students with Behavioral Disorders/Emotional Disturbance 0371			
978-1-60787-035-7	PRAXIS Early Childhood 020, 022			
978-1-60787-041-8	Educational Leadership 0410			
978-1-60787-048-7	Elementary Education 0011, 0012, 0014, 0016			
978-1-60787-044-9	English Language, Literature, and Composition 10041			
978-1-60787-053-1	French Sample Test 0173			
978-1-60787-042-5	Fundamental Subjects 0511			
978-1-60787-032-6	School Guidance & Counseling 20420			
978-1-58197-268-9	General Science 10435			
978-1-60787-039-5	Library Media Specialist 0310			
978-1-60787-049-4	Mathematics 10061, 20063			
978-1-58197-269-6	Middle School English Language Arts 10049			
978-1-58197-343-3	Middle School Mathematics 20069			
978-1-58197-263-4	Middle School Social Studies 0089			
978-1-60787-040-1	Physical Education 10091			
978-1-60787-047-0	Physics 0265			
978-1-60787-038-8	ParaPro Assessment 0755			
978-1-60787-036-4	PPST I: Basic Skills 0710, 0720, 0730			
978-1-58197-054-8	Government/Poltical Science 10930			
978-1-58197-577-2	Principals of Learning and Teaching 30521, 30522, 30523,			
978-1-60787-034-0	Reading 0200, 0201, 0202			
978-1-58197-696-0	Social Studies 10081			
978-1-58197-718-9	Spanish 10191, 30194			
978-1-60787-057-9	353 Exceptional Student Core Content Knowledge (New)			
978-1-60787-055-5	382 Education of Exceptional Students - Learning Disability			
978-1-60787-056-2	542 Ed Students Disabilities Mild to Moderate disabilities			
	Shipping $8.70 1 book, $11.00 2 books, $15.00 3			
	TOTAL			

LaVergne, TN USA
20 May 2010
183412LV00001B/7/P